Student Activities in
GEOGRAPHY
for Christian Schools®

Michael D. Matthews

Teacher's Edition

Bob Jones University Press
Greenville, SC 29614

NOTE:
The fact that materials produced by other publishers are referred to in this volume does not constitute an endorsement by Bob Jones University Press of the content or theological position of materials produced by such publishers. The position of Bob Jones University Press, and the University itself, is well known. Any references and ancillary materials are listed as an aid to the student or the teacher and in an attempt to maintain the accepted academic standards of the publishing industry.

Student Activities in GEOGRAPHY for Christian Schools®
Teacher's Edition

Michael D. Matthews, M.Ed.

Produced in cooperation with the Bob Jones University Department of History of the College of Arts and Science, the School of Religion, and Bob Jones Academy.

for Christian Schools is a registered
trademark of Bob Jones University Press.

ISBN 0-57924-301-0

15 14 13 12 11 10 9 8 7 6 5 4 3 2

Contents

How to Use the Activities Manual

These activities are designed to give you maximum flexibility. We have provided a "menu" of activities from which you can select the ones that will help you achieve your instructional goals. Before you begin each chapter, look over the activities and decide how you want to assign them. The *activity* codes and *skill* codes at the bottom of each page will help you decide.

Activity Codes

Each chapter has four to six activities. The *activity* code tells you which sections of the chapter each activity covers. The code also tells you whether the activity is good for reinforcement, enrichment, or review.

- *Reinforcement* activities are based solely on the information in the textbook. They help students (1) to recognize and recall major terms and concepts in the chapter and (2) to "put it all together." Some reinforcement activities, such as charts and time lines, cover the entire chapter. (Students can complete them as they read through the chapter or as they review for tests.) Other reinforcement activities apply to a specific section of the chapter. (Students can complete them as they read the section.)
- *Enrichment* activities go beyond the textbook. They help students (1) to apply information from the chapter, (2) to pursue subjects they find interesting, and (3) to develop special skills. Every student can benefit from these activities, but the activities are particularly useful for students who need a challenge. Most enrichment activities are related to a specific section in the chapter.
- *Chapter review* activities help students to prepare for the chapter test. They include crossword puzzles, games, and other interesting activities that review the chapter.

Alternative Uses of the Activities

Activities are useful for more than just homework. You can make them an integral part of your classroom discussion. Your students will especially appreciate your help in completing the more difficult activities.

- Homework—The students complete the activity at home.

- Class activity—The students complete the activity in class by themselves or in groups.

- Class discussion—You help the class complete the activity together in a classroom discussion. (See "Special Note" below.)

- Lecture—You complete the activity on the chalkboard or overhead projector during your lecture, while the students take notes.

- Game—The students answer each question in a competition that pits team against team or "every man for himself."

☆ SPECIAL NOTE ABOUT THE CLASS DISCUSSION ICON

This icon signifies activities that assess students' general recall and comprehension. They give you an excellent opportunity to ask a series of thought-provoking questions. At least one student will usually have the answer. If everyone is stumped, then you can supply the answer from the teacher manual without extra work on the students' part. Only the most exceptional student, who loves geography and relishes a challenge, will benefit from doing these time-consuming activities as homework.

Skill Codes

Every activity focuses on one of eighteen skills that history students need to learn. Some activities teach specific skills—such as mapping. Others teach basic thinking skills, such as recognizing terms. The activities for each skill increase in variety and difficulty over the year. *Note: Each number in the chart below corresponds to the activity number for that chapter.*

Chapter	1	2	3	4	5	6	7	8	9	10	11	12	13	14	15	16	17	18	19	20	21	22	23	24	25	26	27	28
1. Maps	3,4,5	1	1	1	1,2	1	1,3	1	1,2,3	1	2,3,4	1,5	1,3,4	1,3,4	1,2	1	1,2	1	1,2	1	1,2,3,5	1	1,2,3	1,2	1,2	1,2,CR	1	2
2. Charts		2,3	2		5,6	5	2	3		2				5			5										3	
3. Outlining				2		2	3							2														4
4. Time Line	2									4	5																	
5. Graphs			3					4																				
6. Original Sources	1			4				4				3	2		4				3,5	2						3,4		1
7. Cause and Effect																												
8. Using Resources											6	2							3				3	4,5	4,5			
9. Bible Study				3	4								3	4						2					3			
10. Writing																2	4	4										
11. Vocabulary																						4						
12. Test-taking				4																	6							
13. Recognition	6	4	CR	5	CR	6	5	5	6	3,CR	7	6,CR		4,5,CR	6	6	2,4,CR			5	CR	5	6,CR	4	6	5	4	
14. Comprehension				5	2,3,7								5	6									7					3,4
15. Application				4	5										5					4				6				
16. Analysis							2,4	2			1	4			4	3			3	4	2						2	
17. Synthesis															3						5	2		2,3				
18. Evaluation																				5						CR		

*CR means "Cumulative Review"

Alternatives to Grading and Burdensome Records

You don't need to grade all the activities. You can complete some of them in class discussions, games, and lectures, as mentioned above. Or you can use some of the ideas below.

- Check marks—Give simple pluses and minuses. You can use this information to decide borderline grades or—if you use them—"effort" grades.
- Extra credit—Let students do activities for extra credit, if they wish.
- Sporadic grades—Grade every third or fourth activity, but do not let students know which activities will be graded.
- Notebook—Make students keep their activities in a notebook. Collect the notebooks quarterly and grade them for neatness, completeness, and accuracy.

Geography

The Travels of Marco Polo

Marco Polo traveled through Asia during the thirteenth century and recorded his adventures in *The Travels of Marco Polo.* His thrilling account helped to spark the great Age of Exploration, which forever changed the world. Read the following excerpts from his book; then answer the questions.

If you wish to wait, this activity would be good to do while studying Chapter Eighteen.

Of the City of Kamadin and its Ruins; also Touching the Karaunah Robbers

After you have ridden downhill two days, you find yourself in a vast plain, and at the beginning thereof there is a city called Kamadin [near the Zagros Mountains in Iran—see text, p. 491], which formerly was a great and noble place, but now is of little consequence, for the Tartars [warlike tribes from Central Asia] in their incursions have several times ravaged it. The plain whereof I speak is a very hot region.

In this plain there are a number of villages and towns which have lofty walls of mud, made as a defense against the bandits, who are very numerous, and are called Karaunahs. This name is given them because they are the sons of Indian mothers by Tartar fathers. And you must know that when these Karaunahs wish to make a plundering incursion, they have certain devilish enchantments whereby they do bring darkness over the face of day, insomuch that you can scarcely discern your comrade riding beside you; and this darkness they will cause to extend over a space of seven days' journey. The old men who they take they butcher; the young men and the women they sell for slaves in other countries; thus the whole land is ruined, and has become well nigh a desert.

Marco himself was all but caught by their bands in such a darkness as that I have told you of; but, as it pleased God, he got off and threw himself into a village that was hard by, called Conosalmi. However he lost his whole company except seven persons who escaped along with him. The rest were caught, and some of them sold, some put to death.

Of the Wearisome and Desert Road that Has Now to Be Traveled

On departing from the city of Kerman [city in southern Iran—see text, p. 491] you find the road for seven days most wearisome; and I will tell you how this is. The first three days you meet with no water, or next to none. And what little you do meet with is bitter green stuff, so salty that no one can drink it. Hence it is necessary to carry water for the people to last these three days; as for the cattle, they must needs drink of the bad water I have mentioned, as there is no help for it, and their great thirst makes them do so. But it scours them to such a degree that sometimes they die of it. In all those three days you meet with no human habitation; it is all desert [the Dasht-E-Lut in Iran—see text, p. 491], and the extremity of drought. Even of wild beasts there are none, for there is nothing for them to eat.

Of an Ascent for Three Days, Leading to the Summit of a High Mountain

When you ride three days northeast of Wakhan [in Central Asia], always among mountains, you get to such a height that it is said to be the highest place in the world! And when you have got to this height you find a great lake between two mountains, and out of it a fine river runs through a plain clothed with the finest pastures in the world; insomuch that a lean beast there will fatten to your heart's content in ten days.

The region [of the Pamir Mountains—see text, p. 415] is so lofty and cold that you do not even see any birds flying. And I must notice also that because of this great cold, fire does not burn so brightly, nor give out so much heat as usual, nor does it cook food so effectually.

1. An important part of understanding original sources is the ability to discern facts from exaggeration. What incident from the above excerpts shows that Marco Polo included some "tall tales" in his writings? Which parts of this incident might be true?   *His report of bandits with devilish enchantments is farfetched; bandits may have attacked travelers and taken slaves, perhaps attacking only at dusk or when the sky was overcast during storms.*

2. What do we know today as the highest place in the world (see page 441)? Was Polo actually at the world's highest spot (see maps in the text, pages 415 and 430)? *Mt. Everest; no*

3. The effects mentioned in the last paragraph are the typical results of high altitude on cooking. Lower air pressure enables water to boil at a lower temperature. How would this cause food to cook less "effectually"? *It would take longer to cook food since the water was boiling at a lower temperature.*

4. What hardships did Marco Polo face during his travels? *losing some of his men to bandits, heat and lack of drinking water in the desert, cold in the mountains, weak fire for cooking food*

Concerning the Palace of the Great Khan

You must know that it is the greatest palace that ever was. The palace itself has no upper story, but it is all on the ground floor. The roof is very lofty, and the walls of the palace are all covered with gold and silver. They are also adorned with representations of dragons sculptured and gold, beasts and birds, knights and idols, and sundry other subjects. And on the ceiling too you see nothing but gold and silver painting. On each of the four sides there is a great marble staircase leading to the top of the marble wall, and forming the approach to the palace.

The hall of the palace is so large that it could easily dine six thousand people; and it is quite a marvel to see how many rooms there are besides. The building is altogether so vast, so rich and so beautiful, that no man on earth could design anything superior to it. The outside of the roof also is all colored with vermilion [red dye] and yellow and green and blue and other hues, which are fixed with a varnish so fine and exquisite that they shine like crystal, and lend a resplendent luster to the palace as seen for a great way round. This roof is made too with such strength and solidity that it is fit to last forever.

5. What was Marco Polo's opinion of the palace of Kublai Khan? *He thought it was the greatest palace that had ever existed.*

6. What types of precious materials were used to construct the palace? *gold, silver, marble*

Concerning the Black Stones that Are Dug in Cathay, and Are Burned for Fuel

It is a fact that all over the country of Cathay [northeastern China] there is a kind of black stones existing in beds in the mountains, which they dig out and burn like firewood. If you supply the fire with them at night, and see that they are well kindled, you will find them still alight in the morning; and they make such excellent fuel that no other is used throughout the country. It is true that they have plenty of wood also, but they do not burn it, because those stones burn better and cost less.

Moreover with that vast number of people, and the number of hot baths that they maintain—for every one has such a bath at least three times a week, and in winter if possible every day while every nobleman and man of wealth has a private bath for his own use—the wood would not suffice for the purpose.

7. What are the "black stones" that burn? *coal*

8. When describing the unusual black stones, why does Polo say "It is a fact"? *He knew that people who had never seen or heard of coal would question his description.*

Geography

Famous Men in the History of Geography

Complete the chart. Choose from the people, dates, and facts of interest listed below the chart. Then answer the questions that follow.

Person	Date	Accomplishment(s)	Significance
Alexander the Great *(p. 3)*	reigned 336–323 B.C.	conquered Persia and marched into India	expanded Greek knowledge about world geography
Eratosthenes (pp. 3-4)	*ca. 276– ca. 195 B.C*	calculated the circumference of the earth; wrote *Geography*	*first to use the term geography*
Hipparchus *(p. 3)*	*second century B.C.*	*drew a map grid*	*made locating places on maps easy*
Ptolemy *(p. 3)*	*second century A.D.*	drew a famous ancient world map; *promoted the geocentric theory*	devised a map and a theory of the universe that was unchallenged for almost fourteen centuries
Copernicus (p. 4)	1543	*promoted the heliocentric theory*	revolutionized ideas about the revolution of the earth and sun
Mercator *(pp. 4-5)*	*1569*	drew a modern world map	*set a new standard of excellence in cartography*

Copernicus
Eratosthenes
ca. 276–ca. 195 B.C.
second century B.C.
second century A.D.
1569

drew a map grid
first to use the term *geography*
made locating places on maps easy
promoted the geocentric theory
promoted the heliocentric theory
set a new standard of excellence in cartography

1. What empire produced the earliest surviving map (a clay tablet)? *Babylonian (p. 3)*

2. Who were the first ancient people to study the earth extensively? *Greeks (p. 3)*

3. What country calculated the meter? *France (p. 5)*

4. What sea power became the world's leading mapmaker in the eighteenth century? *England (p. 5)*

5. What military power is the world's leading mapmaker today? *United States (p. 5)*

Geography

Find It!

Apollo 11 has returned to earth, and you need to find it as quickly as possible. Different reports give the following different locations. With the help of the world relief map on page 1, name the body of water or the continent where *Apollo 11* was sighted.

This activity would be good as a timed drill. See the suggestion on page 7 of the teacher's manual.

1. 20°S, 140°W   *Pacific Ocean*
2. 40°S, 80°E   *Indian Ocean*
3. 80°N, 80°E   *Kara Sea*
4. 60°N, 100°W   *North America*
5. 0°, 60°W   *South America*
6. 20°N, 0°   *Africa*
7. 0°, 0°   *Gulf of Guinea*
8. 90°S, 180°W   *Antarctica*

Name the physical feature at each location below.

9. 0°, 20°E   *Congo Basin*
10. 20°N, 90°W   *Yucatan Peninsula*
11. 20°S, 130°E   *Great Sandy Desert*
12. 40°N, 6°W   *Iberian Peninsula*
13. 10°N, 40°E   *Ethiopian Highlands*
14. 40°N, 80°W   *Appalachian Mountains*
15. 70°S, 65°W   *Antarctic Peninsula*
16. 23°S, 23°E   *Kalahari Desert*

Give the approximate latitude and longitude of each location. **Answers need to be accurate within 10°.**

17. New Zealand   *40°S, 170°E*
18. Gobi Desert   *42°N, 102°E*
19. Hawaiian Islands   *20°N, 158°W*
20. Tasmania   *43°S, 146°E*
21. Alps   *47°N, 10°E*
22. Lake Victoria   *3°S, 33°E*

Geography

Map Projections

Below are two projections of the United States, one Mercator and the other conic. Compare the maps and answer the questions that follow.

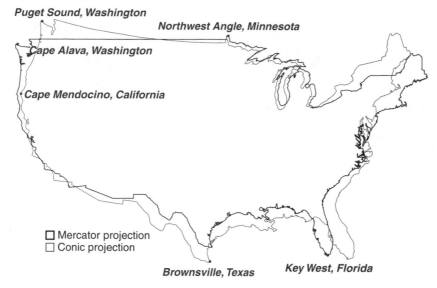

Puget Sound, Washington

Northwest Angle, Minnesota

Cape Alava, Washington

Cape Mendocino, California

☐ Mercator projection
☐ Conic projection

Brownsville, Texas   Key West, Florida

1. Compare the northern border of the United States, from the west coast to Minnesota. Which map makes the border appear as a straight line? How does the border differ on the other map?   *Mercator; the border on the conic projection appears curved*

2. Which projection shows direction most accurately?   *Mercator*

   On this map, mark the southernmost point, the northernmost point, and the westernmost point of the forty-eight United States. Now mark what *appears* to be these points on the other map projection.

   The textbook includes samples of all the projections discussed in your textbook. What projection is found on the following pages?

3. page 45   *Mercator's*

4. page 48   *Robinson's*

5. page 94   *Goode's*

6. page 218   *azimuthal projection*

7. page 597   *conic projection*

   Find an example of each of the projections in the chapters below. Give the page number and the subject of the map.

8. Mercator's in Chapter 13   *p. 303; time zones*

9. Goode's in Chapter 4   *p. 64; major world mines*

10. Robinson's in Chapter 8   *p. 183; wheat-producing regions*

11. azimuthal in Chapter 29   *p. 631; Antarctica*

12. conic in Chapter 6   *p. 117; Northeastern United States; note the straight lines of longitude*

13. How many maps can you find in Chapter 5 that have Robinson's projection?   *four*

Geography

Contour Lines

Match each side view with the correct relief map.

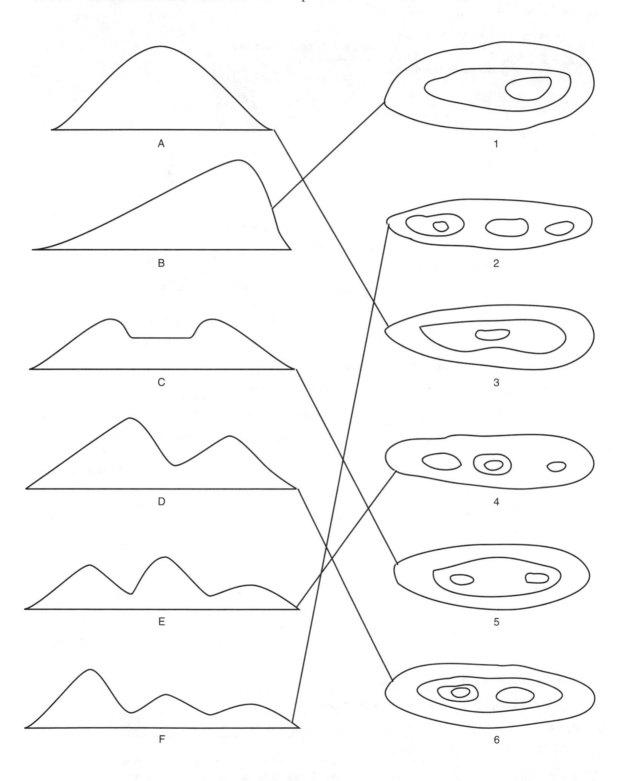

Geography

Crossword Puzzle

Down

1. book by Eratosthenes *(p. 3)*
2. inaccuracy in a map *(p. 9)*
3. relief color for land below sea level *(p. 13)*
5. the leading mapmaker today (initials) *(p. 5)*
8. "description" (suffix) *(p. 3)*
10. detailed land features *(p. 12)*
11. Mercator's projection *(p. 10)*
13. cartographer from Flanders *(p. 4)*
15. line that divides the Northern and Southern Hemispheres *(p. 6)*
16. regular pattern of intersecting lines *(p. 3)*
17. area, distance, direction, and ____ *(p. 9)*
20. author of heliocentric theory (initials) *(p. 4)*
21. Mercator's map distorts the ____ of Antarctica *(p. 10)*
22. "earth" (prefix) *(p. 3)*

Across

4. planar projection *(p. 11)*
6. ____ circle that divides the earth *(p. 7)*
7. official American surveyors (initials) *(p. 5)*
9. strip on a globe *(p. 9)*
12. mapmaking *(p. 4)*
14. half of the earth's sphere *(p. 6)*
18. 660 feet square *(p. 9)*
19. base meridian in a township *(p. 8)*
23. promoted the geocentric theory *(p. 3)*
24. line of latitude *(p. 6)*

¹G		²D										³B			
E	⁴A	Z	I	⁵M	U	T	H	A	L			L			
O		S		S								U			
⁶G	R	E	A	T		⁷U	S	⁸G	S		⁹G	O	¹⁰R	E	
R		O		T				R		¹¹C			E		
A		¹²C	A	R	T	O	G	R	A	P	H	Y		L	
P		T		P				P		L				I	¹³M
H		I		O		¹⁴H	E	M	I	S	P	H	E	R	E
Y	¹⁵E	O		G		Y		N			F		R		
	Q	N		R	¹⁶G			D					C		
¹⁷S	U		¹⁸A	C	R	E		¹⁹P	R	²⁰I	N	C	I	P	A	L
H	A	²¹A		P	I			I		C			T		
A	T	R		H	I	D		C		²²G			O		
²³P	T	O	L	E	M	Y		²⁴P	A	R	A	L	L	E	L
E	R	A			L					L			O		

Geography

The Main Features of the Earth

Refer to the physical maps on pages 1 and 218 to complete the map on the next page. The top-ten lists of various geographic features are scattered throughout the chapter.

1. Number each of the ten largest islands (p. 21).

2. Number each of the ten longest rivers (p. 26).

3. Number each of the ten largest lakes (p. 28).

4. Number each of the ten largest seas (p. 30).

5. Label the following:

   • Mountain Ranges—Appalachians, Rockies, Andes, Alps, Urals, Tien Shan, Himalayas, Atlas, Great Dividing Range

   • Plains—Great Plains, Pampas, Amazon Basin, Northern European Plain, Congo Basin

   • Plateaus—Brazilian Highlands, Guiana Highlands, Central Siberian Plateau, Deccan Plateau, Tibet, Ethiopian Highlands

6. Label and number each of the four oceans by size (p. 21).

7. Put a label beside each of the seven continents and number each of them by size (p. 20).

8. With a red pencil, shade the largest island, the longest river, and the largest lake. Label these three features.

Features of the World

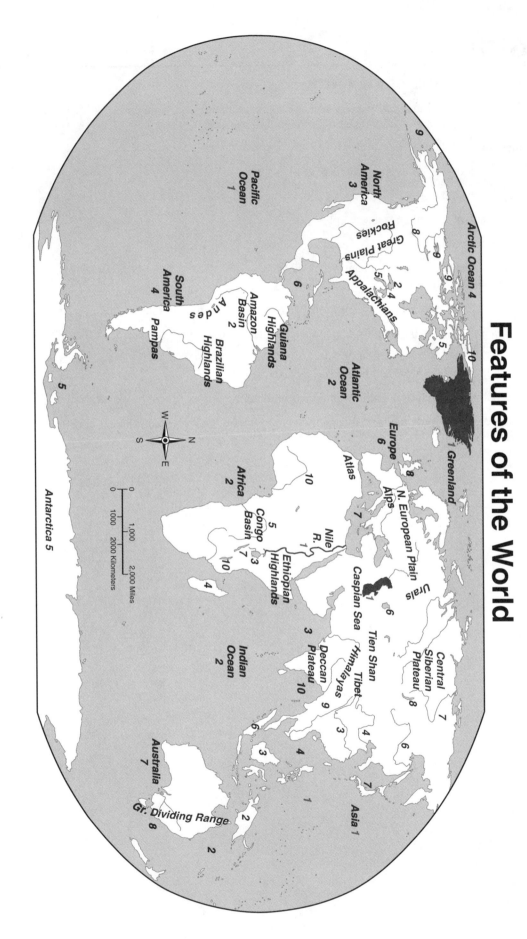

Geography

Statistical Highlights

This chapter has several tables that rank various geographic features. Find the tables and answer the questions about them. You will be studying more about these features in later chapters, but it is helpful to put them in their world context first.

Many of these questions appear in the teacher's manual. They are provided here in case you do not prefer to ask them orally.

Continents, p. 20

1. Which continent is largest in area? smallest? **Asia, Australia**

2. Which continent has the highest "high point"? **Asia**

3. Which continent has the shortest mountains? **Australia**

4. Which continent has the lowest "low point"? **Asia**

5. What is the only continent that never falls below sea level? **Antarctica**

6. How many Australias would fit in Asia? **almost six**

💡 Which continent has the longest drop from its high point to its low point?

How many feet is this drop? **Asia; 30,324 ft.**

Islands, p. 21

1. How many islands are above 100,000 square miles in area? **six**

2. Which two oceans have three islands on the list? **Arctic and Pacific**

3. Which island is about half the size of Sumatra? **Victoria**

💡 How many Ellesmere Islands would fit on Greenland? **eleven**

Oceans, p. 21

1. What are the largest and smallest oceans? **Pacific, Arctic**

2. What ocean has half of all the earth's ocean water? **Pacific**

3. Which ocean is shallowest? **Arctic**

4. What is the lowest point in the world's oceans? **Mariana Trench**

💡 How many Arctic Oceans would fit in the Pacific Ocean? **almost 13**

Rivers, p. 26

1. Which continent has the most rivers on the list? Which continents are not on the list? **Asia;**

   Europe, Australia, Antarctica

2. Which river has the largest discharge? the least discharge? **Amazon, Huang He**

3. Which river has the second largest discharge in the world? **Congo**

4. Which river has the largest drainage area? the smallest? **Amazon, Huang He**

💡 Compare the discharge of the Amazon River to the total discharge of the other nine rivers.

   6,350,000 cu. ft./sec. to 4,920,900 cu. ft./sec.

Lakes, p. 28

1. Which continent has the most lakes on the list? Which continents are not on the list? *North America;*

   South America, Europe, Australia, Antarctica

2. Which lake has the greatest depth? the least depth? *Baykal, Huron*

3. What lake has the greatest volume? the least volume? *Caspian Sea, Aral Sea*

💡 Compare the area of the Caspian Sea to the total area of the next seven largest lakes. *about the*

   same, 143,244 to 143,590 sq. mi.

Seas, p. 30

1. Which ocean has the most seas on the list? Which ocean is not on the list? *Pacific, Arctic*

2. How many seas exceed one million square miles? *five*

3. Which sea is not called a sea? *Bay of Bengal*

💡 Find the Philippine Sea and the Coral Sea on the world relief map. What land features appear to mark

   the boundaries of these huge seas? *The Philippine Sea is bordered by the Philippine Islands and the*

   Islands of Micronesia, while the Coral Sea is bordered by Australia and the Solomon Islands.

Geography

Tiny Tables

Fill in each tiny table.

Phases of the Earth's History, pp. 17-18	Main Forces of Change
1. *Creation*	*God's miraculous intervention*
2. *Flood*	*God's miraculous intervention, floodwater, fountains of the deep, and water pressure*
3. modern world	earthquakes, volcanic forces, weathering, erosion
4. future world	God's miraculous intervention with fire; new heaven and earth

List the Oceans (by size), p. 21
Pacific
Atlantic
Indian
Arctic

Divisions of the Earth Today, p. 19	Description
atmosphere	*air that surrounds the planet*
lithosphere	*solid part of the earth*
hydrosphere	*water on the earth*

List the Continents (by size), p. 20
Asia
Africa
North America
South America
Antarctica
Europe
Australia

Layers of the Lithosphere, pp. 19-20	Depth in Miles	State of Matter (liquid or solid)
crust	*3-37*	*solid rock*
mantle	*1,800*	*fluid*
core	*2,156*	*liquid outer, solid inner*

Major Types of Landforms, pp. 22-23	Description	Advantage for Man	Disadvantage for Man
mountain	*rugged land that rises high above the surrounding landscape*	*mineral riches, defensible border*	*hindrance to travel, poor soil*
plain	*wide, level areas*	*rich soil, easy travel*	*floods, no defensible borders*
plateau	*wide, level areas that rise abruptly above surrounding lands*	*grass for livestock, easy to travel*	*poor soil, few natural resources*

Ways to Compare Rivers, pp. 26–27	Unit of Measure	World Leader
length	*miles*	*Nile River*
discharge	*cubic feet per second*	*Amazon River*
drainage area	*square miles*	*Amazon River*
navigability	miles	Amazon River

Types of Wetlands, p. 29	Distinctive Characteristics
bog	*spongy areas that look dry but are covered with wet organic materials*
marsh	*standing water where grasses and small water plants grow*
swamp	*standing water dominated by large trees*

Forces of Change, pp. 31-35		Manifestations	Resulting Landforms
Internal	tectonic activity	*faults and folds*	*deformational mountains*
	volcanic forces	volcanoes	depositional (volcanic) mountains
External	weathering	*breakdown of rocks (by temperature changes, water, plant roots, and ice)*	unusual rock formations
	erosion	natural removal of weathered rock materials (by wind, waves, glaciers, and running water)	*sand dunes, terminal moraines, sea caves, sea arches, sandbars, barrier islands, gullies*

Geography

Distinguishing Terms

Underline the word or phrase that best completes each sentence.

1. According to II Peter 3:5, modern man is "(willingly ignorant, deceived)" about Creation and the Flood.

2. Christians believe most of the earth's features were changed as a result of (a cataclysm, uniformitarianism).

3. The water on the earth's surface is called the (lithosphere, hydrosphere).

4. The (mantle, core) is the fluid layer of rock located under the earth's crust.

5. Some geographers debate whether (Europe, Australia) is really a continent.

6. The largest islands in the world are (continental, oceanic) islands.

7. The largest continental landmass is (Africa, Eurasia).

8. The four oceans are the Atlantic, Pacific, Indian, and (Arctic, Antarctic).

9. The largest ocean in the world is the (Atlantic, Pacific) Ocean.

10. (Mount Everest, Mount McKinley) rises higher than any other mountain on earth.

11. The most influential physical feature in the development of climate and culture is (mountain ranges, river systems).

12. The best agricultural land is found on the world's (plains, plateaus).

13. Plateaus are sometimes called (basins, tablelands).

14. The longest river in the world is the (Nile, Amazon).

15. The Amazon River has the largest (drainage basin, volume of trade) in the world.

16. One of the most important measurements of a river's value for mankind is its (discharge, navigability).

17. The largest lake in the world is (the Caspian Sea, Lake Baykal).

18. Seas are (larger, smaller) than oceans.

19. A (fault, depositional mountain) is an example of tectonic activity.

20. According to the (continental drift, plate tectonics) theory, the earth was once united into a supercontinent, called Pangaea.

21. (Weathering, Erosion) carries away sand and soil to form sand dunes and barrier islands.

22. Decayed substances produced by living organisms are called (alluvium, humus).

Geography

Climate of the World

Complete the map on the next page and then answer the questions below.

1. Use a blue pencil to trace and label all of the cold currents that are *named* on the ocean current map (p. 45).

2. Look at the climate map on pages 48-49. Use a yellow pencil to shade all of the desert regions near a cold current. Include all of the Sahara.

3. Use a red pencil to shade all of the regions in South America and Africa that have a tropical wet climate (map on pp. 48-49).

4. Look at the map of prevailing winds on page 42. Use a green pencil to draw a series of arrows showing the *prevailing winds* in the United States, South America, and Africa. (Note that some will be westerlies and others will be trade winds.) Also label the doldrums green.

5. Label these lines of latitude: equator, tropic of Capricorn, tropic of Cancer, Arctic Circle, Antarctic Circle (map on pp. 48-49).

6. Look at the map of latitude zones on page 39. Label the Tropics, Temperate Zones, and polar regions.

7. Which direction does the wind blow over the deserts on the west coast of South America and southern Africa? __*southeasterly (moving in a northwest direction over the continent before it reaches the coast)*__

8. What are the prevailing winds in the tropical wet regions of South America and central Africa?

   __*doldrums (the water rises and falls by convection)*__

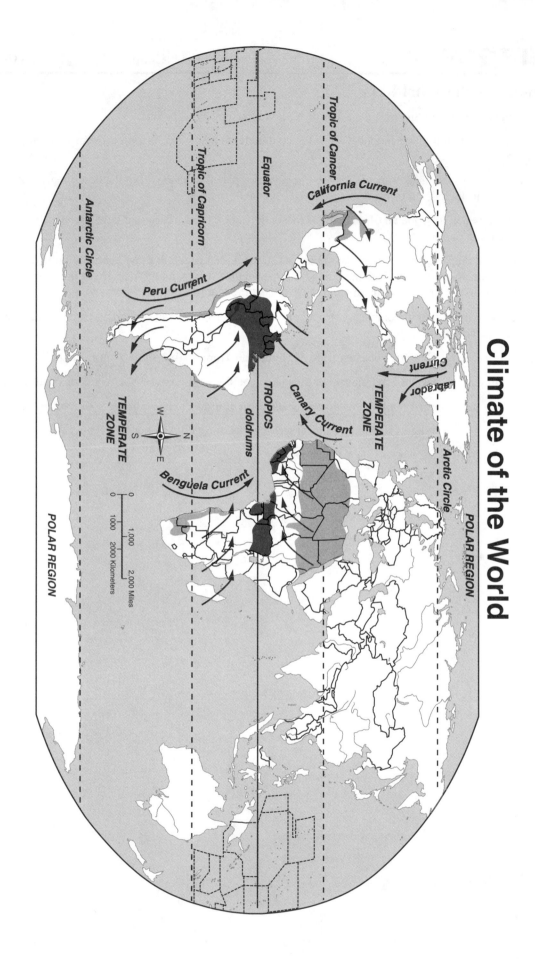

Climate of the World

Tropic of Cancer

California Current

Equator

Tropic of Capricorn

Antarctic Circle

Peru Current

TROPICS

TEMPERATE ZONE

Labrador Current

doldrums

Canary Current

TEMPERATE ZONE

Benguela Current

Arctic Circle

POLAR REGION

POLAR REGION

N
W   E
S

0   0
1,000   1,000
2000 Kilometers   2,000 Miles

Geography

Statistical Averages of the Climates

Answer the questions below based on the statistical table.

Average Statistics for the Climates of the World					
Climate	**Temperature (°F)**		**Precipitation (avg. in.)**		
	Summer	**Winter**	**Annual**	**Summer Months**	**Winter Months**
Tropical Rainy					
Tropical Wet	79	79	100	8	8
Tropical Wet and Dry	79	79	50	10	0.5
Dry					
Tropical and Temperate Dry	81	55	5	0.6	0.1
Semiarid	78	51	18	3.4	0.2
Moderate					
Marine West Coast	60	42	45	2.5	5.5
Mediterranean	72	52	23	0.4	3.8
Humid Continental	66	21	27	3.2	1.6
Humid Subtropical	77	47	50	6.2	2.8
Cold					
Icecap	32	−14	8	1.0	0.4
Polar	40	0	16	1.9	1.2
Subpolar	56	−8	17	1.8	1.2

1. Which climate has the highest summer temperature? *tropical and temperate dry*

2. Which climate has the highest winter temperature? *tropical rainy (tropical wet and tropical wet and*

   dry)

3. Which climate has the lowest temperature? *icecap*

4. Which climate has the highest variation between summer and winter temperatures? *subpolar*

5. Which climates have no variation between summer and winter temperatures? *tropical wet, tropical*

   wet and dry

6. What is the only moderate climate whose average temperature dips below freezing (32°F) in winter?

   humid continental

7. Which climate has the highest annual precipitation? *tropical wet*

8. Which climate has the lowest annual precipitation? *tropical and temperate dry (desert)*

9. Which climate has the highest variation between summer and winter precipitation? *tropical wet*

   and dry

10. Which climate has no variation between summer and winter precipitation? _tropical wet_

11. What is the monthly precipitation in the summer for a mediterranean climate? _0.4 inches_

12. What is the monthly precipitation in the summer for a tropical and temperate dry climate? _0.6 inches_

13. Which moderate climate gets the most rainfall in the summer? _humid subtropical_

14. Which moderate climate gets the most winter rainfall? _marine west coast_

15. What cold climate receives about the same amount of precipitation as a tropical and temperate dry climate? _icecap_

16. What two climates have an annual precipitation about the same as a semiarid climate? _polar and subpolar_

17. If a city has an average temperature of 80°F and 3.5 inches of rain in the summer months, in what climate region is it likely to be? _semiarid_

18. If a city has an average temperature of 50°F and 4.0 inches of rain in the winter months, in what climate region is it likely to be? _mediterranean_

Climimographs Around the World

Your textbook gives sample climographs for various types of climate. Look up the climographs and answer the questions below. You may need to use a ruler.

Moose Factory, Canada, has a subpolar climate (p. 230).

1. What is the average temperature in the hottest month?   *over 60°F* _____

2. What is the average temperature in the coldest month?   *about 0°F* _____

3. Does Moose Factory get more precipitation in the summer or the winter?   *summer* _____

Goiás, Brazil, has a tropical wet and dry climate (p. 292).

4. During which four months is the monthly rainfall below one inch?   *May through August* _____

5. During which three months does rainfall exceed twelve inches?   *December through February* _____

6. What is the hottest month?   *September* _____

Manaus, Brazil, has a tropical wet climate (p. 295).

7. What is the lowest monthly rainfall?   *just under two inches in August* _____

8. Compare the temperatures of Manaus and Goiás. Which has more variation?   *Goiás* _____

9. Compare the amounts of rainfall in Manaus and in Goiás. Does Goiás ever get more rain than

   Manaus?   *yes, during the rainy season (December through February)* _____

Paris, France, has a marine west coast climate (p. 326).

10. Does the precipitation of Paris appear to be steady all year long?   *yes* _____

11. Compare the temperatures of New York City (p. 50) and Paris, which is farther north. Which city has

    the lowest temperature in any single month?   *New York City* _____

12. Which city has the highest temperature in any single month, New York City or Paris?   *New York City,*

    note the effect of the Gulf Stream _____

Rome, Italy, has a mediterranean climate (p. 356).

13. During which two months does Rome receive the most rain?   *October and November (late fall)* _____

14. What is the average temperature in the hottest month?   *about 75°F* _____

15. Which city (discussed above) appears to have the opposite pattern of rains?   *Moose Factory, Canada* __

Moscow, Russia, has a humid continental climate (p. 396).

16. How many degrees Fahrenheit does the temperature drop between July and January?   *over 60°F* ____

17. Compare the amount of rainfall in New York City to that in Moscow. Which city has the higher

    average rainfall?   *New York City* _____

18. Which city has the lowest temperature in any single month, Moscow or New York City?   *Moscow* ___

Tselinograd, Kazakhstan, has a semiarid climate (p. 418).

19. During what three months does precipitation rise above one inch? *June through August*

20. How many degrees Fahrenheit does the temperature drop between August and January? *around 70°*

21. During how many months is the average temperature below freezing (32°F)? *five or six months,*

from November to March or April

Bombay, India, has a tropical wet and dry climate (p. 435).

22. Which month has the highest average rainfall? *July*

23. How many inches of rainfall does Bombay receive at the height of the rainy season? *28+ inches*

24. Compare the amount of rainfall in Bombay to that in Goiás, Brazil, another city with a tropical wet and dry climate. When rainfall is heaviest in Bombay, what is the weather like in Goiás? *dry season*

Cairo, Egypt, has a dry desert climate (p. 532).

25. During which four months does Cairo receive no measurable rainfall? *June through September*

26. Does the rainy season coincide with the highest temperatures in Cairo? *No, it comes in December.*

27. What is the average temperature in the hottest month? *about 85°F*

Eismitte, Greenland, has an icecap climate (p. 632).

28. Does the average temperature ever rise above freezing? *no*

29. What month has the lowest average temperature? *February (–50°F)*

30. What is the average precipitation each month? *0 inches*

Geography

Writing Your Own Glossary

A glossary is a list of important terms with their definitions. Write a short description of each term below. Your description should include the words in parentheses.

Example:

horse latitudes (30° latitude, winds, calm)   *a permanent high-pressure area around 30° latitude*

where the winds are usually calm (p. 42)

Heat Distribution

1. air mass (area, temperature)   *a large area of air that has a similar temperature and moves together*

    (p. 40)

2. Coriolis effect (rotation, direction)   *the influence of the rotation of the earth on wind direction, making*

    wind appear to veer away from its true direction (p. 41)

3. trade winds (Tropics, northeasterly)   *the common northeasterly winds of the Tropics (p. 41)*

4. westerlies (prevailing winds, middle latitudes)   *the prevailing winds in the middle latitudes that blow*

    from the west (p. 41)

5. low pressure (air mass, hot)   *an air mass with relatively hot, rising air (p. 43)*

6. high pressure (air mass, cold)   *an air mass with relatively cold, sinking air (p. 43)*

7. El Niño (Pacific, warm)   *a phenomenon that occurs when waters in the Pacific warm up, moving east to*

    the coast of Chile and then north, changing the weather patterns (p. 44)

8. gyre (circular, current)   *the circular flow of an ocean current (p. 44)*

9. lapse rate (elevation, 3½°F)   *because molecules are thinner at higher elevation, temperatures drop*

    3½°F for every 1,000 feet one climbs in altitude (p. 51)

Water Distribution

10. evaporation (water, vapor)   *the process of liquid changing into water vapor (p. 46)*

11. condensation (vapor, liquid)   *the process of water vapor changing into liquid (p. 46)*

12. humidity (vapor, air)   *the amount of water vapor in the air (p. 46)*

13. dew point (water, condensation)   *the point at which water begins condensation (p. 46)*

14. precipitation (water, earth)   *the fall of water to earth in any form (p. 46)*

15. ground water (slow-moving, under)   *slow-moving water that has seeped under the soil (p. 47)*

16. orographic (precipitation, mountains)   *precipitation that occurs as a humid air mass moves over mountains (p. 47)*

17. front (line, air masses)   *the line where two air masses collide (p. 47)*

18. convection (rise, hot surface)   *the rise of warm air over a hot surface (p. 47)*

Vegetation

19. vegetation (plants, region)   *plants that grow in a region (p. 51)*

20. biome (region, plants, animals)   *large region where distinct populations of plants and animals are found living together (p. 51)*

21. conifer (tree, seeds, cone)   *a tree that produces its seeds in a cone (p. 52)*

22. deciduous (tree, leaves, season)   *a tree that loses its leaves during a particular season of the year (p. 53)*

23. grassland (dry, grasses)   *a dry region that cannot support trees but has plenteous grass (p. 54)*

24. savanna (grasslands, tropical)   *grasslands in tropical regions that offer open areas with scattered trees (p. 54)*

25. steppe (grasslands, temperate)   *grasslands in temperate regions (p. 54)*

26. tundra (poles, limited)   *cold regions near the poles that support only limited vegetation (p. 55)*

27. permafrost (soil, frozen)   *soil that remains frozen all year long (p. 55)*

Geography

Name _____

A Second Look: The World as God Made It

With the help of the world relief map in your student text, page 1, name the body of water or the continent at each location.

1. 40°S, 80°E   *Indian Ocean* _____
2. 0°, 60°W   *South America* _____
3. 20°N, 0°   *Africa* _____
4. 0°, 0°   *Gulf of Guinea* _____
5. 90°S, 180°W   *Antarctica* _____

List the four main phases in the earth's history.

6. *Creation* _____
7. *Flood* _____
8. *modern world* _____
9. *future world* _____

List the seven continents in the first column. List the four oceans in the second column.

10. *Asia*   17. *Pacific*
11. *Africa*   18. *Atlantic*
12. *North America*   19. *Indian*
13. *South America*   20. *Arctic*
14. *Antarctica*
15. *Europe*
16. *Australia*

Underline the word or phrase that best completes each sentence.

21. The two main branches of geography are human and (physical, systematic).
22. The most common world map projection found in your textbook is (Robinson's, Goode's).
23. Evolutionists believe most of the earth's features were changed as a result of (a cataclysm, uniformitarianism).
24. The air above the earth's surface is called the (hydrosphere, atmosphere).
25. The largest landmass is (North America, Eurasia).
26. The largest ocean in the world is the (Atlantic, Pacific).
27. (Mount Aconcagua, Mount Everest) is the highest mountain on earth.
28. The longest river in the world is the (Nile, Amazon).
29. The largest lake in the world is (Lake Superior, the Caspian Sea).
30. (Weathering, Erosion) washes away soil to form barrier islands.

Cumulative Review   **Skill: Recognition**   25

31–34. On the map, label the equator, Tropics, Temperate Zones, and polar regions.

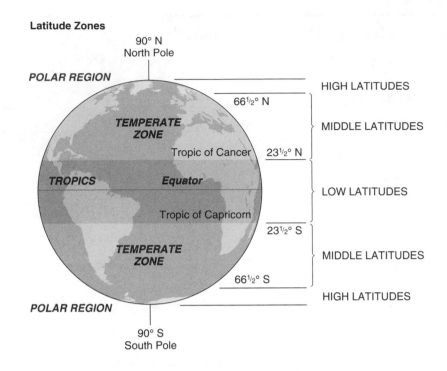

Latitude Zones

Give the term that fits each description.

35. the effect of the earth's rotation on wind direction, making wind appear to veer away from its true

   direction   *Coriolis effect*

36. the prevailing winds in the middle latitudes   *westerlies*

37. the fall of water to earth in any form   *precipitation*

38. precipitation that occurs as a humid air mass moves over mountains   *orographic*

39. grasslands in tropical regions that offer open areas with scattered trees   *savanna*

40. vegetation in cold regions near the poles that support only limited vegetation   *tundra*

Geography

Industry Around the World

Complete the map and then answer the questions that follow.

Industry of the World

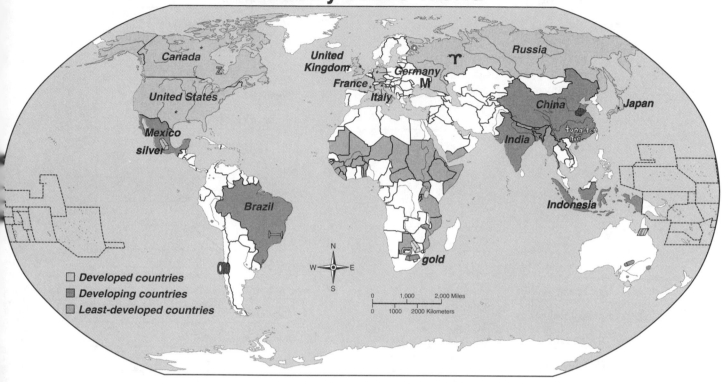

☐ **Developed countries**
■ **Developing countries**
☐ **Least-developed countries**

1. Look at the land-use map on pages 62-63. Color in red all the regions of manufacturing and trade in South America, Africa, and Australia.

2. Look at the mining map on pages 64-65. Then with the help of the table on page 66, draw the symbol of every metal and fossil fuel on the country that is its leading producer. (Some countries will have more than one mine, but draw only one. Two metals—tin and tungsten—are not shown on the map, so simply write the names somewhere in the correct countries. Draw a gas flame for natural gas. Draw a fertilizer bag with either "ph," "ni," or "po" for phosphates, nitrates, and potash.)

3. Look at the map of developing countries on page 81. Shade blue those countries that are least developed in the world.

4. Look at the table of countries with high GDPs on page 81. Write the name of the thirteen countries with the highest GDPs in the world. Put an asterisk inside the G-7 countries. Then color these countries with separate colors for developed and developing countries.

5. Which continent has only one major region of manufacturing and trade? _**Africa**_

6. Which continent has the largest number of least developed countries? _**Africa**_

7. Which continent has the largest number of G-7 countries? _**Europe**_

Geography

Simple Outlining

Look at the headings for Chapter 4, and then complete the outline.

Becoming familiar with outlines will help students' reading skills. This activity gives students practice in outlining and shows them the purpose of the chapter's structure. (Compare the outline to the chart on p. 61.)

Chapter 14: Industry

I.   Primary Industries

   A. Agriculture

      1. Farming

      2. *Animal Husbandry* _____

   B. *Fishing and Forestry* _____

   C. Mining

      1. Metals

         a. Precious Metals

         b. *Common Metals* _____

         c. *Alloys* _____

      2. Nonmetal Minerals

      3. *Fossil Fuels* _____

II. Secondary Industries

   A. *Construction* _____

   B. *Manufacturing* _____

      1. *Industrial Revolution* _____

      2. *Durable and Nondurable Manufacturing* _____

      _____

III. Tertiary Industries

   A. *Infrastructure* _____

      1. *Utilities* _____

      2. *Transportation* _____

         a. *Water Transportation* _____

         b. *Land Transportation* _____

         c. *Air Transportation* _____

      3. *Communication* _____

         a. *Print Media* _____

         b. *Electronic Media* _____

   B. *Trade* _____

   C. *Finance* _____

   D. *General Services* _____

   E. *Government* _____

IV. *The Wealth of Nations* _____

   A. *Who Makes the Choices?* _____

      1. *Capitalism* _____

      2. *Socialism* _____

      3. *Mixed Economies* _____

   B. *How Nations Measure Wealth (GDP)* _____

      _____

   C. *Distribution of Wealth Among Nations* _____

      _____

      1. *Developed and Developing Countries* _____

      _____

      2. *Division of Labor* _____

      3. *The Hope of Prosperity* _____

   D. *Trade Wars* _____

Geography

What God Says About the Environment

1. *Environmentalism* is the modern effort to protect the environment from the impact of human industry. Environmentalists reject the traditional interpretation of God's dominion mandate, given in Genesis 1:28. Even a growing number of Christians advocate "Christian environmentalism," arguing that man has a duty to "serve the creation." The Bible is the only sure guide for understanding the purpose of the environment. Use your Bible to answer these questions about (1) the purpose of the environment, (2) man's responsibility to the environment, and (3) mistaken views about the environment.

   - Who owns the earth (Job 41:11; Ps. 24:1; 50:12)? __*God*__

   - What is one of God's purposes for all animals and plants (Gen. 9:3)? __*food for man*__

   - Has God given dominion over all creation to man (Ps. 8:4-8)? __*yes*__

   - Are people more valuable than animals (Matt. 10:31; 12:11-12)? __*yes*__

   - When did God intervene to destroy the environment (II Pet. 3:5-6)? __*Flood*__

   - With whom did God make a covenant not to destroy the earth again by water (Gen. 9:12-16)? __*every living creature*__

   - What cataclysm will destroy the earth some day, and who will be responsible (II Pet. 3:10)? __*fire; God*__

2. The environmentalist movement has taken off in Christian circles. In 1993 the newly formed Evangelical Environmental Network (EEN) published a sixteen-hundred-word "Evangelical Declaration on the Care of Creation," signed by many Christian leaders. "We repent of the way we have polluted, distorted, or destroyed so much of the Creator's work," the declaration says, and it warns that "we are pressing against the finite limits God has set for creation." It calls on Christians and churches to become "centers of creation's care and renewal." Interestingly, the Bible does not say anything about the government's duty to protect the "environment," but it says a lot about private individuals' obligation to use private property wisely.

   - What is our first responsibility to the environment (Gen. 1:28)? __*Subdue it*__

   - What is another basic responsibility, according to the following verses: John 6:12; Proverbs 12:27; Proverbs 18:9? __*Be frugal, not wasteful.*__

   - What should workers take care of (Prov. 12:10)? __*their beasts of burden*__

   - Which trees could not be cut down by the Israelites during a siege (Deut. 20:19-20)? Why? __*fruit trees; their long-term value for man*__

   - What wild animals are mentioned in Deuteronomy 22:6-7? Why were Israelites commanded not to kill them? __*mother birds; apparently to ensure the survival of birds*__

   - What unfair treatment of animals did God forbid in Exodus 23:19? in Deuteronomy 25:4? __*seethe a kid in its mother's milk; muzzle an ox while he grinds grain*__

   - What will be forgotten some day (Isa. 65:17)? __*modern heaven and earth*__

   - Should Christians ever "serve" the creation (Rom. 1:24-25)? __*no*__

   - What is more valuable than the whole earth (Matt. 16:26)? __*one human soul*__

   - According to Peter, what should be our present attitude, now that we know the earth's future (II Pet. 3:11)? __*Live godly lives.*__

3. Senator Al Gore, a Southern Baptist who was elected vice president in 1992, became a leading spokesman for environmentalism after the publication of his book *Earth in the Balance* (1992). Gore attended the launch of the Evangelical Environmental Network in 1993. His book made several controversial claims. For instance, he said that the modern lesson of Noah and the ark is "Thou shalt preserve biodiversity." He said the first instance of pollution in the Bible occurred when Cain slew Abel and his blood fell on the ground, rendering the ground useless. Gore's concern was so great that he claimed, "We must make the rescue of the environment the central organizing principle for civilization."

- According to Psalm 104:1-5, would you describe the environment as unstable or stable?

  stable, v. 5

- Is it possible for human industry to disrupt the seasons (Gen. 8:22)? *no*

- Environmentalists say God told all mankind to "keep" the earth. But to whom was this command given, and what was he to keep (Gen. 2:15)? *Adam; the garden of Eden*

- Environmentalists quote a warning in Revelation 11:18 that God will "destroy them which destroy the earth." But what is God condemning in this verse? Who will be the one destroying the earth?

  sin that requires judgment; God

Geography

Foreign Products at Home

Almost every home has several products that came from foreign manufacturing plants. Try to find as many products as you can from the countries listed at the bottom of the page.

Of course it is not necessary for students to find every product.

1. Check your home for each of the products listed below. Give the name of the company that manufactured the product, if known, and give where the company is located (city or a country).

Nondurable Manufacturing

☐ peanut butter _____

☐ tuna _____

☐ flour _____

☐ leather belt _____

☐ aspirin _____

☐ book _____

☐ pencil _____

☐ shirt _____

☐ silk tie _____

☐ pants or dress _____

☐ woven basket _____

☐ rug _____

☐ toy (describe the toy) _____

_____

☐ toy (describe the toy) _____

_____

Durable Manufacturing

☐ dinner plate _____

☐ drinking glass _____

☐ clock _____

☐ wristwatch _____

☐ reclining chair _____

☐ wooden chair _____

☐ folding chair _____

☐ screwdriver _____

☐ can opener _____

☐ steel knife _____

☐ automobile _____

☐ computer _____

☐ washing machine _____

2. List items found at your home that were manufactured in the foreign countries below (the top-ten U.S. trade partners). You can include items from the question above. (You may not find something from every country.)

Note: These trade partners are discussed in more detail on page 486 of the student text.

☐ Canada _____

☐ Japan _____

☐ Mexico _____

☐ United Kingdom _____

☐ South Korea _____

☐ Germany _____

☐ Taiwan _____

☐ Netherlands _____

☐ Singapore _____

☐ China _____

☐ other _____

☐ other _____

Geography

Terms from Industry

Identify the terms described below.

1. type of farmer who produces only enough for his household   *subsistence (p. 62)*

2. type of farmer who produces large cash crops for profit   *commercial (p. 62)*

3. aluminum ore   *bauxite (p. 67)*

4. a combination of metals, such as steel   *alloy (p. 67)*

5. three basic fertilizers: phosphorus, nitrogen, and   *potassium (p. 68)*

6. gaseous fossil fuel   *natural gas (p. 69)*

7. liquid fossil fuel   *petroleum (p. 69)*

8. mineral fuel   *uranium (p. 68)*

9. the application of science to industry   *technology (p. 70)*

10. basic energy and equipment needs of industries   *infrastructure (p. 72)*

11. any type of energy resource that will run out some day   *nonrenewable (p. 74)*

12. sending messages through electronic impulses   *telecommunications (p. 77)*

13. type of business that buys goods in large quantities from producers to sell in smaller quantities to other businesses   *wholesale (p. 78)*

14. type of business that sells goods directly to the customer   *retail (p. 78)*

15. money used to build industries   *capital (p. 78)*

16. economic system under which the government owns the major industries   *socialism (p. 79)*

17. economic system under which private individuals or corporations build most industries   *capitalism (p. 78)*

18. the people or businesses that buy products from an industry   *market (p. 84)*

19. goods received from other countries   *imports (p. 84)*

20. taxes on imports and exports   *tariffs (p. 84)*

Identify the terms described below.

21. order from the Lord to subdue the earth   *dominion mandate (p. 60)*

22. subsistence husbandry   *nomadic herding (p. 62)*

23. natural resources extracted by primary industries   *raw materials (p. 70)*

24. opposite of protectionism   *free trade (pp. 78-79)*

25. goods shipped to other countries   *exports (p. 84)*

Geography

Population of the World

Complete the map on the next page.

1. Look at the map of culture regions on pages 58-59. Label and draw borders around the eight culture regions of the world.

2. Look at the religion map on pages 94-95. Shade gray the areas of the world where most of the people follow Christianity. Shade orange those parts where most of the people are Islamic. Shade green those parts where the people follow Eastern religions. Shade yellow those parts where the people follow tribal religions. (Note: The interior of South America follows tribal religions.)

3. Look at the population map on pages 106-7. Label the ten largest cities in the world (chart on p. 103).

4. Label the ten largest countries in the world, using a blue pencil (chart on p. 96).

5. Label the ten most populous countries in the world, using a green pencil (chart on p. 104). Underline the countries that are also among the ten largest. (Note: Pakistan is found on p. 430.)

6. Draw a tank in the ten countries with the largest armies in the world (chart on p. 110).

7. Place the initials of the United Nations (UN) within the five countries that are permanent members of the Security Council (found on p. 111).

8. If possible, get a list of the missionaries that your church supports, and draw a cross in each of the countries where they serve. How many of the eight culture regions are unreached?

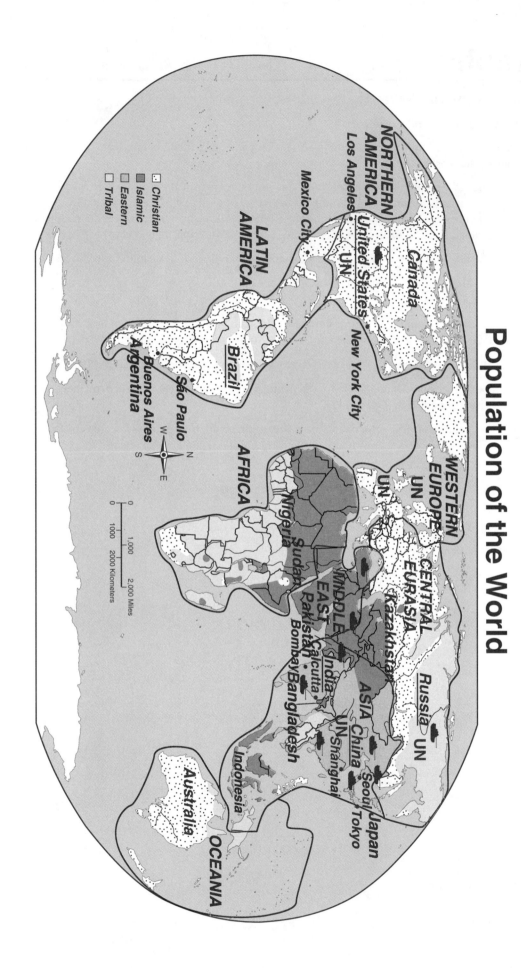

Population of the World

Legend:
- Christian
- Islamic
- Eastern
- Tribal

NORTHERN AMERICA
- Canada
- United States — UN
- Los Angeles
- Mexico City
- New York City

LATIN AMERICA
- Brazil
- São Paulo
- Buenos Aires
- Argentina

WESTERN EUROPE — UN

CENTRAL EURASIA — UN
- Russia — UN
- Kazakhstan

AFRICA
- Nigeria
- Sudan

MIDDLE EAST
- Pakistan

ASIA — UN
- India
- Bombay
- Calcutta
- Bangladesh
- China — UN
- Shanghai
- Seoul
- Japan
- Tokyo
- Indonesia

OCEANIA
- Australia

Scale: 0 1,000 2,000 Miles / 0 1000 2000 Kilometers

Compass: N S E W

Geography

A Closer Look at the World Culture Regions

Look at the culture map on pages 58-59 to answer the following questions about the eight world culture regions.

1. List all of the cultural subregions under each main region.

   • Northern America   *Canada, United States*

   • Latin America   *Middle America, South America*

   • Western Europe   *British Isles, Scandinavia, Continental Europe, Mediterranean Europe*

   • Central Eurasia   *Eastern Europe, Russia, Central Asia*

   • Asia   *South Asia, East Asia, Southeast Asia*

   • Middle East   *Persian Gulf, Eastern Mediterranean*

   • Africa   *North Africa, West Africa, Central Africa, East Africa, Southern Africa*

   • Oceania   *Australia, New Zealand, Pacific Islands*

2. Which culture region has the most countries?   *Africa*

3. Which culture region has the fewest countries?   *Northern America*

4. What two world culture regions share part of the continent of North America?   *Northern America, Latin America*

5. Which world culture region includes part of three continents?   *Middle East*

6. Which continent has three world culture regions?   *Asia*

7. Which world culture region is broken up into the most subregions?   *Africa*

8. How many individual countries are listed as subregions? List them.   *five—Canada, Russia, the United States, Australia, and New Zealand*

9. How many subregions include a compass direction, such as East, in their names? List them.

   ten—South America, Eastern Europe, South Asia, Southeast Asia, East Asia, Eastern Mediterranean, North Africa, West Africa, East Africa, Southern Africa

10. How many regions or subregions include the word *central* or *middle*?   *five—Middle America, Central Eurasia, Central Asia, Middle East, Central Africa*

11. How many regions or subregions are named after a specific body of water? List them.   *four—Mediterranean Europe, Eastern Mediterranean, Pacific Islands, Persian Gulf*

   Look at the table on page 87 to answer the following questions about the eight world culture regions.

12. Which world culture region has the largest population?   *Asia*

13. Which world culture region has the highest population density?   *Asia*

14. Which world culture region has the largest area?   *Africa*

15. Which world culture region has the smallest population and the lowest population density?

   Oceania

16. Which world culture region has the smallest area?   *Europe*

Geography

Complete an Encyclopedia Entry on "Culture"

Use these words to complete the encyclopedia entry on "culture."

Arabs	English	group	medieval
cultural convergence	Enlightenment	Indo-European	nationalism
culture	European	institutions	nuclear
culture regions	extended	language	religion
dialects	Greeks	language families	traditions

(1) _____Culture_____ is a society's total way of life. It includes (2) _____traditions_____ (the products of human thought and deeds) and (3) _____institutions_____ (organizations that society uses to transmit traditions). The world is divided into eight (4) _____culture regions_____ , each with its own basic culture.

God's division of (5) _____languages_____ at Babel became the foundation of separate cultures. Today, ninety-nine percent of all people speak a language under one of the ten major (6) _____language families_____ . The most widely spoken language family is (7) _____Indo-European_____ . The single most-spoken language is Mandarin (Chinese), but the most common second language is (8) _____English_____ . In many cases, people speak a single language but their speech patterns vary considerably, resulting in different (9) _____dialects_____ .

There are four institutions that transmit culture—the family, (10) _____religion_____ , volunteer community organizations, and the nation. In general, Western institutions worship the individual, while Eastern institutions worship the (11) _____group_____ . For example, Western societies focus on the (12) _____nuclear_____ family—a man, his wife, and their children. But Eastern societies focus on the (13) _____extended_____ family, which includes grandparents, aunts, and uncles.

Cultures have gone through three major periods in history—ancient, (14) _____medieval_____ , and modern. Most of the world culture regions arose during ancient history, including the (15) _____Greeks_____ and Romans, whose ideas became the foundation of Western civilization. The (16) _____Arabs_____ spread across the Middle East during the medieval period. Around 1500, a series of (17) _____European_____ nations spread their culture around the world. But the eighteenth-century philosophy called the (18) _____Enlightenment_____ argued that the government's power came from the "will of the people," and it eventually brought an end to European imperialism. A new movement arose, called (19) _____nationalism_____ , which argued that every nation has a right to establish its own government. With the defeat of the Soviet Union during the Cold War, the nations have been adopting Western ways, leading to (20) cultural _____convergence_____ .

Geography

How to Witness to Anyone

Over the course of this school year, you will have a chance to survey all the major religions of the world. You will learn about their holy books, their key doctrines, and the Bible's response to their errors. Your studies will expose you to *all* the religions that make a serious claim to be "the truth." Anyone who says that he needs to study many religions before he can decide which one to follow is just making excuses. God has not hidden His message. You can tell people with confidence that biblical Christianity is the *only* religion that offers salvation by grace, not works, based on the love and sacrificial work of the Son of God, not based on the personal merit of sinners.

You do not need to know all about world religions before you can begin witnessing. God does not expect you to learn many different messages. Your duty is to be growing in the knowledge of God, studying the Bible, and living a godly life. The gospel is a simple message. It can be understood by citizens of every nation and followers of every religion.

Know Why You Might Be Afraid to Speak. Believers are timid about sharing the gospel for several reasons. Look up each passage and explain in your own words why each fear is unjustified.

1. *Fear of Ridicule* (Matt. 5:11-12)   **Jesus said that persecution is a blessing that should bring great joy because it results in great rewards; persecution should be expected among prophets (those who speak God's truth). [Discuss Matthew 10:23-35.]**

2. *Fear of Embarrassment* (Mark 8:34-38)   **Jesus called Christians to a life of self-sacrifice; it is shameful for Christians to give less value to the opinion of Christ than to the opinions of this wicked generation.**

3. *Fear of Being Asked a Question You Cannot Answer* (Matt. 10:19)   **If we are faithful to walk with God each day, as the disciples did, then the Holy Spirit will bring to mind the words we need. (See John 16:13.)**

4. *Fear That No One Will Listen* (Isa. 55:11)   **God promises that His Word will be heard. Discuss the parable of the sower (Matthew 13)—some seed will fall on good soil.**

5. *Fear of Saying the Wrong Thing* (I Cor. 2:1-5)   **Paul did not use complicated arguments to convert sinners, but instead he kept the message simple and relied on the Holy Spirit for guidance.**

Know the Gospel. Every believer should memorize key verses that give the basics of the gospel. One popular list of verses is known as the "Romans Road." Look up the passages from Romans and answer the questions.

6. How many people have a sin problem? (Rom. 3:10)   **All people have a sin problem; no one is righteous.**

7. What is sin? (Rom. 3:23)   **failure to live by God's standard of righteousness**

8. What originally caused the sin problem? (Rom. 5:12)   **Adam's sin**

9. What are the consequences of sin? (Rom. 6:23a)   **The wages of sin is death.**

10. What did Christ do to prevent us from suffering the consequences of sin (Rom. 5:8)?   **He was without sin and died on our behalf.**

11. What can I do to receive the benefits of Christ's sacrifice? (Rom. 10:9-13) *agree (confess) that*

Jesus is the Christ (the Messiah, or anointed one) and believe in Him

Know God's Role in Witnessing. Christians who witness for Christ can be assured of success because God is with them. Look up each passage below and explain in your own words the things that are God's concern, not ours, in witnessing.

12. John 14:26 *The Holy Spirit will guide us into all truth. Discuss John 16:13-14.*

13. John 15:26 *The Holy Spirit will testify of Christ.*

14. John 6:44 *No man can come to Christ on his own (because man is spiritually dead), but the Father must first draw him.*

15. Acts 1:8*a* *God will give us power through the Holy Spirit.*

16. II Timothy 1:7 *God will take away our fear and give us power, love, and a sound mind.*

17. John 16:7-12 *The Holy Spirit will convict of the sin of unbelief and convince sinners of the true nature of Christ and the certainty of judgment.*

18. I Corinthians 3:5-8 *God will cause fruit to grow from seeds sown by believers; if no one responds to our witness, then we have still done our duty.*

19. Ephesians 2:1 *God will quicken (give life to) spiritually dead sinners.*

Geography

Demographic Statistics

The sections on "Demography" in your textbook have several tables that illustrate demographic statistics. Find the tables and answer the questions about them. *Many of these questions appear in the teacher's manual. They are provided here in case you do not prefer to ask them orally.*

Population Growth Statistics, p. 101

1. Which of the listed countries has the highest crude birth rate?   *Bangladesh*

2. Which country has the highest crude death rate?   *Russia*

3. Which country has the highest rate of natural increase?   *Mexico*

4. Which countries have a negative rate of natural increase?   *Germany, Russia*

5. Contrast the natural increase for developed and developing countries.   *lower rates in developed countries (0.5–0.6 versus 1.0–2.1)*

Do you see any differences between the death rates for developed and developing countries? Explain what you see.   *There are no clear patterns. Modern medicine has wiped out some of the differences in death rates. Developing countries usually have a higher infant mortality, but developed countries typically have a larger elderly population that boosts their death rate.*

Ten Most Populous Countries, p. 104

6. Which country is the most populous?   *China*

7. Which country has the largest area?   *Russia*

8. Which country has the highest population density per square mile?   *Bangladesh*

9. Which country has the highest physiological density per square mile?   *Japan*

10. Compare this list to the ten largest countries on page 96. Which countries appear on both lists?

    Russia, China, United States, Brazil, and India

Can you guess why five nations do not appear on both lists?   *The total amount of arable land (area times percent arable land) is relatively small in these five countries. (Direct students to these five countries in the following table.)*

Complete the missing information on the table below.

Country	Crude Birthrate	Crude Death Rate	Rate of Natural Increase
Honduras	33	6	*2.7*
Kazakhstan	19	10	*0.9*
Netherlands	12	*9*	0.3
Sweden	10	*11*	−0.1
Vietnam	*22*	7	1.6

Below is a chart of the world's largest cities, according to the United Nations's definition of "urban agglomerations." Find the cities on the map on pages 106-7, and then answer the questions about the table.

Fifteen Largest Cities			
City	Pop.	Pop. Growth Rate	% of Total Pop.
1. Tokyo, Japan	26,959,000	1.5%	22%
2. Mexico City, Mexico	16,562,000	1.8%	18%
3. São Paulo, Brazil	16,533,000	1.8%	10%
4. New York City, U.S.A.	16,332,000	0.3%	6%
5. Bombay, India	15,138,000	4.2%	2%
6. Shanghai, China	13,584,000	0.4%	1%
7. Seoul, South Korea	12,609,000	1.9%	26%
8. Los Angeles, U.S.A.	12,410,000	1.6%	5%
9. Calcutta, India	11,923,000	1.8%	1%
10. Buenos Aires, Argentina	11,802,000	1.2%	34%
11. Beijing, China	11,299,000	0.9%	1%
12. Osaka, Japan	10,609,000	0.2%	8%
13. Lagos, Nigeria	10,287,000	5.7%	9%
14. Rio de Janeiro, Brazil	10,181,000	1.0%	6%
15. Delhi, India	9,948,000	3.9%	1%

Projected Fifteen Largest Cities in 2015	
City	Population
1. Tokyo, Japan	28,800,000
2. Bombay, India	26,200,000
3. Lagos, Nigeria	24,600,000
4. São Paulo, Brazil	20,300,000
5. Dhaka, Bangladesh	19,400,000
6. Karachi, Pakistan	19,300,000
7. Mexico City, Mexico	19,100,000
8. Shanghai, China	17,900,000
9. New York City, U.S.A.	17,600,000
10. Calcutta, India	17,300,000
11. Delhi, India	16,800,000
12. Beijing, China	15,500,000
13. Manila, Philippines	14,600,000
14. Cairo, Egypt	14,400,000
15. Los Angeles, U.S.A.	14,200,000

11. How many cities listed on the chart are in the Western Hemisphere? *five*

12. How many European cities are on the list? *none*

13. Which of these cities are in developed nations? *Tokyo, New York City, Los Angeles*

14. Which city is home to one-third of the nation's total population? *Buenos Aires*

15. Which city is projected to double its population by 2015? *Lagos*

16. What four cities will drop off the list of the fifteen largest cities by 2015? *Seoul, Buenos Aires, Osaka, Rio de Janeiro*

Calculate the population density and physiological density for each country in the table below. To find population density, divide population by the area. To find physiological density, divide population density by the percent arable land.

Country	Population	Area (sq. mi.)	Percent Arable Land	Population Density (per sq. mi.)	Physiological Density (per sq. mi.)
Canada	29,000,000	3,849,674	9%	*8*	*84*
Honduras	6,000,000	43,433	14%	*138*	*987*
Kenya	29,000,000	224,961	3%	*129*	*4,297*
Venezuela	22,000,000	352,144	3%	*62*	*2,082*
Vietnam	75,000,000	127,816	22%	*587*	*2,667*

Geography

Politics

Complete the chart, which classifies all basic types of government. Then answer the questions that follow.

Type of Government	Definition
I. Anarchy	*no government (p. 107)*
II. Authoritarian Government	*a government that holds power by claiming an authority higher than the people it governs (p. 108)*
A. Absolute Monarchy	*rule by a monarch who receives his authority by birth and rules as he pleases (p. 108)*
B. Dictatorship	*rule by a dictator who rules by the authority of the military (pp. 108-9)*
C. Totalitarian Government	*rule by leaders who believe they should make decisions about every detail of their people's lives for the good of the whole (p. 109)*
III. Elected Government	*a government that relies on the consent of the people to keep its position (p. 109)*
A. Direct (Pure) Democracy	*a government in which the whole population rules (p. 109)*
B. Indirect (Representative) Democracy	*a government that gives the people an opportunity to vote for politicians of their choice, to voice their opinions, and to run for office (p. 109)*
1. Constitutional Monarchy	*a government whose monarch's power is limited by law and whose real power belongs to an elected legislature; the leader of the legislature heads the bureaucracy (p. 109)*
2. Republic	*a government that elects both a legislature and a separate national leader (president) who supervises the bureaucracy (p. 109)*

1. What are the two basic duties of government?   *justice and defense (p. 108)*

2. What three types of countries are the main concern of U.S. foreign policy: (1) the seven world powers that spend the most on military technology, (2) ___*militarized (p. 110)*___ states that spend a large percentage of their GDP on weapons and (3) ___*rogue (p. 110)*___ nations that ignore fundamental principles of international relations.

3. What are the two basic types of treaties?   *peace treaty and military alliance (pp. 110-11)*

4. Name the five members of the UN Security Council.   *United States, United Kingdom, France, China, Russia (p. 111)*

5. Contrast the right of self-determination and the right of territorial integrity.   *the belief that all peoples have a right to vote for the type of government they will have; the right of every nation to defensible borders even if they must ignore the wishes of a minority for self-government (p. 112)*

Geography

Modified True/False

If the statement is true, write the word *true* in the blank. If it is false, change the underlined words to make the statement true.

Culture (p. 86)	1. <u>Dialect</u> is a society's total way of life.
true (p. 87)	2. The world is divided into <u>eight</u> main culture regions.
convergence (p. 99)	3. The growing similarity between cultures is called cultural <u>divergence</u>.
true (p. 88)	4. The man-centered system of thinking that began at Babel is known as <u>humanism</u>.
dialects (p. 89)	5. Regional variations in the speech patterns of a single language are called <u>language families</u>.
Indo-European (p. 89)	6. The most widely spoken language family is <u>Austro-Asiatic</u>.
true (p. 91)	7. Developed countries usually have a <u>high</u> literacy rate.
a nuclear (pp. 91–92)	8. A man, his wife, and their children make up <u>an extended</u> family.
true (p. 92)	9. Religious statistics usually list <u>Eastern</u> religions as one of the five major religious groups.
ancient (p. 96)	10. Most of the world culture regions arose during the <u>medieval</u> period of history.
Imperialism (p. 98)	11. Europeans fought each other to establish empires over the peoples of Asia and Africa during the Age of <u>Exploration</u>.
true (p. 99)	12. <u>Nationalism</u> is the Enlightened concept that every nation has a right to establish its own government.
census (p. 101)	13. A <u>survey</u> is an official government count of the entire population of a nation.
crude death rate (p. 101)	14. The rate of natural increase is calculated by subtracting <u>life expectancy</u> from the crude birthrate.
true (p. 105)	15. Physiological density compares the population to the amount of <u>arable land</u> in a country.
true (p. 109)	16. A Communist government is one form of <u>totalitarian</u> government.
a republic (p. 109)	17. The United States government is an example of <u>anarchy</u>.
NATO (p. 111)	18. The <u>United Nations</u> was the most successful military alliance of the twentieth century.
true (p. 95)	19. The United States shares a <u>geometric</u> boundary with Canada.
true (p. 110)	20. Radical Muslim nations that ignore fundamental principles of international relations are known as <u>rogue nations</u>.

Geography

A Second Look: The World as Man Subdues It

List the four main phases in the earth's history.

1. _Creation_

2. _Flood_

3. _modern world_

4. _future world_

List the seven continents in the first column. List the eight culture regions in the second column.

5. _Asia_

6. _Africa_

7. _North America_

8. _South America_

9. _Antarctica_

10. _Europe_

11. _Australia_

12. _Africa_

13. _Asia_

14. _Central Eurasia_

15. _Europe_

16. _Latin America_

17. _Middle East_

18. _Northern America_

19. _Oceania_

20-23. On the map, label the equator, Tropics, Temperate Zones, and polar regions.

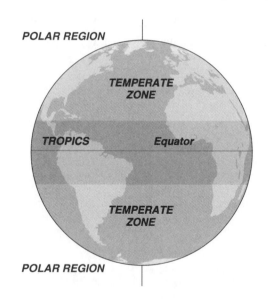

Underline the word or phrase that best completes each sentence.

24. The two main branches of geography are human and (physical, <u>systematic</u>).

25. Rain that falls when a humid air mass moves over mountains is (<u>orographic</u>, convection) precipitation.

26. The smallest ocean in the world is the (Indian, <u>Arctic</u>).

27. Agriculture is a (<u>primary</u>, secondary) industry.

28. Urbanization is a (vital, <u>community</u>) statistic.

Give the term that fits each description.

29. aluminum ore   *bauxite*

30. economic system under which individuals or corporations build most industries   *capitalism*

31. goods received from other countries   *imports*

32. the order from the Lord to subdue the earth   *dominion mandate*

33. the order from the Lord to fill the earth with people   *cultural mandate*

Use geography terms to complete the paragraph on culture.

(34) _____*Culture*_____ is a society's total way of life. God's division of languages at (35) _____*Babel*_____ became the foundation of separate cultures. Today the most widely spoken language family is (36) _____*Indo-European*_____ . There are four basic types of institutions that transmit culture—the family, (37) _____*religion*_____ , volunteer community organizations, and the nation. In general, Western institutions worship the individual, while Eastern institutions worship the (38) _____*group*_____ . Western societies focus on the (39) _____*nuclear*_____ family—a man, his wife, and their children, but Eastern societies focus on the (40) _____*extended*_____ family.

Geography

Map of the Northeastern United States

Refer to the relief map on page 117 to complete the map below.

1. Label these features of physical geography:
   Rivers—Allegheny River, Connecticut River, Delaware River, Hudson River, Mohawk River
   Bays—Chesapeake Bay, Delaware Bay, Massachusetts Bay
   Mountains—Adirondack Mountains, Berkshire Hills, Green Mountains, White Mountains
   Miscellaneous—Aroostook Valley, Delmarva Peninsula, Niagara Falls, Pine Barrens

2. Label these features of human geography:
   Cities—Baltimore, Boston, New York City, Philadelphia, Washington, D.C.
   Miscellaneous—Erie Canal

3. Label all the states and their capitals in the Northeastern United States.

4. Label the Mason-Dixon Line and trace over it in red. (See interest box on p. 136)

Optional Activities *Answers are found in the running text of the chapter.*

5. Draw these figures in the appropriate state.

   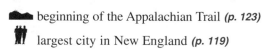 beginning of the Appalachian Trail *(p. 123)*    largest city in the United States *(p. 126)*

   largest city in New England *(p. 119)*   Cradle of American Industry (state) *(p. 120)*

6. Draw these figures in the appropriate location.

   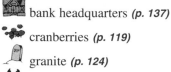 bank headquarters *(p. 137)*   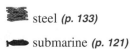 steel *(p. 133)*

   cranberries *(p. 119)*   submarine *(p. 121)*

   granite *(p. 124)*   truck farms *(p. 135)*

   lobster *(p. 125)*

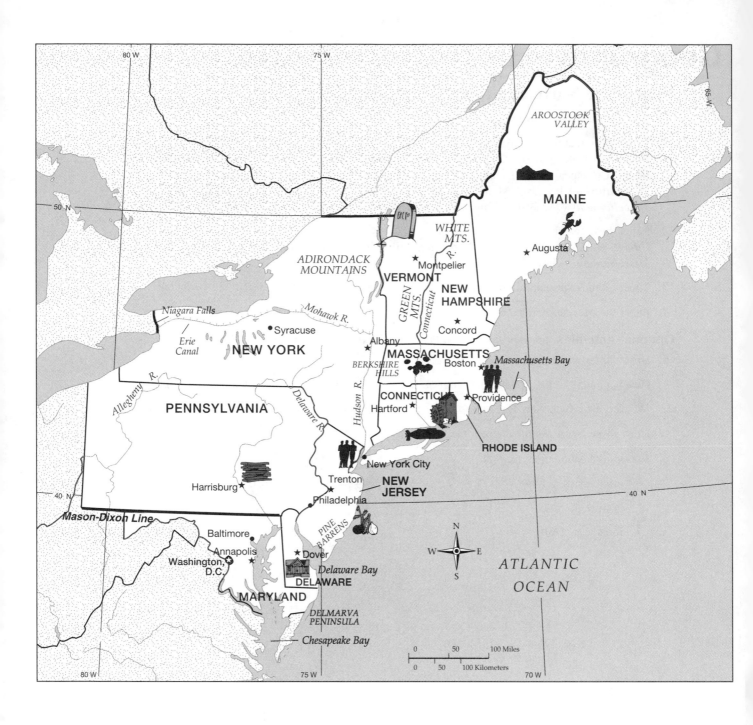

80 W · 75 W · 50 N · 40 N · 40 N · 75 W · 70 W · 65 W

AROOSTOOK
VALLEY

MAINE

Augusta

WHITE
MTS.

ADIRONDACK
MOUNTAINS

Montpelier

VERMONT

NEW
HAMPSHIRE

Connecticut R.

GREEN MTS.

Concord

Niagara Falls

Mohawk R.

Erie
Canal

Syracuse

NEW YORK

Albany

MASSACHUSETTS

Boston

Massachusetts Bay

BERKSHIRE
HILLS

Allegheny R.

Delaware R.

Hudson R.

CONNECTICUT

Hartford

Providence

RHODE ISLAND

PENNSYLVANIA

New York City

Trenton

NEW
JERSEY

Harrisburg

Philadelphia

40 N

Mason-Dixon Line

Baltimore

PINE
BARRENS

Annapolis

Washington,
D.C.

Dover

Delaware Bay

DELAWARE

MARYLAND

DELMARVA
PENINSULA

Chesapeake Bay

ATLANTIC
OCEAN

N
W   E
S

0   50   100 Miles

0   50   100 Kilometers

Geography

Taking a Closer Look at Cultural Subregions

Beginning with this chapter, your book is organized by geographic regions and subregions, not by periods of history or by general subjects. You need to become familiar with this type of outlining because it will help you find information and study for tests.

Culture Regions of Northern America

The culture maps at the beginning of each unit give you valuable clues about the outline of the chapters. Look at the culture map of Northern America on page 114. Then answer the following questions.

1. What are the two main subregions of Northern America? (Hint: Each is a country.) __*United States,*__

    Canada

2. The United States is divided into what four subregions? (Hint: Each is the title of a separate chapter.)

    Northeast,   South,   Midwest,   West

3. The Northeastern United States is divided into what two subregions? (Hint: These subregions form the

    two **master headings** in Chapter 6, found on pages 116 and 125.) *New England,   Middle Atlantic*

Cultural Subregions of the Northeast

The headings within each chapter point you to ever-smaller cultural subregions. One of the most obvious cultural boundaries is state borders (because residents of each state follow different laws and leaders). But there are other regional divisions as well.

A Closer Look at New England

4. New England is divided into what two subregions? (Hint: These subregions form the two **a-level**

    headings under New England, found on pages 118 and 122.) *Lower New England,   Upper New*

    England

5. Lower New England is divided into what three states? (Hint: These subregions form the **b-level**

    headings under lower New England, found on pages 119-21.) *Massachusetts,   Rhode Island,*

    Connecticut

6. Upper New England is divided into what three states? (Hint: These subregions form the **b-level**

    headings under upper New England, found on pages 122-24.) *New Hampshire,   Vermont,   Maine*

A Closer Look at the Middle Atlantic

7. The Middle Atlantic is divided into what *four* subregions? (Hint: These subregions form the four

    a-level headings under the Middle Atlantic, found on pages 126, 133, 136, and 138.) *New York,*

    States on the Delaware River,   Border States,   District of Columbia

8. How is the outline of New York different from all the other states in the chapter? Give the two main

    subregions of New York. *New York is an a-level heading all by itself, but the others are b-level headings;*

    the two main subregions are the megalopolis (N.Y. metropolitan area) and the Upstate.

Geographic Subregions Within Each Northeastern State

The breakdown of the Northeast into cultural subregions does not end at the state level. Every state is divided into geographic subregions. But these subregions rarely have a heading, so you must look for them within the paragraphs. Understanding how paragraphs are organized will help you find the key points under each heading. Look at the map on page 147 and answer these questions about the Northeastern states.

9. What are the three geographic subregions in New England states? __Coastal Lowlands,   New England Upland,   Appalachian Mountains__

10. List the four New England states that include all three subregions above. __Massachusetts, Connecticut,   New Hampshire,   Maine__

11. List the two New England states that include only two geographic subregions. Give the subregions within each state. __Rhode Island—Coastal Lowlands and New England Upland, Vermont—New England Upland and Appalachian Mountains__

12. New York is divided into five main geographic regions. The megalopolis is located in the Atlantic coastal plain and in the Piedmont. Name three other geographic regions in New York. __Appalachian Mountains (and Adirondacks),   Allegheny (Appalachian) Plateau,   Great Lakes (Central) Plain__

13. Delaware has only two geographic regions. Name them. __Atlantic Coastal Plain,   Piedmont__

Culture Map of the Northeastern United States

When you read about cultural subregions, it helps to see the divisions on a map. Follow the directions below to create your own "Culture Map of the Northeastern United States." It should look like a mini-version of the "Culture Map of Northern America" on page 114.

14. Color New England in red, and color the Middle Atlantic in blue; then label these two regions (putting the name out in the ocean next to the region).

15. Label the following subregions, and draw thick, black lines to separate them: Lower New England, Upper New England, New York, States on the Delaware River, Border States, and the District of Columbia.

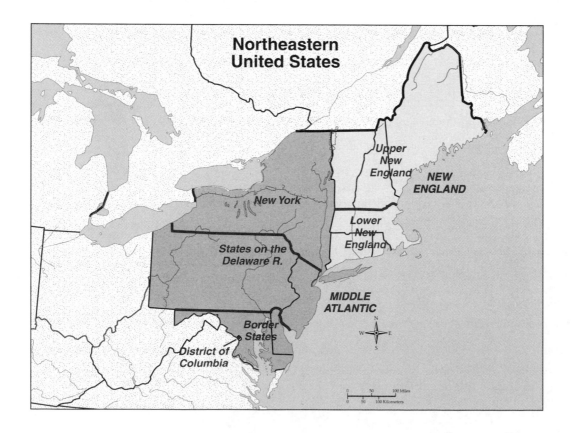

Geography

Franklin and Emerson

The Northeast produced several writers whose works left a lasting mark on the ideas of American culture. Among the most influential were Benjamin Franklin and Ralph Waldo Emerson. With the spread of U.S. culture around the world, these men's ideas have literally changed the world. Read the following excerpts and answer the questions that follow.

Benjamin Franklin's *The Way to Wealth*

Perhaps the most influential American writer of the eighteenth century was Benjamin Franklin, a Philadelphia printer who grew rich publishing Poor Richard's Almanac. His sayings have entered everyday speech—"Time is money," "God helps them that help themselves," and "Little strokes fell great oaks." Franklin compiled the most famous sayings of "Poor Richard" in *The Way to Wealth,* published in 1758. It sets forth Franklin's commonsense ideals that came to dominate Yankee thinking.

It would be thought a hard government that should tax its people one-tenth part of their time, to be employed in its service. But idleness taxes many of us much more, if we reckon all that is spent in absolute sloth, or doing of nothing, with that which is spent in idle employments or amusements, that amount to nothing. *Sloth, like rust, consumes faster than labor wears; while the used key is always bright,* as Poor Richard says. *But dost thou love life, then do not squander time, for that's the stuff life is made of,* as Poor Richard says. . . .

If we are industrious, we shall never starve; for, as *Poor Richard says, At the working man's house hunger looks in, but dares not enter.* . . . But with our industry, we must likewise be steady, settled, and careful, and oversee our own affairs with our own eyes, and not trust too much to others; for, as Poor Richard says,

I never saw an oft-removed [moved many times] tree,
Nor yet an oft-removed family,
That throve so well as those that settled be.

And again, *Three removes is as bad as a fire;* and again, *Keep thy shop, and thy shop will keep thee;* and again, *If you would have your business done, go; if not, send.* And again. . . . *Not to oversee workmen, is to leave them your purse open.* Trusting too much to other's care is the ruin of many; for, as the Almanac says, *In the affairs of this world, men are saved, not by faith, but by the want of it* . . . and farther, *If you would have a faithful servant, and one that you like, serve yourself.*

Ralph Waldo Emerson's "Self-Reliance"

Ralph Waldo Emerson was one of the most influential American writers and thinkers of the nineteenth century. Born in Boston in 1803, he was educated at Harvard and Cambridge, and he served as a Unitarian minister for a few years. After he left the church, he gave lectures and wrote essays on transcendentalism, a belief that man is good, the Bible is irrelevant, an "over-soul" pervades the world, and truth can be found apart from the five senses—in nature. His essay "Self-Reliance," which details his doctrine of individualism, greatly influenced American thought.

In the first paragraph, Emerson argues that every man must choose for himself what principles he will live by. In the second famous paragraph he argues that our search for truth requires us to be free to change our minds from day to day. The third paragraph defends a radical individualism that rejects all ties to family and friends. Who has the right to stand in the way of an individual's quest for truth?

Warn students that Emerson is hard to read. Two or three readings are required to make the meaning clear.

Whoso would be a man, must be a nonconformist. He who would gather immortal palms must not be hindered by the name of goodness, but must explore if it be goodness. Nothing is at last sacred but the integrity of our own mind. Absolve you to yourself, and you shall have the suffrage [approval] of the world. I remember an answer which when quite young I was prompted to make to a valued

adviser who was wont to [accustomed to] importune [harass] me with the dear old doctrines of the church. On my saying, "What have I to do with the sacredness of traditions, if I live wholly from within?" my friend suggested,—"But these impulses may be from below, not from above." I replied, "They do not seem to me to be such; but if I am the devil's child, I will live then from the devil." No law can be sacred to me but that of my nature. Good and bad are but names very readily transferable to that or this; the only right is what is after my constitution; the only wrong what is against it.

A foolish consistency is the hobgoblin of little minds, adored by little statesmen and philosophers and divines [gods]. With consistency a great soul has simply nothing to do. He may as well concern himself with his shadow on the wall. Out upon your guarded lips! Sew them up with packthread, do. Else if you would be a man speak what you think today in words as hard as cannon balls, and tomorrow speak what tomorrow thinks in hard words again, though it contradict every thing you said today. Ah, then, exclaim the aged ladies, you shall be sure to be misunderstood! Misunderstood! It is a right fool's word. Is it so bad then to be misunderstood? Pythagoras [Greek philosopher] was misunderstood, and Socrates, and Jesus, and Luther, and Copernicus, and Galileo, and Newton, and every pure and wise spirit that ever took flesh. To be great is to be misunderstood. . . .

Check this lying hospitality and lying affection. Live no longer to the expectation of these deceived and deceiving people with whom we converse. Say to them, O father, O mother, O wife, O brother, O friend, I have lived with you after appearances hitherto. Henceforward I am the truth's. Be it known unto you that henceforward I obey no law less than the eternal law. I will have no covenants but proximities. I shall endeavor to nourish my parents, to support my family, to be the chaste husband of one wife—but these relations I must fill after a new and unprecedented way. I appeal from your customs. I must be myself. I cannot break myself any longer for you, or you. If you can love me for what I am, we shall be happier. If you cannot, I will still seek to deserve that you should. I must be myself. I will not hide my tastes or aversions. I will so trust that what is deep is holy, that I will do strongly before the sun and moon whatever inly rejoices me and the heart appoints. If you are noble, I will love you; if you are not, I will not hurt you and myself by hypocritical attentions. If you are true, but not in the same truth with me, cleave to your companions; I will seek my own. I do this not selfishly but humbly and truly. It is alike your interest, and mine, and all men's, however long we have dwelt in lies, to live in truth. Does this sound harsh today? You will soon love what is dictated by your nature as well as mine, and if we follow the truth it will bring us out safe at last.—But so may you give these friends pain. Yes, but I cannot sell my liberty and my power, to save their sensibility. Besides, all persons have their moments of reason, when they look out into the region of absolute truth; then will they justify me and do the same thing. . . .

Nothing can bring you peace but yourself. Nothing can bring you peace but the triumph of principles.

1. How does Franklin describe the Yankee work ethic? *industry (hard work), not being lazy, using your* *time wisely, doing the work yourself*

2. Both Franklin and Emerson write about trust. Whom do they believe you should trust the most?
   yourself

3. What good advice does Emerson give? *Don't conform to what others say; search out what is good.*

4. Explain why most of Emerson's advice is unbiblical. *He says to search out what is good using* *yourself, not God's Word, as the measure. If you believe something is good, then it is.*

5. Both Franklin and Emerson influenced American thought. What advice do they give that is still a part of American thought today? *Franklin—hard work is the way to wealth and success. Emerson—be true* *to yourself and follow your feelings.*

Geography

City Demographics

Below are tables for cities and metropolitan areas in each of the four regions of the United States. Under each category, color the highest number red and the lowest number blue. Then answer the questions that follow.

Students may enjoy a discussion of these charts in relation to the population map on page 128. You may want to refer to this activity in later chapters or save it for a later chapter.

Top-Ten Cities in the Northeast (city proper)

City	Population	Area (sq. mi.)	Pop. Growth Rate	Per Capita GDP	Pop. Density (per sq. mi.)
New York	7,333,253	309	0.1%	$30,896	23,740
Philadelphia	1,524,249	135	−3.9%	$26,959	11,282
Baltimore	702,979	81	−4.5%	$25,347	8,700
Washington	567,094	61	−6.6%	$30,824	9,236
Boston	547,725	48	−4.6%	$28,564	11,317
Pittsburgh	358,883	56	−3.0%	$24,071	6,455
Buffalo	312,965	41	−4.6%	$22,645	7,708
Newark	258,751	24	−6.0%	$32,346	10,872
Rochester	231,170	36	0.4%	$24,566	6,457
Jersey City	226,022	15	−1.1	$23,561	15,169

Top-Ten Metropolitan Areas in the Northeast

New York	19,800,000
Washington	7,050,000
Philadelphia	5,960,000
Boston	5,500,000
Pittsburgh	2,400,000
Buffalo	1,190,000
Hartford	1,150,000
Providence	1,130,000
Rochester	1,090,000
Albany	880,000

Top-Ten Cities in the South (city proper)

City	Population	Area (sq. mi.)	Pop. Growth Rate	Per Capita GDP	Pop. Density (per sq. mi.)
Houston	1,702,086	540	4.4%	$25,449	3,153
Dallas	1,022,830	342	1.5%	$26,803	2,987
San Antonio	998,905	333	6.8%	$20,034	3,000
Jacksonville	665,070	759	4.7%	$22,617	877
Memphis	614,289	256	−0.7%	$23,640	2,400
El Paso	579,307	245	12.4%	$13,702	2,361
Austin	514,013	218	10.4%	$22,185	2,360
Nashville	504,505	473	3.3%	$25,077	1,066
New Orleans	484,149	181	−2.6%	$21,374	2,681
Oklahoma City	463,201	608	4.2%	$20,139	762

Top Metropolitan Areas in the South (over one million population)

Dallas	4,360,000
Houston	4,100,000
Miami	3,410,000
Atlanta	3,330,000
Tampa	2,160,000
Norfolk	1,530,000
San Antonio	1,440,000
Orlando	1,360,000
New Orleans	1,310,000
Charlotte	1,260,000
Greensboro	1,110,000
Nashville	1,070,000
Memphis	1,060,000
Oklahoma City	1,010,000

Top-Ten Cities in the Midwest (city proper)

City	Population	Area (sq. mi.)	Pop. Growth Rate	Per Capita GDP	Pop. Density (per sq. mi.)
Chicago	2,731,743	227	–1.9%	$28,177	12,024
Detroit	992,038	139	–3.5%	$26,889	7,152
Indianapolis	752,279	362	2.9%	$24,664	2,080
Columbus	635,913	191	0.5%	$24,132	3,331
Milwaukee	617,044	96	–1.8%	$25,906	6,421
Cleveland	492,901	77	–2.5%	$25,303	6,401
Kansas City, Mo.	443,878	312	2.1%	$24,576	1,425
St. Louis, Mo.	368,215	62	–7.2%	$25,170	5,948
Cincinnati	358,170	77	–1.6%	$24,199	4,640
Minneapolis	354,590	55	–3.7%	$27,436	6,459

Top Ten Metropolitan Areas in the Midwest (over one million population)

Chicago	8,530,000
Detroit	5,260,000
Cleveland	2,900,000
Minneapolis	2,690,000
St. Louis	2,540,000
Cincinnati	1,890,000
Kansas City	1,650,000
Milwaukee	1,640,000
Indianapolis	1,460,000
Columbus	1,420,000

Top-Ten Cities in the West (city proper)

City	Population	Area (sq. mi.)	Pop. Growth Rate	Per Capita GDP	Pop. Density (per sq. mi.)
Los Angeles	3,448,613	469	–1.1%	$23,501	7,348
San Diego	1,151,977	324	3.7%	$23,263	3,555
Phoenix	1,048,949	420	6.6%	$21,839	2,498
San Jose	816,884	171	4.4%	$31,487	4,769
San Francisco	734,676	47	1.5%	$36,989	15,732
Seattle	520,947	84	0.9%	$28,773	6,209
Denver	493,559	153	5.5%	$27,069	3,220
Portland	450,777	125	2.7%	$24,553	3,615
Tucson	434,726	156	6.4%	$19,556	2,781
Long Beach	433,852	50	1.1%	$23,501	8,677

Top Ten Metropolitan Areas in the West (over one million population)

Los Angeles	15,300,000
San Francisco–San Jose	6,510,000
Seattle	3,230,000
San Diego	2,500,000
Phoenix	2,470,000
Denver	2,190,000
Portland	1,980,000
Sacramento	1,590,000
Salt Lake City	1,180,000
Las Vegas	1,080,000

Compare all the cities (city proper) to find the city that fits each description below.

1. largest area   __Jacksonville (759 sq. mi.)__

2. highest population growth rate   __El Paso (12.4%)__

3. lowest population growth rate (negative number)   __St. Louis, Missouri (–7.2%)__

4. highest per capita GDP   __San Francisco ($36,989)__

5. highest population density   __New York (23,740 people per sq. mi.)__

6. lowest population density   __Oklahoma City (762 people per sq. mi.)__

Compare the cities (city proper) and name the U.S. region (Northeast, South, Midwest, West) that fits each description below.

7. most cities with a population above 1,000,000 _West (three)_

8. most cities with a population above 500,000 _South (eight)_

9. most cities with a per capita GDP above $26,000 _Northeast (five)_

10. most cities with a per capita GDP below $22,000 _South (four)_

11. most cities with a population growth rate above 3.0% _South (seven)_

12. most cities with a population growth rate below 0% _Midwest (eight)_

13. most cities with a population density above 6,000 people per sq. mi. _Northeast (ten)_

14. most cities with a population density below 3,500 people per sq. mi. _South (ten)_

Compare the metropolitan areas and name the U.S. region (Northeast, South, Midwest, West) that fits each description below.

15. most metro areas above 4,000,000 _Northeast (four)_

16. most metro areas above 1,000,000 _South (fourteen)_

Use the tables above to compile a list of the top-ten cities and metropolitan areas in the entire United States. Next, under each category, color the highest number red and the lowest number blue. Then answer the questions that follow.

Top-Ten Cities in the United States (city proper)					
City	Population	Area (sq. mi.)	Pop. Growth Rate	Per Capita GDP	Pop. Density (per sq. mi.)
1. New York	7,333,253	309	0.1%	$30,896	23,740
2. Los Angeles	3,448,613	469	–1.1%	$23,501	7,348
3. Chicago	2,731,743	227	–1.9%	$28,177	12,024
4. Houston	1,702,086	540	4.4%	$25,449	3,153
5. Philadelphia	1,524,249	135	–3.9%	$26,959	11,282
6. San Diego	1,151,977	324	3.7%	$23,263	3,555
7. Phoenix	1,048,949	420	6.6%	$21,839	2,498
8. Dallas	1,022,830	342	1.5%	$26,803	2,987
9. San Antonio	998,905	333	6.8%	$20,034	3,000
10. Detroit	992,038	139	–3.5%	$26,889	7,152

Top Ten Metropolitan Areas in the United States	
1. New York	19,800,000
2. Los Angeles	15,300,000
3. Chicago	8,530,000
4. Washington	7,050,000
5. San Francisco	6,510,000
6. Philadelphia	5,960,000
7. Boston	5,500,000
8. Detroit	5,260,000
9. Dallas	4,360,000
10. Houston	4,100,000

17. How many of the top-ten cities (city proper) are in the Northeast? _two_

18. How many of the top-ten metropolitan areas are in the Northeast? _four_

19. Which of the top-ten metropolitan areas are not even on the list of top cities? Why might this be so?

Washington, San Francisco, and Boston; these cities are relatively small, but they have numerous

suburbs and sister cities.

Geography

Where Am I?

Read each phrase and decide the place it describes. Write the correct answer in the blank.

Erie Canal (p. 130)	1. canal that made New York the trade capital of the world
New England uplands (p. 118)	2. low, rocky plateau in Massachusetts and Connecticut
Piedmont (p. 126)	3. low, hilly plateau near the coast of the Middle Atlantic
Aroostook Valley (p. 125)	4. potato-producing valley in Maine
Manhattan (p. 129)	5. borough with the main skyscrapers of New York City
Connecticut (p. 121)	6. the Constitution State
Maryland (p. 137)	7. border state on the Chesapeake Bay
Berkshire Hills (p. 120)	8. hills of Massachusetts
Green Mountains (p. 124)	9. mountains of Vermont
White Mountains (p. 122)	10. mountains of New Hampshire
Maine (pp. 124–25)	11. last state in upper New England to join the Union
Pennsylvania (p. 133)	12. state known for steel
Vermont (p. 124)	13. state with the lowest population in the Northeast
Rhode Island (p. 120)	14. state where the textile industry began
Delaware River (p. 133)	15. river that divides Pennsylvania and New Jersey
Finger Lakes (p. 132)	16. lakes in New York's Allegheny Plateau
Pine Barrens (p. 135)	17. wooded wilderness in New Jersey

What Am I?

Read each phrase and decide the thing it describes. Write the correct answer in the blank.

alpine zone (p. 122)	18. area above the timber line with stunted vegetation
township (p. 118)	19. political division in New England that allowed local communities to run their own affairs
Smithsonian Institution (p. 139)	20. largest museum in America
mass production (p. 121)	21. efficient industrial process developed by Eli Whitney
notch (p. 122)	22. New England term for a pass through a mountain range
suburb (p. 127)	23. residential community outside the city proper
Fall Line (p. 126)	24. line where the Piedmont drops to the coastal plain
monadnock (p. 123)	25. any solitary mountain
panhandle (p. 138)	26. part of a state that forms a long, narrow strip

Geography

Map of the Southern United States

Refer to the relief map on page 143 to complete the map on the next page.

1. Label these features of physical geography:
   Rivers—Mississippi River, Red River, Rio Grande, Tennessee River
   Mountains—Appalachian Mountains, Great Smoky Mountains
   Miscellaneous—Atlantic Coastal Plain, Bluegrass, Cumberland Plateau, Everglades (p. 190), Gulf Coastal Plain, Ozark Plateau

2. Label these cities—Dallas, Houston, Memphis, Miami, New Orleans

3. Label all the states and their capitals in the Southern United States.

4. Look at the map of the "War Between the States" on page 143. Shade blue the state in the Southern United States that was a Union state during the American Civil War. Shade yellow the state that was a border state.

5. Look at the religion map on page 151. Shade orange those sections of the Southern United States that are predominately Roman Catholic.

Optional Activities *Answers are found in the running text of the chapter.*

6. Draw these figures in the appropriate state.

   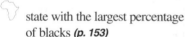 main Confederate capital *(p. 144)*

   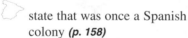 highest mountain east of the Mississippi *(p. 146)*

    state with the most Indians *(p. 164)*

    state with the largest percentage of blacks *(p. 153)*

   state that was once a Spanish colony *(p. 158)*

    Cajuns *(p. 162)*

   state with the most Civil War battles *(p. 145)*

    $ state with the highest per capita GDP *(p. 144)*

   largest city in the Upper South *(pp. 152–53)*

   largest city in the South (city proper) *(p. 165)*

7. Draw these figures in the appropriate location.

    thoroughbred horses *(p. 149)*

   Z zinc *(p. 152)*

    peanuts *(p. 156)*

    catfish *(p. 158)*

   oranges *(p. 160)*

    chicken *(p. 162)*

    helium *(p. 164)*

    beef *(p. 165)*

   sheep *(p. 166)*

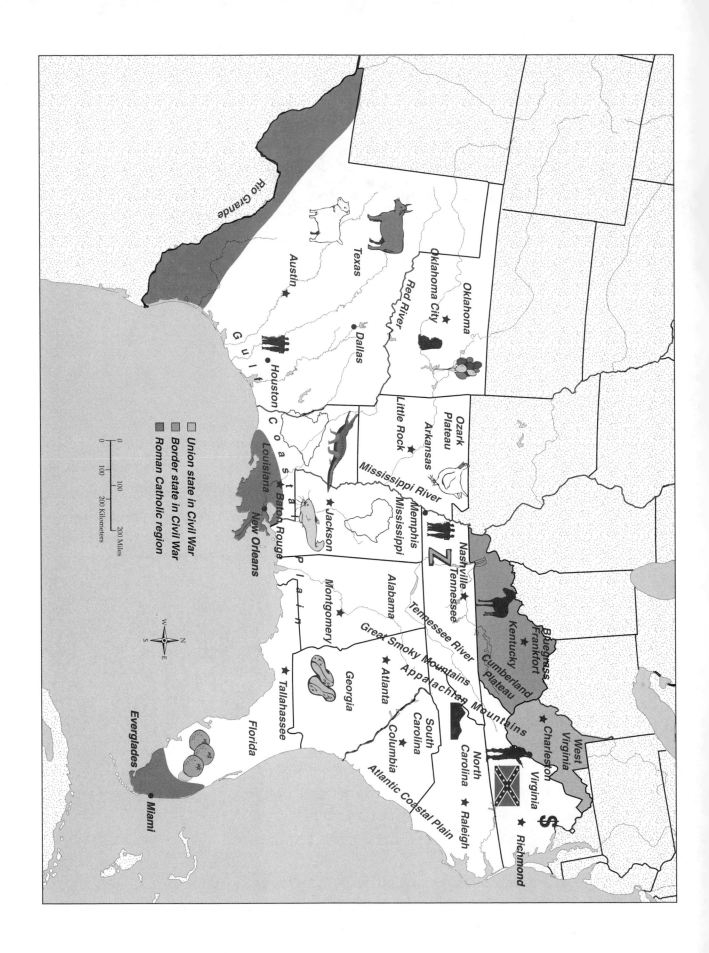

Union state in Civil War
Border state in Civil War
Roman Catholic region

0   100   200 Miles
0   100   200 Kilometers

Rio Grande

Texas
Austin
Dallas
Houston
Gulf Coastal Plain

Oklahoma
Oklahoma City
Red River

Ozark Plateau
Arkansas
Little Rock
Mississippi River

Mississippi
Memphis
Jackson

Louisiana
Baton Rouge
New Orleans

Alabama
Montgomery
Great Smoky Mountains

Georgia
Atlanta

Tennessee
Nashville
Tennessee River
Appalachian Mountains

Kentucky
Frankfort
Cumberland Plateau
Bluegrass

West Virginia
Charleston
Virginia
Richmond

North Carolina
Raleigh
South Carolina
Columbia
Atlantic Coastal Plain

Florida
Tallahassee
Everglades
Miami

N
W   E
S

Geography

Name _____

Chapter 7   Activity 2

Plan a Trip—Distance Charts

Examine the distance chart and answer the questions that follow. *This activity is a building block for the unit project on planning an "Imaginary Vacation." (See page 115 in the teacher manual.)*

	Atlanta, Ga.	Boston, Mass.	Chicago, Ill.	Dallas, Tex.	Denver, Colo.	Detroit, Mich.	Houston, Tex.	Indianapolis, Ind.	Kansas City, Mo.	Los Angeles, Calif.	Memphis, Tenn.	Milwaukee, Wisc.	New Orleans, La.	New York, N.Y.	Philadelphia, Pa.	Pittsburgh, Pa.	San Francisco, Calif.	Seattle, Wash.	Tulsa, Okla.	Washington, D.C.
Atlanta, Ga.		1037	674	795	1398	699	789	493	798	2182	371	761	479	841	741	687	2496	2618	772	608
Boston, Mass.	1037		994	1748	1949	695	1804	906	1391	2979	1296	1050	1507	206	296	574	3095	2976	1537	429
Chicago, Ill.	674	994		917	996	266	1067	181	499	2054	530	87	912	802	738	452	2142	2013	683	671
Dallas, Tex.	795	1748	917		781	1143	243	865	489	1387	452	991	496	1552	1452	1204	1753	2078	257	1319
Denver, Colo.	1398	1949	996	781		1253	1019	1058	606	1059	1040	1029	1273	1771	1691	1411	1235	1307	681	1616
Detroit, Mich.	699	695	266	1143	1253		1265	278	743	2311	713	353	1045	637	573	287	2399	2279	909	506
Houston, Tex.	789	1804	1067	243	1019	1265		987	710	1538	561	1142	356	1608	1508	1313	1912	2274	478	1375
Indianapolis, Ind.	493	906	181	865	1058	278	987		485	2073	435	268	796	713	633	353	2256	2194	631	558
Kansas City, Mo.	798	1391	499	489	600	743	710	485		1589	451	537	806	1198	1118	838	1835	1839	248	1043
Los Angeles, Calif.	2182	2979	2054	1387	1059	2311	1538	2073	1589		1817	2087	1883	2786	2706	2426	379	1131	1452	2631
Memphis, Tenn.	371	1296	530	452	1040	713	561	435	451	1817		612	390	1100	1000	752	2125	2290	401	867
Milwaukee, Wis.	761	1050	87	991	1029	353	1142	268	537	2087	612		994	889	825	539	2175	1940	757	758
New Orleans, La.	479	1507	912	496	1273	1045	356	796	806	1883	390	994		1311	1211	1070	2249	2574	647	1078
New York, N.Y.	841	206	802	1552	1771	637	1608	713	1198	2786	1100	889	1311		106	368	2934	2815	1344	233
Philadelphia, Pa.	741	296	738	1452	1691	573	1508	633	1118	2706	1000	825	1211	106		288	2866	2751	1264	143
Pittsburgh, Pa.	687	574	452	1204	1411	287	1313	353	838	2426	752	539	1070	368	288		2578	2465	984	221
San Francisco, Calif.	2496	3095	2142	1753	1235	2399	1912	2256	1835	379	2125	2175	2249	2934	2866	2578		808	1760	2799
Seattle, Wash.	2618	2976	2013	2078	1307	2279	2274	2194	1839	1131	2290	1940	2574	2815	2751	2465	808		1982	2684
Tulsa, Okla.	772	1537	683	257	681	909	478	631	248	1452	401	757	647	1344	1264	984	1760	1982		1189
Washington, D.C.	608	429	671	1319	1616	506	1375	558	1043	2631	867	758	1078	233	143	221	2799	2684	1189	

1. What is the farthest city from Atlanta?   *Seattle, Washington*

2. What is the closest city to Atlanta?   *Memphis, Tennessee*

3. How far is the trip from Atlanta to the U.S. capital?   *608 mi.*

4. How far is the trip from San Francisco to the U.S. capital?   *2799 mi.*

5. Why are some of the distances blank on the chart?   *Each city has an index to itself.*

6. If you live in Indianapolis and want to visit the South, which of the following cities would be closest: Atlanta, Dallas, Memphis, or New Orleans?   *Memphis*

7. If you travel 700 miles per day from San Francisco to the U.S. capital, how many days will your trip take?

    4 days

Enrichment: Sections 1-6   **Skill: Charts/Analysis**   57

8. If you travel from Denver to Atlanta in two days, stopping at a motel in Kansas City, how many miles will you be on the road each day?   _600 mi., 798 mi._

9. Pretend you live in Houston and want to take a trip to see four big cities in the Northeast—Washington, D.C.; Philadelphia; New York; and Boston. Answer the following questions about your trip.

   • How many miles will you travel on the way to Boston, stopping at the other cities along the way?

     _1375 + 143 + 106 + 206 = 1830 mi._

   • If you take the most direct route home from Boston, how many miles will you travel on the return trip?   _1804 mi._

   • If you travel a maximum of 460 miles per day, how many days will you spend traveling from your home to Washington, D.C.? How many days will the trip home from Boston take?   _1375/460 = 3 days;   1830/460 = 4 days_

   • After you reach Washington, D.C., you will want to stay two more days touring that city. You also want to set aside two days for each of the other cities (travel and touring time). How many days will the whole trip take?   _3 + 2 + 2 + 2 + 2 + 4 = 15 days_

Geography

Region Review

One of the most valuable lessons you can learn from each chapter is the scheme, or outline, of the regions. You can carry this scheme with you for the rest of your life. Once you know how to break the world down into a memorable scheme, then you will have a "mental file cabinet" where you can store current news about foreign countries or events in the United States. The more you know about each region, the easier it will be to understand the causes and probable consequences of current events.

Fill in the scheme below for the Southern United States. Give at least one characteristic that is distinctive about each region. (These distinctives are usually described in the paragraphs directly under the heading.) In the blanks under each state, write all the geographic regions in the state **using the map on page 147.**

I. The Upper South

Distinctive(s):   (1) The Upper South has five states with mountains that exceed four thousand feet. (2) Mountains have played a major role in the region's history.

A. The Tobacco States of the Atlantic

Distinctive(s):   (1) These two states of the original colonies in the South have a long coastline/shoreline on the Atlantic Coastal Plain. (2) The warm climate and fertile soil is ideal for growing tobacco.

1. Virginia

Geographic Regions

Atlantic Coastal Plain (Tidewater)

Piedmont

Appalachian Mountains

Appalachian Plateau

2. North Carolina

Geographic Regions

Atlantic Coastal Plain

Piedmont

Appalachian Mountains

B. Beyond the Appalachians

Distinctive(s):   *(1) Three Southern states have Appalachian Mountains but no coastline. (2) They share the Appalachian*

Plateau. (3) They share famous mountain traditions along with a struggle against poverty.

1. West Virginia

Geographic Regions

Appalachian Mountains

Appalachian (Allegheny) Plateau

2. Kentucky

Geographic Regions

Appalachian Mountains

Appalachian (Cumberland) Plateau

Bluegrass

Pennyroyal

Gulf Coastal (or Mississippi) Plain

3. Tennessee

Geographic Regions

Appalachian Mountains

Appalachian (Cumberland) Plateau

Nashville Basin

Mississippi Plain

II. The Lower South

Distinctive(s):   *(1) The region has five states with wide coastal plains along the Atlantic Ocean and Gulf of Mexico. (2) The economy, once based on cotton, has diversified. (3) This region was first to join the Confederacy and later became the focus of the civil rights movement.*

A. Colonial States of the Lower South

Distinctive(s): *(1) The colonial states of the Lower South were the farthest south of the original thirteen colonies, and (2) their ports on the Atlantic rivaled Boston and Philadelphia.*

1. South Carolina

Geographic Regions

Atlantic Coastal Plain

Piedmont

Appalachian Mountains

2. Georgia

Geographic Regions

Gulf Coastal Plain

Atlantic Coastal Plain

Piedmont

Appalachian Mountains

Cumberland Plateau

B. Gulf States

Distinctive(s): *(1) Alabama and Mississippi share the Gulf Coastal Plain and the Gulf Intercoastal Highway. (2) Both once were part of the Mississippi Territory.*

1. Alabama

Geographic Regions

Gulf Coastal Plain

Piedmont

Appalachian Mountains

Cumberland Plateau

Low Interior Plateau

2. Mississippi

Geographic Regions

Gulf Coastal Plain

Low Interior Plateau

C. Florida

Geographic Regions

Atlantic Coastal Plain

Gulf Coastal Plain

III. The South Central States

Distinctive(s): *(1) The four South Central states lie west of the Mississippi River and have weak ties to the Deep South. (2) Oil is the most important product.*

A. Louisiana

Geographic Region

Gulf Coastal Plain

B. Interior South Central States

Distinctive(s): *Both interior states lack coasts and share low mountain ranges unrelated to the Appalachians.*

1. Arkansas

Geographic Regions

Gulf Coastal Plain

Ozark Plateau

Ouachita Mountains

2. Oklahoma

Geographic Regions

Gulf Coastal Plain

Ozark Plateau

Ouachita Mountains

Central Plains

Great Plains

C. Texas

Geographic Regions

Gulf Coastal Plain

Central Plains

Great Plains

Rio Grande Basin (or Rockies)

Culture Map of the Southern United States

It helps to see the divisions of the South on a map. Follow the directions below to create your own "Culture Map of the Southern United States." It should look like a mini-version of the "Culture Map of Northern America" on page 114.

- Color the Upper South in yellow, the Lower South in red, and the South Central states in green. Then fill in the key with the correct colors.

- Draw the borders between the geographic regions in the South (found on the map on page 147 of the student text), and label the regions.

- Match the following cultural subregions with the correct letter on the map.

__A__	1. tobacco states of the Atlantic
__E__	2. states beyond the Appalachians
__B__	3. colonial states of the Lower South
__D__	4. Gulf States
__C__	5. Florida
__G__	6. Louisiana
__F__	7. interior South Central states
__H__	8. Texas

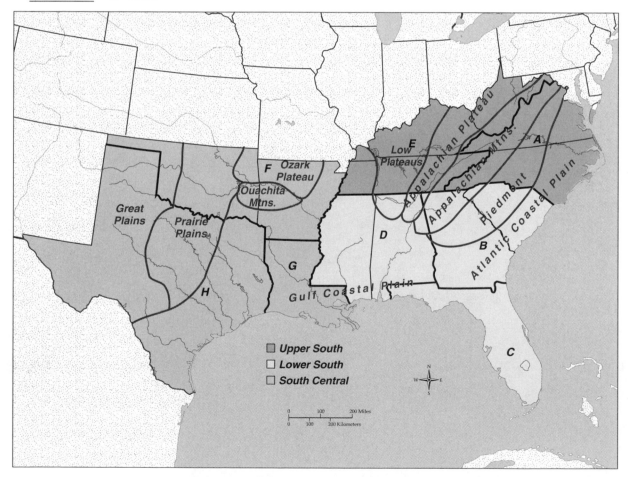

Geography

How Were Cities Founded?

Below is an illustration of ten types of locations where cities are founded. From your reading about the United States, give an example of a city founded in each location. Some answers are already provided for you from other places in the world. Note that the two main priorities for the location of cities are (1) access to trade and (2) safety from attack. The second priority was very important in early history, but it lost its value with the development of modern weapons of destruction. *Emphasize that the location of each of the world's great cities is no accident but is a result of God's geographic design.*

1. Mountain Pass (trade)   Innsbruck, Switzerland _____

2. Hill (safety)   Jerusalem, Israel _____

3. Fertile Valley (trade/access to food)   *Hartford, Conn. Answers vary.* _____

4. Lake Shore (trade)   *Rochester, N.Y. Answers vary.* _____

5. River Confluence (trade)   *Pittsburgh, Pa. Answers vary.* _____

6. Fall Line (trade)   *Richmond, Va. See p. 127.* _____

7. River Mouth (trade)   *New York, N.Y. Answers vary.* _____

8. Deep Harbor (trade)   *Norfolk, Va. Answers vary.* _____

9. Peninsula (safety)   *Yorktown, Va. Answers vary.* _____

10. Island (safety/trade)   *Jamestown, Va. Answers vary.* _____

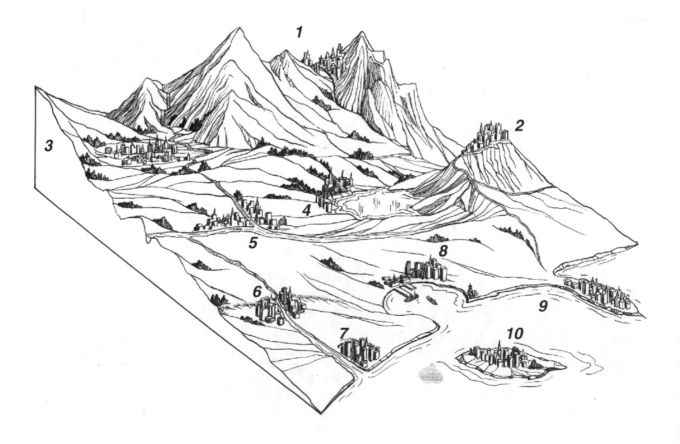

Geography

Matching States

Match the states with the descriptions below. Give *all* the states that fit each description.

A. Alabama   F. Louisiana   K. Tennessee
B. Arkansas   G. Mississippi   L. Texas
C. Florida   H. North Carolina   M. Virginia
D. Georgia   I. Oklahoma   N. West Virginia
E. Kentucky   J. South Carolina

E, H, K, M, N (p. 114)	1. Upper South
A, C, D, G, J (p. 114)	2. Lower South
B, F, I, L (p. 114)	3. South Central
D, H, J, M (pp. 143, 153)	4. one of the original thirteen colonies
D, J (p. 153)	5. one of the colonial states of the Lower South
C (p. 158)	6. former Spanish colony ceded to the United States
F (p. 162)	7. former French settlements
B (p. 162)	8. two capitals at one time during the Civil War
N (p. 148)	9. became part of the Union during the Civil War
G (p. 153)	10. highest percentage of blacks in any state
I (p. 164)	11. highest number of Indians in any state
N (p. 144)	12. lowest population in the South
L (p. 144)	13. highest population in the South
M (p. 144)	14. highest per capita GDP in the South
L (p. 165)	15. most beef
L (p. 165)	16. most cotton
L (p. 161)	17. most oil
C (p. 160)	18. most oranges
C (p. 160)	19. most sugar cane
H (p. 146)	20. most tobacco
F, I, L (p. 161)	21. most natural gas (top three states)
E, H, K, L, M, N (p. 144)	22. mountains above 4,000 feet
B, E, I, K, N (p. 143)	23. no coastline or shoreline
C (p. 158)	24. both Atlantic and Gulf coasts
C, D, H, J, M (p. 147)	25. Atlantic Coastal Plain
E (p. 149)	26. Bluegrass
C (p. 160)	27. Everglades
E, K (p. 152)	28. Great Smoky Mountains

_F (p. 162)_	29. Mississippi Delta
_H (p. 145)_	30. Outer Banks
_B, I (p. 164)_	31. Ozark Plateau
_L (p. 166)_	32. Rio Grande
_M (p. 145)_	33. Shenandoah Valley
_D (pp. 156-57)_	34. Stone Mountain

Geography

Map of the Midwestern United States

Refer to the relief map on page 169 to complete the map on the next page.

1. Label these features of physical geography:
   Bodies of Water—Lake Michigan, Lake Superior, Mississippi River, Missouri River, Ohio River
   Land Features—Badlands, Black Hills, Great Plains, Ozarks

2. Label all the Midwestern states and their capitals.

3. Look at the population map on page 128. Label the five Midwestern cities that have metropolitan areas with a population above 2 million.

4. Look at the map on page 176. Trace in blue the navigable water routes of the Midwest.

5. Look at the climate map on page 184. Shade in orange the Midwestern region that has a semiarid climate.

6. Shade the Corn Belt yellow (map on p. 170), and shade the Dairy Belt in green (the region north of the Corn Belt on the product map, p. 211).

Optional Activities *Answers are found in the running text of the chapter.*

7. Draw these figures in the appropriate state.

   two largest cities in the Midwest *(pp. 173, 176)*

   two states with over 10 million people *(p. 171)*

   busiest airport in the world *(p. 175)*

   unicameral legislature *(p. 183)*

   Gateway Arch *(p. 179)*

   Great Serpent Mound *(p. 172)*

   home state of Mark Twain *(p. 179)*

   boyhood home of Abe Lincoln *(p. 171)*

8. Draw these figures in the appropriate location.

   dairy products *(pp. 177, 178)*

   corn *(pp. 180, 181)*

   winter wheat *(p. 182)*

   summer wheat *(pp. 183, 187)*

   iron ore *(p. 181)*

   hogs *(p. 180)*

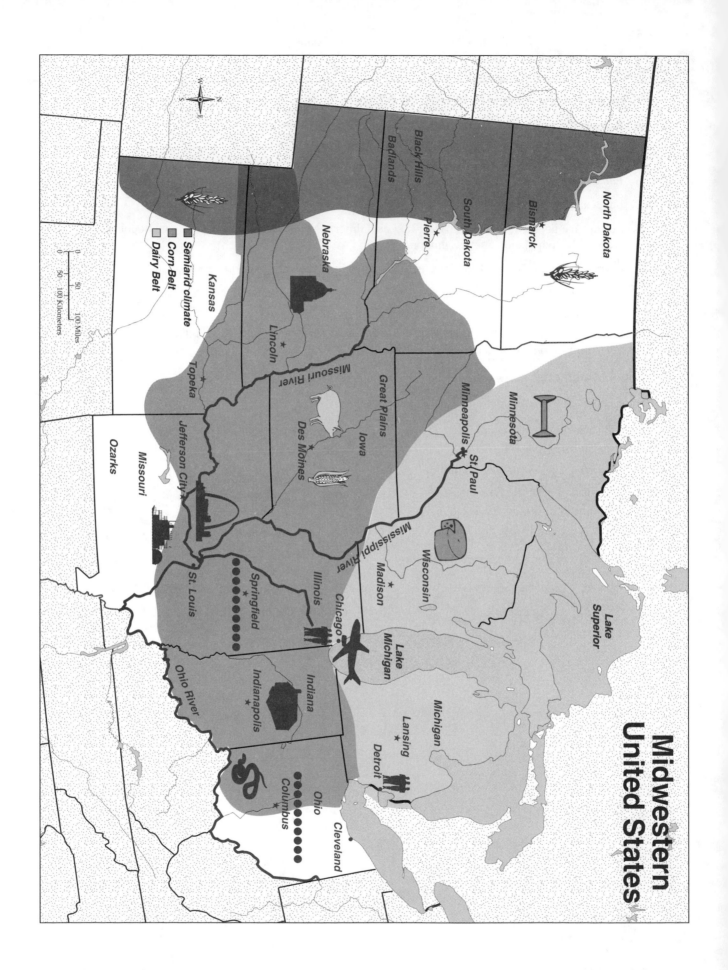

Midwestern United States

Legend:
- Semiarid climate
- Corn Belt
- Dairy Belt

Scale:
0 50 100 Miles
0 50 100 Kilometers

Labels on map:

North Dakota
Bismarck ★
South Dakota
Pierre ★
Badlands
Black Hills
Nebraska
Lincoln ★
Kansas
Topeka ★
Ozarks
Missouri
Jefferson City ★
St. Louis
Great Plains
Iowa
Des Moines
Missouri River
Minnesota
Minneapolis
St. Paul ★
Mississippi River
Wisconsin
Madison ★
Lake Superior
Lake Michigan
Michigan
Lansing ★
Detroit
Illinois
Springfield ★
Chicago
Indiana
Indianapolis ★
Ohio
Columbus ★
Cleveland
Ohio River

Geography

Distinctives of U.S. Cultural Subregions

A combination of history, geography, and traditions helps to create the distinctive traits of different peoples. As you study Geography, be alert to the factors that make people different. Consider the distinctives of regions within the United States. For each word or phrase below, give the region it is associated with: Northeast (N), South (S), or Midwest (M).

Geography

_S_ 1. Great Smoky Mountains

_S_ 2. wide, fertile coastal plain

_M_ 3. dry Central Plains

_N_ 4. rocky coast

_S_ 5. humid subtropical climate

Population

_S_ 6. Atlanta

_M_ 7. Chicago

_N_ 8. New York City

_N_ 9. megalopolis

_S_ 10. multitude of small towns close together

_M_ 11. nodal cities

History

_N_ 12. Jonathan Edwards

_S_ 13. Robert E. Lee

_M_ 14. Abraham Lincoln

_S_ 15. Civil War

_N_ 16. War for Independence

_M_ 17. political reforms for the "common man"

Views

_N_ 18. national independence

_S_ 19. state's rights

_M_ 20. universal manhood suffrage

_N_ 21. religious liberalism

_S_ 22. religious conservativism

Industry and Products

_S_ 23. cotton and tobacco

_M_ 24. wheat and corn

_M_ 25. automobiles

_N_ 26. newspapers and banking

This activity provides an excellent opportunity to discuss the bitterness and misunderstandings that false stereotypes can cause. But stereotypes also help us to make sense of a complex world—a quick flip through the book will reveal "stereotypical" pictures that are identified with each region of the world. The duty of the Christian is to discern the limits of stereotypes.

Geography

Compare the Great Lakes

Answer the following questions about the chart on the Great Lakes. You will also need to look at the maps on student text pages 117 and 169 and the text of the chapter. **Elevations may vary slightly.**

Lake	Area (sq. mi.)	Depth (ft.)	Volume (cu. mi.)	Elevation (ft. above sea level)
Superior	31,700	3,363	2,916	602
Huron	23,000	220	827	578
Michigan	22,300	750	1,161	578
Erie	9,910	210	116	572
Ontario	7,340	802	393	246

1. Which of the Great Lakes cover an area less than one-third the area of Lake Superior?   **Erie, Ontario**

2. Lake Superior has the greatest depth. What Great Lake has the second greatest depth? How does its depth compare to Lake Superior's depth?   **Ontario; the depth of Lake Ontario is less than one-fourth the depth of Superior.**

3. Lake Superior has the greatest volume. What Great Lake has the second greatest volume? How does its volume compare to Lake Superior's volume?   **Michigan; Lake Michigan has only about one-third the volume of Superior.**

4. Which Great Lake has the shortest depth and the smallest volume? Does it also have the smallest area?   **Erie; no**

5. Lake Huron covers a greater area than Lake Michigan, but it has much less volume. Why is this?
   Lake Michigan is three times as deep, and volume is calculated by a combination of depth and surface area.

6. Which of the Great Lakes touches *four* states? Name the states.   **Lake Michigan; Illinois, Indiana, Michigan, Wisconsin**

7. Which two of the Great Lakes touch *three* states? Name the two lakes and the states each touches.
   Lake Erie; Ohio, New York, Pennsylvania
   Lake Superior; Michigan, Minnesota, Wisconsin

8. Which two of the Great Lakes touch only *one* state? Name the two lakes and the state each touches.
   Lake Ontario—New York; Lake Huron—Michigan

9. Which state touches the largest number of Great Lakes?   **Michigan (four)**

10. Which Great Lake lies entirely within the United States and does not share a border with Canada?
    Michigan

11. Look at the map of Canada on page 224. Which of the Great Lakes has the same name as a Canadian province? How many of the Great Lakes does this province touch?   **Ontario; four**

💡 If you want to ship a load of iron ore by water from the Mesabi Range (upper Minnesota) to New York City, what cities will the ore pass?   **Duluth, Minn.; Sault Sainte Marie and Detroit, Mich.; Buffalo, Rochester, and Albany, N.Y. (Also accept Marquette, Wisc., and Alpena, N.Y.)**

Geography

Bar Graphs: U.S. Agriculture

Fill in these bar graphs based on the information supplied by the U.S. Department of Agriculture.

Top-Ten Soybean-Producing States: The soybean has many uses—source of oil, feed for livestock, food for man, and industrial byproducts. Farmers in the Midwest often alternate planting soybeans and corn because soybeans restore nitrogen to the soil. On the graph below, mark the amount of soybeans produced by each state and fill it in. (It should look similar to the graphs in Chapter 8 of your textbook.)

State	Iowa	Ill.	Minn.	Ind.	Ohio	Mo.	Nebr.	Ark.	S.Dak.	Kans.
Soybeans (millions of bushels)	416	399	224	204	157	150	135	112	91	74

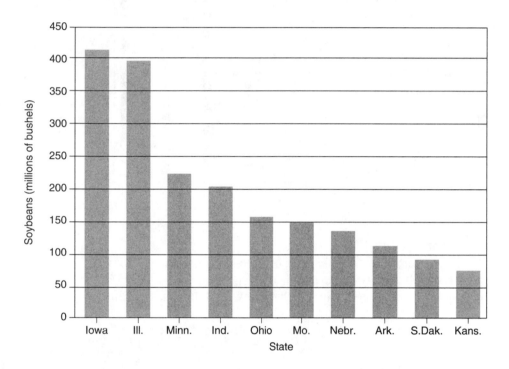

Changing Prices for Farm Products: Farmers are at the mercy of wild fluctuations in market prices. Prices of farm products continue to fall compared to the cost of other products. (The cost of non-farm products, such as cars, has increased over 500% since 1940.) Complete the following graph to see what has happened to three basic farm prices. Use three colored pencils to mark the amount farmers were paid for a bushel of each product.

	1940	1950	1960	1970	1980	1990	1998
Corn	$0.62	$1.52	$1.00	$1.33	$3.11	$2.28	$2.22
Wheat	$0.67	$2.00	$1.74	$1.33	$3.91	$2.61	$2.94
Soybeans	$0.89	$2.47	$2.13	$2.85	$7.57	$5.74	$5.51

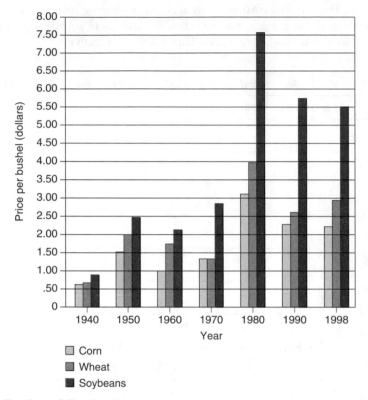

Decline of Family Farms: Sometimes you can combine two types of graphs on one chart to contrast the pattern of change. Use a line graph to show the shift in the number of farms, and use a bar graph to show the size of average farms.

Year	1940	1950	1960	1970	1980	1990	1997
Number of Farms (millions)	6.2	5.7	3.9	2.9	2.3	2.1	2.1
Size of Average Farm (acres)	174	213	297	374	425	460	470

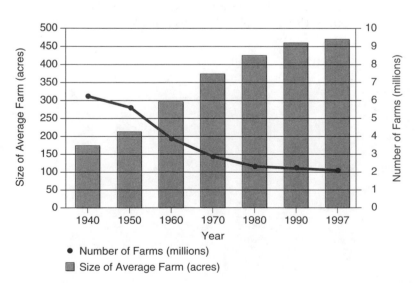

Geography

Land of Lincoln

Abraham Lincoln gave what is considered to be the most memorable speech about American ideals. To find what the name of the speech is, complete the puzzle below.

1. name for the arch of St. Louis
2. direct vote by the people on a new law
3. plains shared by all Midwestern states
4. president from Missouri who fought the Cold War
5. Great Commoner from Nebraska
6. huge territory that the U.S. purchased from France
7. two-house legislature
8. steep riverbank

9. dry plains west of the Central Plains
10. college built using gifts of federal land
11. rolling plains with high grasses
12. famous urban evangelist from Chicago
13. main agricultural industry in the far north
14. election to nominate party candidates
15. typical culture of America
16. tall building, such as the Sears Tower
17. range with the nation's leading iron ore mines

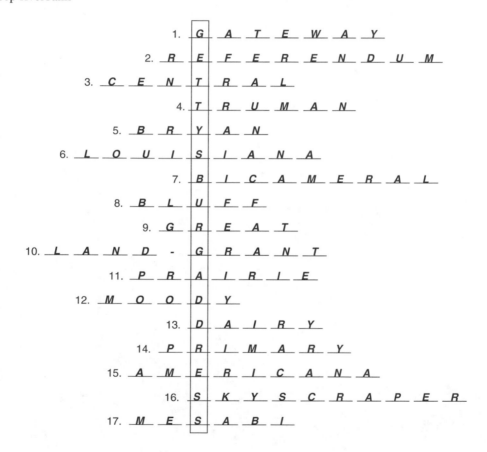

1. G A T E W A Y
2. R E F E R E N D U M
3. C E N T R A L
4. T R U M A N
5. B R Y A N
6. L O U I S I A N A
7. B I C A M E R A L
8. B L U F F
9. G R E A T
10. L A N D - G R A N T
11. P R A I R I E
12. M O O D Y
13. D A I R Y
14. P R I M A R Y
15. A M E R I C A N A
16. S K Y S C R A P E R
17. M E S A B I

Geography

Map of the Western United States

Fill in each blank with the correct letter or number from the map. States are uppercase letters (A, B, C); cities are lowercase letters (a, b, c); special features are numbers (1, 2, 3). Refer to pages 195, 217, and 220.

States

_M_	1.	Alaska
_J_	2.	Arizona
_C_	3.	California
_I_	4.	Colorado
_L_	5.	Hawaii
_E_	6.	Idaho
_F_	7.	Montana
_D_	8.	Nevada
_K_	9.	New Mexico
_B_	10.	Oregon
_H_	11.	Utah
_A_	12.	Washington
_G_	13.	Wyoming

Cities

_k_	14.	Denver
_h_	15.	Las Vegas
_b_	16.	Los Angeles
_i_	17.	Phoenix
_e_	18.	Portland
_d_	19.	Sacramento
_g_	20.	Salt Lake City
_a_	21.	San Diego
_c_	22.	San Francisco
_f_	23.	Seattle
_j_	24.	Tucson

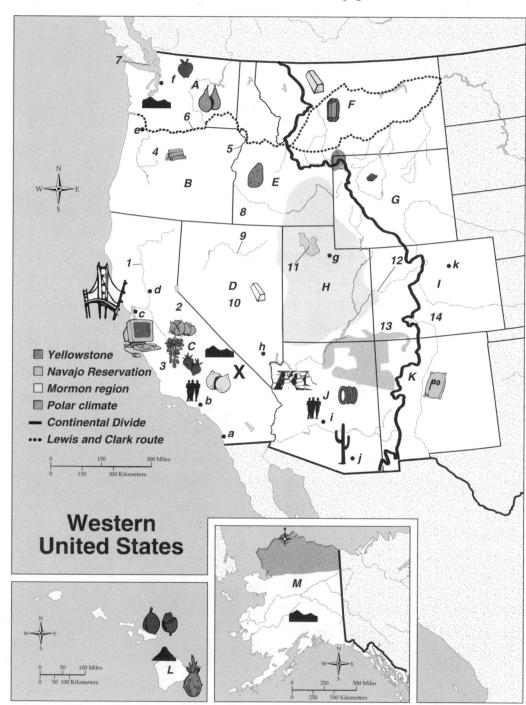

Yellowstone
Navajo Reservation
Mormon region
Polar climate
Continental Divide
Lewis and Clark route

Western United States

Special Features

4	25. Cascade Mountains	6	30. Columbia River	1	35. Sacramento River
3	26. Coast Ranges	10	31. Great Basin	14	36. Sangre de Cristo Mountains
13	27. Colorado Plateau	11	32. Great Salt Lake		
12	28. Colorado River	9	33. Humboldt River	2	37. Sierra Nevada
8	29. Columbia Plateau	7	34. Puget Sound	5	38. Snake River

Map Work

39. Look at the national parks map on page 190. Shade yellow Wyoming's Yellowstone National Park.

40. Look at the "Manifest Destiny" map on page 194. Draw the routes Lewis and Clark covered in the Western United States.

41. Look at the map on page 205. Shade purple the Navajo reservation.

42. Look at the religion map on page 151. Shade red the region where Mormonism predominates.

43. Look at the climate map on page 184. Shade blue the region having a polar climate.

44. Draw the continental divide and label it (map on p. 195).

Optional Activities *Answers are found in the running text of the chapter.*

45. Draw these figures in the appropriate state.

  Golden Gate Bridge *(p. 210)*

  Silicon Valley *(p. 210)*

  largest city in the West *(p. 209)*

  largest city in the interior states of the West *(p. 206)*

  desert with saguaro cacti *(pp. 193, 206)*

  longest and widest canyon in the world *(p. 206)*

  highest point in Hawaii *(p. 196)*

  highest point in the contiguous states *(p. 212)*

  highest point in Washington *(p. 196)*

  highest point in North America *(p. 219)*

  X lowest point in North America *(p. 213)*

  northernmost point in the United States *(p. 219)*

46. Draw these figures in the appropriate state.

  platinum and gem sapphires *(p. 197)*

  coal *(p. 197)*

  potatoes *(p. 199)*

  lettuce, grapes, strawberries, and lemons *(p. 210)*

  wood products *(p. 214)*

  apples and pears *(p. 217)*

  coffee and pineapple *(pp. 220–21)*

  silver *(p. 203)*

  copper *(p. 206)*

  potash *(p. 203)*

Geography

Treasure Hunt

The maps in your textbook contain a wealth of information, but maps often require careful study to uncover their treasures. The Western United States is a fascinating place rich in detail. Compare the maps in your chapter to see how much treasure you can find. *Choose a "Treasure Hunt" for your students to do. Many of these questions appear in the teacher's manual. They are provided here in case you do not prefer to ask them orally.*

Hunt #1: Treasures of the West, p. 190

1. The West has thirty-seven national parks. How many are in each of the other regions? __*Northeast has one; Midwest has five; South has nine.*__

2. Does every western state have a national park? __*yes, although the sliver of Yellowstone in Idaho is Idaho's only national park*__

💡 Which two states have the most national parks? How many? Why these states? __*Alaska and California; each has eight; both are large states with scenic areas.*__

Hunt #2: Manifest Destiny, p. 194

Make sure to compare this map with the relief maps on pages 195 and 218.

1. What natural feature formed the following borders?
   - western border of the United States in 1783 __*Mississippi River*__
   - Texas' southwestern border in 1845 __*Rio Grande*__
   - boundary between the Louisiana Purchase and Oregon Country __*Continental Divide*__
   - boundary between the Mexican Cession and the Gadsden Purchase __*Gila River*__

2. What modern city was formed near the following forts?
   - Bent's Fort __*Pueblo, Colo.*__
   - Ft. Hall __*Pocatello, Idaho*__
   - Ft. Vancouver __*Portland, Ore.*__

3. Look closely at the route of Lewis and Clark.
   - What river did they follow from St. Louis to Montana? __*Missouri River*__
   - What subrange of the Rockies did Lewis and Clark cross in order to reach Idaho? __*Bitterroot Mts.*__
   - On the journey home, Clark split off in Montana and took a southerly route. What river did he explore? __*Yellowstone River*__

4. Now look closely at the Oregon Trail and California Trail.
   - What river did wagons follow into the Rocky Mountains? __*Platte River*__
   - What river did wagons first reach on the west side of the Rockies? __*Snake River*__
   - The wagons took a shortcut across northeastern Oregon to the Columbia River. What modern city arose on this shortcut? __*Pendleton*__

- Goldminers heading to California first followed the Oregon Trail across the Rockies. Then they cut off to the south looking for what river? _**Humboldt River**_
- What mountain range did gold miners cross between the Great Basin and Sacramento? _**Sierra Nevada**_

5. Look closely at the Santa Fé Trail.
   - The trail splits at one point, where traders had two routes to choose from. What range did they cross at this point? _**Sangre de Cristo Mts.**_
   - Bent's Fort was the traders' last stop on the Arkansas River. What major river did they seek on the other side of the Continental Divide? _**Rio Grande**_

Hunt #3: Relief Map of the West, p. 195

1. How many western states have no coastline? _**eight**_
2. Which four states include parts of the main Rocky Mountain range? _**Colorado, Montana, New Mexico, and Wyoming**_
3. Name two plateaus west of the Rocky Mountains. What two major river systems begin in the Rockies and cut through each plateau? _**Colorado and Columbia Plateaus; Colorado and Columbia Rivers**_
4. Which state border is defined, in part, by the Continental Divide? _**Idaho**_
5. What three state borders include parts of the Columbia River and its tributaries? What is the only other river that forms a state boundary? _**Idaho, Oregon, and Washington; Colorado River**_
6. Which western state has the largest area with a low (green) elevation? Which two valleys drop below sea level? _**California; Death Valley and Imperial Valley**_
7. What three western states border Mexico? What is the only other state that borders Mexico? _**Arizona, California, and New Mexico; Texas**_
8. What three western states border Canada? _**Idaho, Montana, and Washington**_

   What states are made up entirely of geometric boundaries? What lake was used in the definition of state borders? _**Colorado, New Mexico, Wyoming, and Utah; Lake Tahoe**_

Hunt #4: Indian Reservations, p. 205

1. The Mohawk Indians live in the Eastern Woodlands region. In what region do each of the Indians in the photos belong (p. 204)?
   - Navajo _**Southwestern**_
   - Crow _**Plains**_
   - Aguascaliente (or Agua Caliente) _**California Intermountain**_
2. Which of the four subregions of the United States appears to have the fewest reservations? _**Northeast**_
3. What is the largest reservation? _**Navajo**_

💡 What geographic differences help to explain the five basic divisions between the Indian cultures?

The climate and vegetation required completely different lifestyles to survive—eastern forests, grasslands on the plains, the arid southwest, the isolated valleys of California and the Great Basin, and the rain forest of the Pacific Northwest.

Hunt #5: Hispanic Minority Population, pp. 195, 208

1. Which states in the West have regions with Hispanic populations above 25%?   *Arizona, California, Colorado, New Mexico*

2. What is the only state outside the West that has a Hispanic population over 50% in some areas?
   Texas

3. What two states contain no areas of Hispanic population over 1%?
   Maine, New Hampshire

4. Find the only region in California where Hispanics make up over 50% of the population. What valley is in this region?   *Imperial Valley*

5. What river flows through the region where Hispanics are concentrated in Arizona?   *Gila River*

6. What two rivers help to explain the location of Hispanics in New Mexico?   *Gila River, Rio Grande*

💡 What is the only state east of the Mississippi River with a Hispanic population over 25% in some areas? Why here?   *Florida; Cubans*

Hunt #6: Precipitation in the United States, p. 215

1. Which two western states have *no* regions where precipitation is below 8 inches?   *Montana and Oregon*

2. Which state appears to have the lowest *average* precipitation?   *Nevada (Lake Tahoe is the only region that receives more than 24 inches.)*

3. What is the only state with an area of precipitation above 128 inches? Where is that region located?
   Washington; Cascade Range

4. What spot east of the Rockies has precipitation above 80 inches?   *border of South Carolina, North Carolina, and Georgia (See the last paragraph in the student text on p. 146.)*

5. Find the division between the Central Plains and the Great Plains on page 147. What amount of rainfall appears to mark the division between the two?   *24 in.*

💡 Is California's heaviest rainfall in the mountains or the valleys? Explain why that is true. (Hint: Refer to p. 47.)   *mountains; orographic precipitation*

Geography

U.S. Cultural Subregions

Follow the directions below to create your own "Culture Map of the United States." It should look like a mini-version of the "Culture Map of Northern America" on page 114.

- Choose a different color for each region. Then fill in the key and the respective regions on the map.

- Label on the map the four main U.S. culture regions: Midwest, Northeast, South, and West.

- Match the following cultural subregions with the correct letter on the map.

V 1. Alaska

T 2. California

J 3. Florida

W 4. Hawaii

K 5. Louisiana

C 6. New York

X 7. Texas

S 8. Southwest

U 9. Northwest

E 10. border states

B 11. upper New England

A 12. lower New England

D 13. on the Delaware River

G 14. beyond the Appalachians

Q 15. Rocky Mountains

I 16. Gulf states

P 17. Great Plains

R 18. Great Basin

O 19. upper Mississippi basin

L 20. interior South Central states

H 21. colonial states of the Lower South

M 22. Corn Belt above the Ohio River

N 23. Dairy Belt of the far North

F 24. tobacco states of the Atlantic

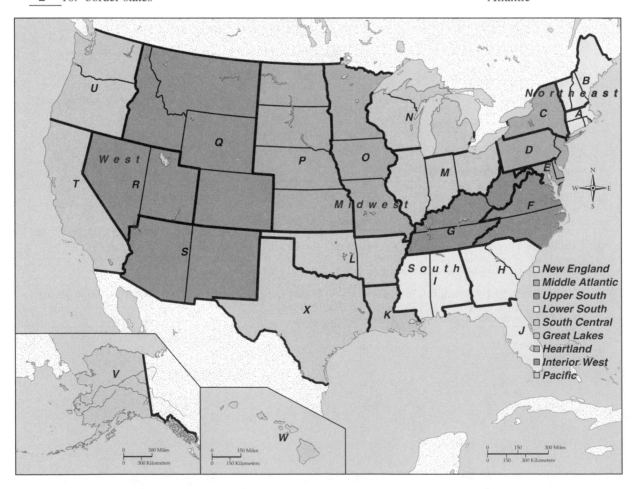

Mormonism

The only major religion founded in the United States, Mormonism has become one of the largest cults in the world. Although Mormons are strongest in the western United States, particularly Utah, their presence is felt in every state and many countries around the world. The study of key Mormon documents and doctrines will enable you to defend your faith and to witness more effectively to Mormons.

When witnessing to a Mormon, be sure to define your terms. Mormons often use terms similar to Christian terms, but they mean different things. Also, Mormons sometimes quote Bible verses to support their beliefs, but they usually take the verses out of context. Show any Mormon to whom you witness the full context of the verses he quotes. Keep in mind that most Mormons have been raised in their church and are grounded in its doctrines. Don't be discouraged if the Mormons you witness to do not respond right away—it is very rare for a Mormon to be converted to true Christianity on the first or second encounter.

Members of the Church of Jesus Christ of Latter-Day Saints (Mormons) use the Bible, the *Book of Mormon,* the *Doctrine and Covenants,* and the *Pearl of Great Price* as their standard doctrinal works. The writings of their own prophets, such as *Gospel Through the Ages, The Teachings of the Prophet Joseph Smith, Mormon Doctrine,* and *Doctrines of Salvation* quoted below, are even more important in determining their beliefs. Carefully read the following excerpts, which show Mormon views on key doctrines. Answer each group of questions after you read the passage(s) under each heading.

Doctrine of the Bible

"Wherefore, thou seest that after the book hath gone forth through the hands of the great and abominable church, that there are many plain and precious things taken away from the book, which is the book of the Lamb of God.

"And after these plain and precious things were taken away it goeth forth unto all the nations of the Gentiles; and after it goeth forth unto all the nations of the Gentiles, yea, even across the many waters which thou hast seen with the Gentiles which have gone forth out of captivity, thou seest—because of the many plain and precious things which have been taken out of the book, which were plain unto the understanding of the children of men, according to the plainness which is in the Lamb of God—because of these things which are taken away out of the gospel of the Lamb, an exceedingly great many do stumble, yea, insomuch that Satan hath great power over them" (I Nephi 13:28-29, *Book of Mormon*)

"Wo[e] be unto him that shall say: We have received the word of God, and we need no more of the word of God, for we have enough!

"For behold, thus saith the Lord God: I will give unto the children of men line upon line, precept upon precept, here a little and there a little; and blessed are those who hearken unto my precepts, and lend an ear unto my counsel, for they shall learn wisdom; for unto him that receiveth I will give more; and from them that shall say, We have enough, from them shall be taken away even that which they have" (II Nephi 28:29-30, *Book of Mormon*).

1. What claim does the first excerpt make about the Bible? How would this help Mormons justify the use of other books to complete Scripture? *The passage claims that the Bible was corrupted. The other books in the Mormon canon supposedly restore the doctrines lost when the Bible was corrupted.*

2. How does the scriptural teaching regarding the Bible contradict Mormon views (I Peter 1:23-25, Isaiah 40:8, Matthew 24:35, Ecclesiastes 3:14)? *God's Word endures forever; no one can add or subtract anything from God's Word.*

3. What does the second excerpt say about those who reject the new Mormon teachings? *They will lose everything, including, perhaps, salvation. (Note the twisting of Matthew 13:12.)*

Doctrine of the Trinity

"The Father has a body of flesh and bones as tangible as man's; the Son also: but the Holy Ghost has not a body of flesh and bones, but is a personage of Spirit. Were it not so, the Holy Ghost could not dwell in us" (*Doctrine and Covenants* 130:22).

"I have always declared God to be a distinct personage, Jesus Christ a separate and distinct personage from God the Father, and that the Holy Ghost was a distinct personage and a Spirit: and these three constitute three distinct personages and three Gods" (*The Teachings of the Prophet Joseph Smith,* compiled by Joseph Smith's nephew Joseph Fielding Smith, p. 370).

4. How does the first passage differ from the biblical teaching of God the Father (John 4:24)?   *It claims that God the Father has a body of flesh and bones like a man.*

5. Explain how Joseph Smith's view of the Trinity contradicts the biblical view. (John 10:30, I John 5:7).

    Smith said that the three members of the Trinity were separate gods.

Doctrine of Christ

"The appointment of Jesus to be the savior of the world was contested by one of the other sons of God. He was called Lucifer, son of the morning. Haughty, ambitious, and covetous of power and glory, this spirit-brother of Jesus desperately tried to become the Savior of Mankind" (Milton R. Hunter, *Gospel Through the Ages,* p. 15).

"Joseph Smith taught that there were certain sins so grievous that man may commit that they will place the transgressors beyond the power of the atonement of Christ. If these offenses are committed, then the blood of Christ will not cleanse them from their sins even though they repent. Therefore their only hope is to have their own blood shed to atone, as far as possible, in their behalf" (Bruce R. McConkie, *Mormon Doctrine,* p. 93).

6. How does Colossians 1:16 disprove Hunter's statement that Jesus is the brother of Lucifer (the Devil)?

    Jesus is the Creator of all things, including Lucifer.

7. What did Joseph Smith teach about the blood of Christ? What does the Bible teach about atonement (John 1:29, I John 1:7)?   *Smith taught that the blood of Christ is not sufficient to atone for certain sins; but the Bible teaches that Christ's blood atoned for all sin, and anyone can enjoy its benefit.*

Doctrine of God and Godhood

"We believe in a God who is Himself progressive, whose majesty is intelligence; whose perfection consists in eternal advancement—a Being who has attained His exalted state by a path which now His children are permitted to follow, whose glory it is their heritage to share. In spite of the opposition of the sects, in face of direct charges of blasphemy, the Church proclaims the eternal truth, 'As man is, God once was; as God is, man may be'" (James E. Talmage, *The Articles of Faith,* p. 430).

"But if we are married for time and for all eternity and it is sealed upon our heads by those who have the authority so to seal, and if we then keep our covenants and are faithful to the end, we shall come forth in the resurrection from the dead and receive the following promised blessings:

'Then shall they be gods, because they have no end; therefore shall they be from everlasting to everlasting, because they continue; then shall they be above all, because all things are subject unto them. Then shall they be gods, because they have all power, and the angels are subject unto them.' (Doctrine and Covenants 132:20)" (quoted in Joseph Fielding Smith, *Doctrines of Salvation,* Vol. 2, p. 62).

". . . and because they [Abraham, Isaac, and Jacob] did none other things than that which they were commanded, they have entered into their exaltation, according to the promises, and sit upon thrones, and are not angels but are gods" (*Doctrine and Covenants* 132:37).

8. How do Psalm 90:2 and Isaiah 43:10 contradict the Mormon view of God? _**The Bible tells us that**_

**God has always been God, and He is the only God—no other gods have ever existed or will exist.**

9. What statement in the first passage describes the Mormon belief that man can become like God, who

is just an exalted man? _**"As man is, God once was; as God is, man may be."**_

Doctrine of Salvation

"This doctrine presents in a clear light the wisdom and mercy of God in preparing an ordinance for the salvation of the dead, being baptized by proxy, their names recorded in heaven and they judged according to the deeds done in the body. This doctrine was the burden of the scriptures. Those Saints who neglect it in behalf of their deceased relatives, do it at the peril of their own salvation" (Joseph Fielding Smith, *The Teachings of the Prophet Joseph Smith,* p. 193).

"That by keeping the commandments they might be washed and cleansed from all their sins, and receive the Holy Spirit by the laying on of the hands of him who is ordained and sealed unto this power" (*Doctrine and Covenants* 76:52).

10. Mormons believe their temple rituals will help them get to heaven. What example is given in the first

passage? _**baptism of the dead**_

11. What phrase in the second excerpt shows the Mormon reliance on works for salvation? Give a Bible

verse that contradicts this view. _**"by keeping the commandments"; important verses on the role of**_

**works include Ephesians 2:8-9**

Additions to Scripture

Although the Mormons use the Bible as part of their canon, the Mormon books and the Mormon prophets can "correct" it by changing, adding to, or subtracting from Scripture. Before his death, Joseph Smith began his own translation of the Bible. Read the following two verses translated by Smith, then answer the questions.

"And no man hath seen God at any time, except he hath borne record of the Son, for except it is through him no man can be saved" (John 1:18).

"No man has seen God at any time, except them who believe. If we love one another, God dwells in us, and His love is perfected in us" (I John 4:12).

12. Compare Smith's translations to the translations in your own Bible. What phrases did Smith add to the

verses? _**except he hath borne record of the Son; except them who believe (Note Revelation 22:18-19 on**_

**adding to Scripture.)**

13. Why would Smith translate these verses this way? _**to justify his claim that God appeared to him and**_

**talked with him face-to-face**

Matching Terms

Match each term with the correct definition or description.

Terms

A. aqueduct	E. hoodoo	H. mission
B. continental divide	F. immigration	I. rainshadow
C. geologic column	G. manifest destiny	J. salt flat
D. geothermal		

_G_ 1. belief that America should expand its borders to the Pacific Ocean

_F_ 2. movement of foreigners into a nation

_A_ 3. canal built to carry drinking water long distances

_D_ 4. underground heat that causes strange features on the surface

_E_ 5. strangely shaped column of rock

_C_ 6. division of the earth's surface into separate layers that appear to display the earth's history

_B_ 7. high ground that separates water drainage into separate oceans

_J_ 8. dried-up lakebed

_I_ 9. dry side of mountains on the far side of the prevailing winds

_H_ 10. building used by Roman Catholic missionaries

Natural Features

A. Central Valley	E. Grand Canyon	H. Rio Grande Valley
B. Colorado Plateau	F. Great Basin	I. Sonoran Desert
C. Columbia Plateau	G. North Slope	J. Willamette Valley
D. Death Valley		

_J_ 11. fertile plain in Oregon

_A_ 12. fertile plain in California

_H_ 13. fertile plain in New Mexico

_G_ 14. coastal plain along the Arctic Ocean

_F_ 15. low bowl of land in the Southwest

_D_ 16. lowest spot in North America

_E_ 17. biggest hole on earth

_I_ 18. home of saguaro cacti in southern Arizona

_B_ 19. highlands of northern Arizona and southern Utah

_C_ 20. highlands of eastern Oregon and Washington

A. Alaska Range   E. Mt. McKinley   H. Sangre de Cristo
B. Brooks Range   F. Mt. Ranier   I. Sawatch Range
C. Cascade Mountains   G. Mt. Whitney   J. Sierra Nevada
D. Mauna Loa

   A   21. highest range in North America

   E   22. highest mountain in North America

   J   23. highest range in the contiguous states

   G   24. highest mountain in the contiguous states

   H   25. high range that rises west of the Great Plains

   B   26. northernmost extension of the Rocky Mountains

   I   27. range of the Rockies that forms the backbone of the continent

   C   28. range of volcanic mountains that forms the backbone of the Pacific Northeast

   F   29. mountain with the most glaciers outside Alaska

   D   30. largest active volcano in the world

Human Features

A. Bay Area   E. Pacific Northwest   H. Seattle
B. Denver   F. Phoenix   I. Silicon Valley
C. Inland Empire   G. Salt Lake City   J. Southwest
D. Los Angeles

   B   31. largest metro area in the Rocky Mountain region

   D   32. largest metro area in the West

   A   33. metro area centered around San Francisco

   F   34. largest city in the West's interior

   H   35. largest city in the Pacific Northwest

   G   36. Mormon capital

   J   37. New Mexico and Arizona

   E   38. Washington and Oregon

   I   39. hub of the computer industry in San Jose

   C   40. hub of the nation's apple and pear industry

Geography

Map of Canada

Refer to the relief map on page 224 to complete the map on the next page.

1. Label these features of physical geography:
    Bodies of Water—Hudson Bay, Mackenzie River, St. Lawrence River
    Miscellaneous—Baffin Island, Canadian Shield, Labrador

2. Label these cities: Calgary, Montreal, Ottawa, Vancouver

3. Label all the provinces, territories, and their capitals.

4. Look at the climate map on page 184. Shade blue those parts of Canada that are tundra.

5. Shade green those areas in Canada having a humid continental climate.

Optional Activities *Answers are found in the running text of the chapter.*

6. Draw these figures in the appropriate place.

     largest city in Canada *(p. 231)*   French majority *(p. 230)*

     largest metro area in Canada *(p. 233)*   Inuit territory *(p. 242)*

     largest port in the Maritimes *(p. 227)*   settled by American Loyalists *(p. 227)*

    busiest port in Canada *(p. 240)*

    .... only province with over 10 million
    people *(p. 225)*

7. Draw these figures in the appropriate province.

     automobiles *(p. 233)*   oil reserves *(p. 238)*

     beef *(p. 238)*   peas *(p. 238)*

     butter *(p. 231)*   potatoes *(p. 228)*

     iron *(p. 226)*   wheat *(p. 238)*

    lumber *(p. 240)*   uranium *(p. 238)*

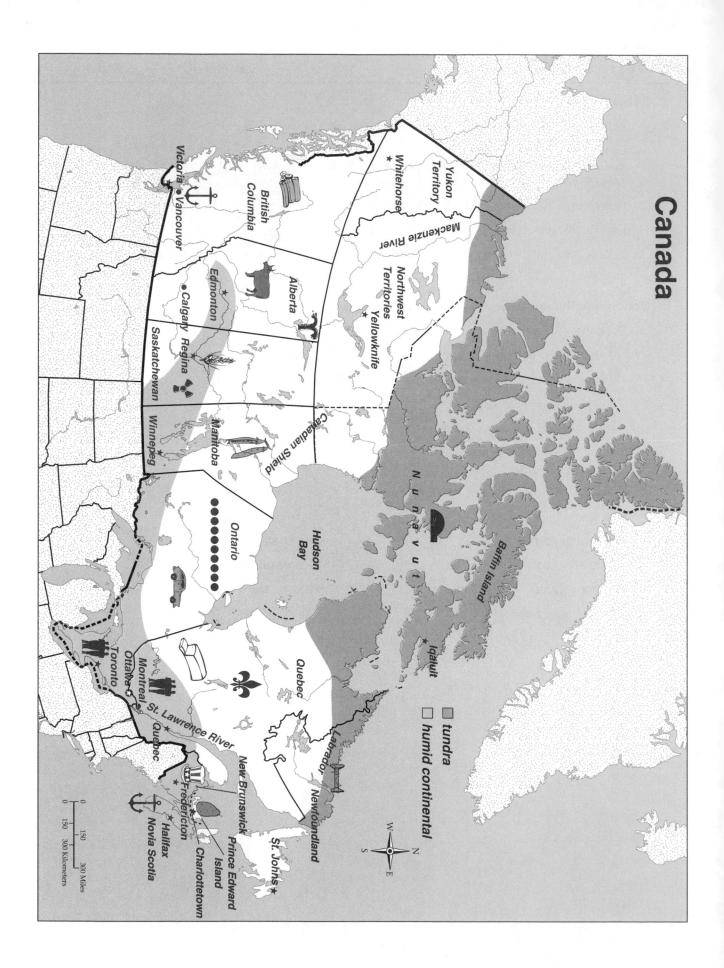

Canada

Yukon Territory
Whitehorse ★
Mackenzie River
Northwest Territories
Yellowknife ★
British Columbia
Victoria ● Vancouver
Alberta
Edmonton ★
● Calgary Regina ★
Saskatchewan
Winnepeg ★
Manitoba
Canadian Shield
Hudson Bay
N u n a v u t
Baffin Island
Iqaluit ★
Ontario
Quebec
Labrador
Newfoundland
St. Johns ★
Toronto ★
Ottawa ★
Montreal ● Quebec
St. Lawrence River
Fredericton ★
New Brunswick
Prince Edward Island
Charlottetown ★
Halifax ★
Nova Scotia

□ tundra
□ humid continental

N
W   E
S

0   150   300 Kilometers
0   150   300 Miles

Geography

☆ ## Comparison of Canada and the United States

Complete the chart showing some of the similarities and differences between Canada and the United States. Don't forget to look at the statistical charts in the student book. ☆ *Class discussion. See page v.*

		United States	Canada
Geography	Climate (p. 184)	*every type of climate (p. 184)*	*colder climates (no desert, mediterranean, or tropical climates) (p. 184)*
	Area	*3,675,031 sq. mi. (p. 138)*	*3,851,790 sq. mi. (p. 234)*
	Main Mountain Ranges	*Appalachians, Ozark-Ouachitas, Pacific Mountain System (three parts—Rockies, Cascades/Sierra Nevada, Coastal Ranges) (pp. 147, 218-19)*	*Appalachians, Pacific Mountain System (two parts—Rockies, Coastal Mountains) (pp. 223, 240)*
	Main Lakes	*Great Lakes (p. 169)*	*Great Lakes (except Michigan), Great Slave Lake, Great Bear Lake (pp. 232, 242)*
	High Point	*Mt. McKinley (20,320 ft.) (p. 219)*	*Mt. Logan (19,524 ft.) (p. 225)*
	Longest River	*Mississippi-Missouri (p. 179)*	*Mackenzie (p. 242)*
Economy	Per Capita GDP (pp. 138, 234)	*$27,607*	*$24,400*
	Major Agricultural Products	*wheat, corn, dairy, tobacco, fruit (pp. 143, 160, 170, 176, 182)*	*fish, wheat, dairy, barley (pp. 226, 231, 237)*
	Major Mining Products (See chart on p. 66.)	*silver, iron, chromium, copper, lead, phosphates, nitrates, sulfur, coal, natural gas*	*gold, silver, iron, copper, zinc, nickel, potash, uranium*
	Major Manufacturing	*textiles, automobiles, computers, etc. (pp. 120, 146, 176, 210)*	*newsprint, automobiles, computers, etc. (pp. 226-27, 233)*
Demography	Population	*267,954,767 (p. 138)*	*29,123,194 (p. 234)*
	Population Density	*72 (p. 138)*	*8 (p. 234)*
	Natural Increase	*0.6% (p. 138)*	*1.2% (p. 234)*
	Life Expectancy	*76 (p. 138)*	*76 (p. 234)*
	Literacy Rate	*96% (p. 138)*	*97% (p. 234)*
	Largest Metro Area	*New York (p. 127)*	*Toronto (p. 233)*
	Most Populous State/Province	*California (31,878,234) (p. 207)*	*Ontario (10,753,573) (p. 225)*
	Least Populous State/Province	*Wyoming (481,400) (pp. 196-97)*	*Prince Edward Island (134,557) (p. 225)*

		United States	Canada
History	First Settlement	*Jamestown (1607) or St. Augustine (1565) (pp. 144-45, 159-60)*	*Port Royal (1604) (p. 227)*
	Creation of the Union	*American War for Independence (1775-83) (p. 119)*	*British North America Act (1867) (p. 234)*
	Civil War	*American Civil War (1861-65) (p. 142)*	*"rebellion" in 1837 (p. 234)*
	Relationship to Great Britain	*revolt in 1775 (p. 119) [member of NATO]*	*member of the British Commonwealth [and NATO] (p. 234)*
Government	Form of Government	*federated republic (p. 138)*	*federated parliament (p. 234)*
	Executive	*president (p. 138)*	*prime minister (p. 234)*
	Number of Political Divisions (States/Provinces)	*fifty states (p. 138)*	*ten provinces (p. 234)*
Society	Cultural Subregions	*Northeast (New England and Middle Atlantic), South, Midwest (Great Lakes and the Heartland), West (pp. 114, 116)*	*Maritime Provinces (similar to New England), Central Provinces (similar to Middle Atlantic and Great Lakes), Western Provinces (Prairie Provinces similar to the Heartland; British Columbia similar to the Pacific states) (pp. 114, 224, 229, 237)*
	Main Language(s)	*English (p. 159)*	*English and French (p. 236)*
	Main Minorities	*black, Hispanic, Asian, Indian (pp. 153, 204, 208-9, 216)*	*French, Indian, Inuit*
	Main Religion	*Protestantism (p. 174)*	*Roman Catholicism (p. 236)*
	Popular Sports	*baseball football rodeo (general knowledge)*	*hockey (others same as the U.S., plus lacrosse) (p. 231)*
	Famous Tall Buildings	*Sears Tower in Chicago, Empire State Building and twin towers of the World Trade Center in NYC (pp. 129, 175)*	*CN Tower in Toronto (pp. 234, 236)*
	First National Park	*Yellowstone, Wyoming (p. 198)*	*Banff, Alberta (p. 238)*

Geography

PassWord

    This game is called "PassWord." Terms are divided into categories. For each term, write three one-word clues *without using any portion of the terms.* Give one clue at a time until your partner comes up with the term. The team that needs the fewest clues wins. (If your partner misses the term after three clues, giving him the answer counts as the fourth "clue.") **Adapt this activity to your class, but make the rules clear.**

Score	Term	Clue 1	Clue 2	Clue 3
Natural Features				
	1. Baffin Island	*See page 242.*		
	2. Canadian Shield	*pp. 229-30, 232, 237-38*		
	3. Grand Banks	*pp. 225-26*		
	4. Insular Mountains	*p. 240*		
	5. Labrador	*p. 226*		
	6. Mackenzie River	*p. 242*		
	7. Newfoundland	*pp. 224-26*		
	8. St. Lawrence River	*pp. 230-34*		
Provinces				
	9. Alberta	*pp. 238-39*		
	10. British Colombia	*pp. 239-41*		
	11. Manitoba	*pp. 237-38*		
	12. New Brunswick	*p. 227*		
	13. Newfoundland	*pp. 224-27*		
	14. Nova Scotia	*p. 227*		
	15. Ontario	*pp. 232-34*		
	16. P.E.I.	*pp. 227-29*		
	17. Quebec	*pp. 230-31*		
	18. Saskatchewan	*p. 238*		
Cities				
	19. Calgary	*pp. 238-39*		
	20. Halifax	*p. 227*		
	21. Montreal	*p. 231*		
	22. Quebec	*p. 231*		
	23. Toronto	*pp. 233-34*		
	24. Vancouver	*p. 240*		

Score	Term	Clue 1	Clue 2	Clue 3
Terms				
	25. archipelago	*p. 242*		
	26. bilingual	*p. 231*		
	27. cordillera	*p. 240*		
	28. demilitarize	*p. 234*		
	29. Inuit	*p. 241*		
	30. lock	*p. 232*		
	31. maritime	*p. 224*		
	32. portage	*p. 230*		
	33. premier	*pp. 236-37*		
	34. ribbon development	*p. 229*		
	35. taiga	*p. 230*		

Skill: Recognition

Geography

History of Canada by Region

Just as U.S. history was broken up and discussed under different regions in the previous chapters, Canadian history is divided under different headings in this chapter. For each event below, write the province/region where it is discussed in the book. *Discuss the importance of these events in Canadian history, and compare them to similar events that Americans study in history class.*

Newfoundland, p. 226	1. John Cabot discovers the Grand Banks in 1497.
Newfoundland, p. 225	2. Great Britain claims the island of Newfoundland in 1583.
Acadia, p. 227	3. France founds Port Royal in 1604.
Quebec, p. 231	4. France founds Quebec in 1608.
Quebec, p. 230	5. The Hudson Bay Company receives a charter in 1670.
Acadia, p. 227	6. Britain drives French Acadians out of Canada in 1755.
Quebec, p. 230	7. Britain conquers French-controlled Quebec in the Seven Years' War (1757-63).
British Columbia, p. 239	8. British ships first sight the shores of British Columbia in 1778.
Ontario, pp. 233-34	9. The United States invades Canada and captures Toronto (York) during the War of 1812.
British Columbia, pp. 239-40	10. The United States and Britain peacefully settle their western borders in the 1840s.
Canada's Capital, p. 234	11. Canadian colonies unite under the British North America Act (1867).
Manitoba, pp. 237-38	12. *Métis* launch the Red River Rebellion in 1867, paving the way for a bill of rights and provincial status for Manitoba in 1870.
Yukon Territory, p. 241	13. The discovery of gold attracts thousands of miners to the Klondike in the 1890s.
Canada's Capital, p. 236	14. Several Protestant denominations unite to form the mainline United Church of Canada in 1925.
Newfoundland, p. 226	15. Newfoundland becomes the last province to join Canada in 1949.
Quebec/Ontario, p. 232	16. Canada and the United States complete major work on the St. Lawrence Seaway in 1959.
Quebec, p. 230	17. Quebec makes French the sole official language in the province in 1974.
Canada's Capital, p. 236	18. Quebec's refusal to sign the 1982 Charter of Rights and Freedoms creates a constitutional crisis that threatens to split the country.
Nunavut, p. 242	19. Nunavut gains self-government in 1999.

Geography

A Second Look: Northern America

List the seven continents in the first column. List the four oceans in the second column.

1. _Asia_

2. _Africa_

3. _North America_

4. _South America_

5. _Antarctica_

6. _Europe_

7. _Australia_

8. _Pacific_

9. _Atlantic_

10. _Indian_

11. _Antarctic_

12-17. On the map, label the equator, Tropics, middle latitudes, and high latitudes. Then draw arrows showing the direction of the trade winds and the westerlies.

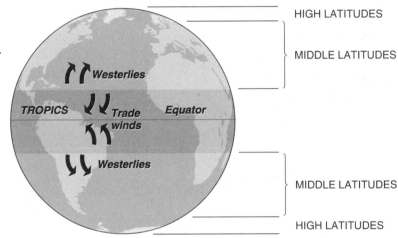

HIGH LATITUDES

MIDDLE LATITUDES

MIDDLE LATITUDES

HIGH LATITUDES

Underline the word or phrase that best completes each sentence.

18. The two main branches of geography are human and (physical, <u>systematic</u>).

19. Rain that falls when a humid air mass moves over mountains is (<u>orographic</u>, convection) precipitation.

20. A line of longitude is sometimes called a (parallel, <u>meridian</u>).

21. Agriculture is a (<u>primary</u>, secondary) industry.

Give the term that fits each description.

22. economic system under which private individuals or corporations build most industries   _capitalism_

23. goods received from other countries   _imports_

24. area above the timberline with stunted vegetation   _alpine zone_

25. residential community outside the city proper   _suburb_

26. line where the Piedmont plateau drops to the coastal plain   _Fall Line_

In the blank beside each descriptive phrase, write *C* for Canada, *U.S.* for the United States, or *both* if it describes both countries.

both   27. Rockies

_U.S._   28. federated republic

both   29. wheat

_C_   30. ribbon development

Geography

Statistics on North America's Big Three

Complete the table of statistics from the charts in the student book, pages 138, 234, and 249. Then answer the questions that follow.

	United States	Canada	Mexico
Area (sq. mi.)	3,675,031	3,851,790	761,601
Population	267,954,767	29,123,194	78,000,000
Natural Increase	0.6%	1.2%	2.9%
Life Expectancy	76	76	66
Literacy Rate	96%	97%	74%
Per Capita GDP	$27,607	$24,400	$2,180
Population Density	72	8	102

1. Compare the area of Mexico to the area of the next largest country in North America. *less than one-fourth the area of the United States*

2. Compare the population of Mexico to the population of the United States. *less than one-third*

3. Compare the population of Mexico to the population of Canada. *almost three times larger*

4. Which country has the highest rate of natural increase? Why does this usually reflect a "developing" country? *Mexico; the population usually grows quickly in developing countries, and income cannot keep up*

5. Why do you think the rate of natural increase is so much smaller in the United States than in Canada?
   Answers will vary. Canada has a large minority population, and abortion is rampant in the United States.

6. Is Mexico's life expectancy typical of a "developing" or a "developed" country? *developing*

7. Is Mexico's literacy rate typical of a "developing" or a "developed" country? *developing*

8. Compare Canada's per capita GDP to Mexico's. *more than eleven times larger*

9. Is Mexico's population density typical of a "developing" or a "developed" country? *neither*

Suppose the per capita GDP remained unchanged in the United States, but Mexico's per capita GDP doubled every ten years. In how many years would Mexicans catch up with Americans? *between thirty and forty years! ($4,360 in 10 years, $8,720 in 20 years, $17,440 in 30 years, and $34,880 in forty years)*

Geography

Mexico's Forgotten States

Color in the key and the map with the six cultural subregions in Mexico discussed in your text. The key also gives the number of states within each region. (Note that the Mesa Central includes the federal district around the capital, as well as ten states.) Which Mexican states are terms in the text?

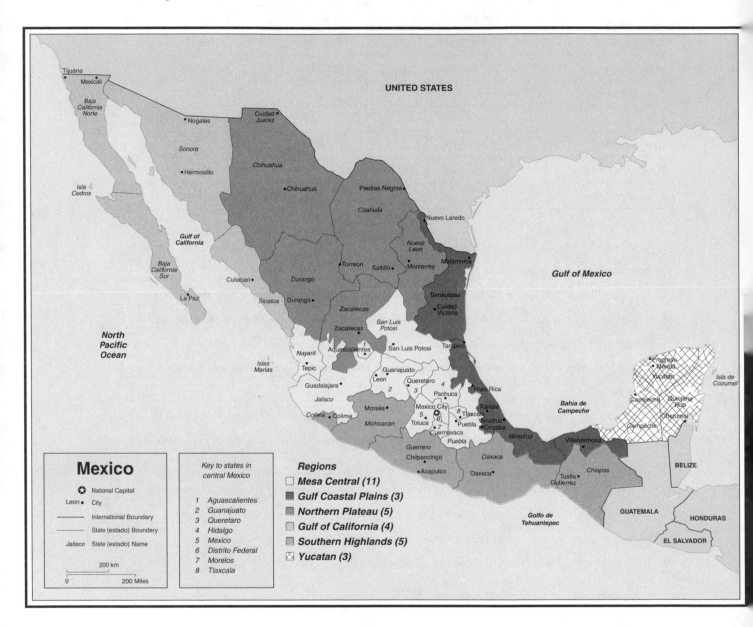

Mexico

✪ National Capital

Leon • City

———— International Boundary

———— State (estado) Boundary

Jalisco State (estado) Name

200 km

0   200 Miles

Key to states in central Mexico

1 Aguascalientes
2 Guanajuato
3 Queretaro
4 Hidalgo
5 Mexico
6 Distrito Federal
7 Morelos
8 Tlaxcala

Regions

☐ **Mesa Central (11)**
■ **Gulf Coastal Plains (3)**
■ **Northern Plateau (5)**
☐ **Gulf of California (4)**
■ **Southern Highlands (5)**
⊠ **Yucatan (3)**

Geography

Map of Mexico

Complete the map below using the relief map in the student text on page 247.

1. Label these features of physical geography:
   Water—Bay of Campeche, Gulf of California, Gulf of Mexico, Lake Chapala, Rio Grande
   Mountains—Sierra Madre Del Sur, Sierra Madre Occidental, Sierra Madre Oriental
   Peninsulas—Baja California, Yucatan
   Deserts—Chihuahuan Desert (in the state of Chihuahua, p. 254), Sonoran Desert (in the state of Sonora)

2. Label these cities: Acapulco, Cancún, Guadalajara, Mérida, Mexico City, Monterrey, Veracruz, Tijuana.

3. Draw a line connecting the Atlantic and Pacific Oceans at the narrowest spot in Mexico.

4. Draw a dotted line where the tropic of Cancer crosses Mexico, and label it.

Optional Activity

5. Draw these figures in the appropriate place.

    largest city in North America *(p. 249)*

    second largest city in Mexico *(p. 247)*

    Aztec capital (Tenochtitlán) *(pp. 249-50)*

    Shrine of Our Lady of Guadalupe *(p. 250)*

    biggest port *(p. 255)*

    center of silver mines *(p. 255)*

    main oil deposit *(p. 255)*

    Mayan ruins in Mexico's Yucatan *(pp. 248, 257)*

    highest peak in Mexico *(p. 251)*

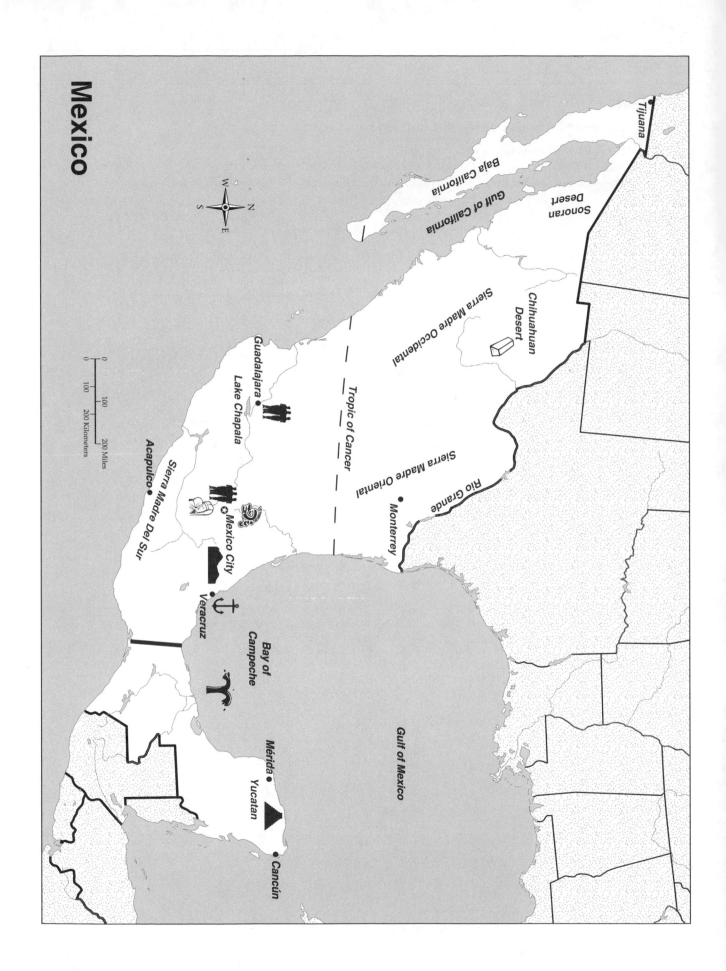

Mexico

Tijuana

Baja California

Gulf of California

Sonoran Desert

Sierra Madre Occidental

Chihuahuan Desert

Tropic of Cancer

Guadalajara

Lake Chapala

Sierra Madre Oriental

Rio Grande

Monterrey

Acapulco

Sierra Madre Del Sur

Mexico City

Veracruz

Bay of Campeche

Gulf of Mexico

Mérida

Yucatan

Cancún

N
W   E
S

0
100
100
200 Kilometers
0
200 Miles

Geography

Map of Central America and the West Indies

Complete the map with the help of the relief map in the student text, page 260.

1. Label these features of human geography:
   Cities—Guatemala City, Havana, Santo Domingo
   Miscellaneous—Panama Canal

2. Label all the countries in Central America and the West Indies.

3. Look at the map on page 261. Shade pink the two countries that are mostly European, red the countries that are mostly Black, and blue the countries that are mostly mulatto.

Optional Activity

4. Draw these figures in the appropriate place.

    U.S. commonwealth *(p. 268)*

    Central American country with British heritage *(p. 259)*

    home of Fidel Castro *(p. 265)*

   Contra Contra rebellion *(p. 262)*

    major bauxite mine *(p. 268)*

   14 ruled by "Fourteen Families" *(p. 261)*

    most densely populated nation in Latin America *(p. 261)*

    poorest country in Latin America *(p. 266)*

   #1 largest nation in the West Indies *(p. 265)*

    oldest European city in Latin America *(p. 267)*

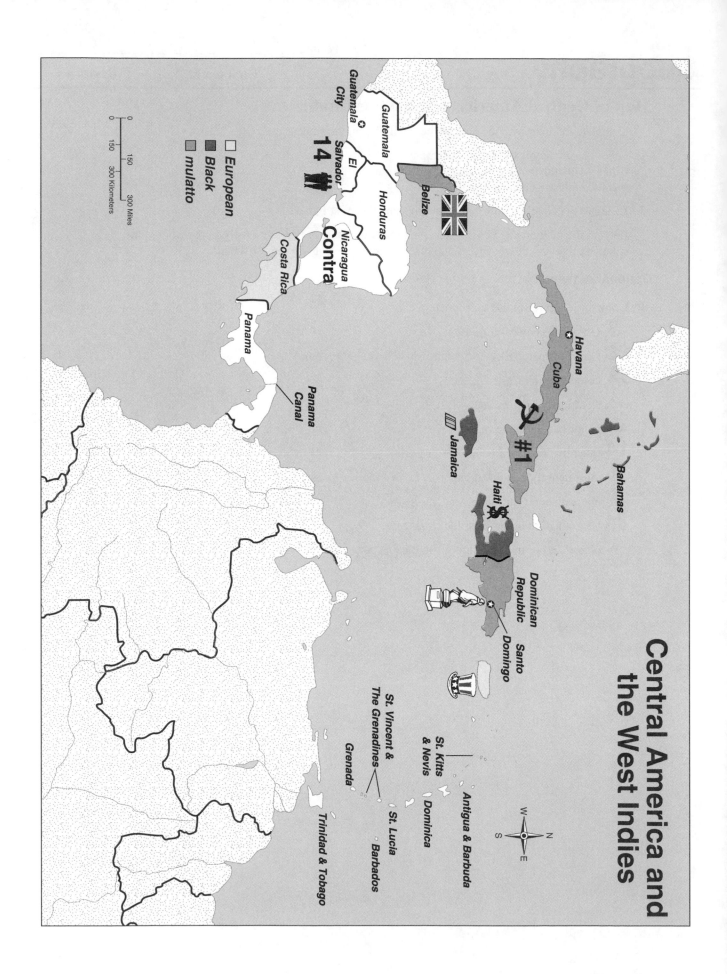

Central America and the West Indies

European
Black
mulatto

0 150 300 Miles
0 150 300 Kilometers

Guatemala City

Guatemala

El Salvador

Honduras

Belize

Nicaragua **Contra**

Costa Rica

Panama

Panama Canal

14

#1

Havana

Cuba

Jamaica

Bahamas

Haiti

Dominican Republic

Santo Domingo

St. Vincent & The Grenadines

Grenada

St. Lucia

Barbados

Trinidad & Tobago

St. Kitts & Nevis

Dominica

Antigua & Barbuda

N
W   E
S

Geography

☆ **Timeline of U.S. Intervention**

The United States has frequently intervened in Middle America. Give the country and circumstances of each intervention. Then answer the questions that follow. ☆ *Class discussion. See page v.*

Dates	Country	Circumstances of Intervention
1835-36	Mexico	Texas War of Independence *(p. 253)*
1846-48	*Mexico*	*Mexican War (p. 254)*
1867	*Mexico*	*U.S. troops chase away French troops who had landed in Mexico (p. 254).*
1898	*Cuba*	*Spanish-American War*
1903	*Panama*	*U.S. warships aid Panama's break from Columbia; the new government allows the United States to build the Panama Canal (p. 264).*
1904-7	Dominican Republic	The United States intervenes to make sure the Dominican Republic can pay its debts.
1912-33	Nicaragua	Marines land to help restore order and stay almost continually until they oversee election of a pro-American president. *(p. 262)*
1914	*Mexico*	*Marines land at the coast to help the revolutionaries during the revolution of 1910-20 (p. 254).*
1915-34	*Haiti*	*Marines land to restore order (p. 266).*
1916	*Mexico*	*The U.S. invades northern Mexico to capture the Mexican bandit Pancho Villa (p. 254).*
1916-24	Dominican Republic	Marines occupy the country to restore order.
1962	Cuba	The United States supports an invasion at the Bay of Pigs by 1,300 Cuban exiles who want to topple Castro.
1965-66	Dominican Republic	After a coup, Marines land to protect American lives and supervise a peaceful election.
1980s	El Salvador	The United States supplies arms and aid to protect El Salvador from Communist rebels supported by Nicaragua.
1980s	Nicaragua	*The United States sends aid to the rebel Contras who opposed the Communist regime (p. 262).*
1983	*Grenada*	*The United States drives out the Communist (Cuban) forces in Grenada (p. 269).*

Dates	Country	Circumstances of Intervention
1988	Honduras	The United States sends 3,200 troops to protect Honduras against the Communists in Nicaragua.
1989	*Panama*	*U.S. invades to overthrow strongman Manuel Noriega (p. 264).*
1994	*Haiti*	*Marines land to restore President Jean-Bertrand Aristide to power (p. 266).*

1. In which two cases did the United States help a country to gain independence? *Cuba in 1898 and Panama in 1903*

2. List all of the countries on the mainland in which the United States has intervened. Which mainland countries have been free of U.S. intervention? *Mexico, Nicaragua, El Salvador, Honduras, Panama; Belize, Costa Rica, Guatemala*

3. List all of the countries in the West Indies in which the United States has intervened. *Cuba, Dominican Republic, Haiti, Grenada*

4. In which of these cases did the Latin American government clearly seek U.S. help? *El Salvador in the 1980s*

5. What appear to be two main reasons for U.S. intervention in Latin America? *Answers will vary. The United States opposes Communists and desires political stability.*

Geography

Report on a Little Country

Pick one country below. Then find as much as you can about it using an encyclopedia, almanac, or other resources. *Assign one country to each student. With larger classes, have students work in teams or assign other countries or islands from the chapter.*

Antigua and Barbuda   Dominica   St. Kitts and Nevis   St. Vincent and the Grenadines
Barbados   Grenada   St. Lucia   Trinidad and Tobago

1. Location among the three island groups of the West Indies _____

    _____

2. Unusual geographic features _____

    _____

3. Type of government _____

4. Main languages _____

5. Religious divisions (with percentages) _____

6. Currency _____

7. Ethnic groups (with percentages) _____

    _____

8. Major industry _____

9. Main trade partners (imports and exports) _____

    _____

10. Description of flag _____

    _____

11. Date of discovery _____

12. Name of discoverer and his nationality _____

13. Name and date of the first European colony _____

14. Date of independence _____

15. Famous person(s) _____

16. Recent natural disaster _____

17. Other interesting facts from history _____

    _____

    _____

    _____

    _____

Geography

Crossword Puzzle

Across

3. poorest country in the Western Hemisphere
4. a council of military and civilian leaders
5. Spanish colony freed during the Spanish-American War
6. religion that mixes black magic and Catholicism
7. local political boss in Mexico
10. large ranch owned by a Spanish nobleman
12. Spanish for "eastern"
15. narrow land bridge
16. form of government in Puerto Rico
18. type of Indian living in the Sierra Madre del Sur
19. person of mixed European and African ancestry
21. alpine zone in Latin America
22. most densely populated nation in the Western Hemisphere
23. Indian group who built Chichen Itza
24. early empire on the Central Mesa that built Tula

25. "small" Antilles
26. trade agreement between Canada, the United States, and Mexico
27. southernmost state in Mexico near Guatemala

Down

1. person of mixed Spanish and Indian blood
2. southern peninsula in Mexico
3. largest city in the West Indies
5. language that mixes French and African words
8. ruling party in Mexico (initials)
9. type of farming required in growing bananas and coffee
11. largest state in Mexico
13. Spanish for "mild"
14. assembly plants in Mexico near the U.S. border
17. main source of jobs in Panama
20. anti-Communist rebels in Nicaragua
21. public square in the center of a Mexican village

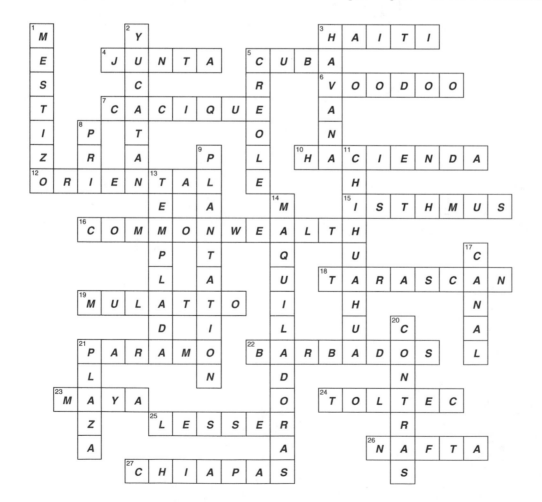

Geography

Map of South America

Complete the map below, referring to the relief map on page 272.

1. Label these features of physical geography:
   Rivers—Amazon River, Orinoco River, Paraná River, Rio de la Plata
   Other bodies of water—Lake Maracaibo, Lake Titicaca, Strait of Magellan
   Plateaus—Brazilian Highlands, Guiana Highlands, Mato Grosso Plateau, Patagonia
   Plains—Altiplano, Gran Chaco, Llanos, Pampas
   Miscellaneous—Atacama Desert, Tierra del Fuego, Angel Falls, Iguaçu Falls

2. Label these cities—Buenos Aires, Cuzco, Lima, Rio de Janeiro, São Paulo

3. Label all the countries and their capitals in South America.

4. Draw and label the equator where it crosses the continent.

5. Look at the map on page 45. Draw a blue line showing the path of the Peru Current. Draw a red line showing the path of the Brazil Current.

6. Look at the map on page 248. Color the Incan Empire brown.

7. Look at the colonial map on page 273. Shade each modern country and territory according to the colonial powers that controlled it: French colony–green; English colony–purple; Dutch colony–red; Portuguese colony–blue; Spanish colony–yellow. (Note: Guyana was once owned by the Dutch but England took it over.)

8. Draw and label the Line of Demarcation (or Line of Tordesillas).

9. Based on your reading in the textbook, write the names of these men in the appropriate countries: Pedro, Perón, Pinochet, Pizarro.

Optional Activity

10. Draw these figures in the appropriate place. (Hint: Many minerals appear on the map on page 287.)

    highest mountain in the Western Hemisphere *(p. 287)*

    reputedly the world's driest desert *(p. 284)*

    #1 largest lake in South America *(p. 275)*

    highest navigable lake in the world *(p. 283)*

    world's highest waterfall *(p. 277)*

    world's widest waterfall *(p. 290)*

    Inca capital *(p. 278)*

    nerve center of the Spanish Empire in South America *(p. 281)*

    largest city in South America *(p. 292)*

    "most charming city" in the New World *(p. 291)*

    two landlocked countries *(pp. 281, 289)*

    S first *two* countries liberated by San Martín *(p. 286)*

    B first *three* countries liberated by Bolívar *(p. 273)*

    gauchos *(p. 288)*

    world leader in iron *(p. 293)*

    world leader in copper *(p. 284)*

    world leader in emeralds *(p. 274)*

    world leader in cocaine *(p. 275)*

    world leader in beef *(p. 293)*

    world leader in coffee *(p. 276)*

    world leader in oranges *(p. 291)*

    Wester Hemisphere's leader in bananas

    and cacao *(p. 291)*

    South America's leader in oil *(pp. 275-76)*

    South America's leader in gold *(p. 293)*

    South America's leader in tin *(p. 295)*

    South America's leader in bauxite *(p. 295)*

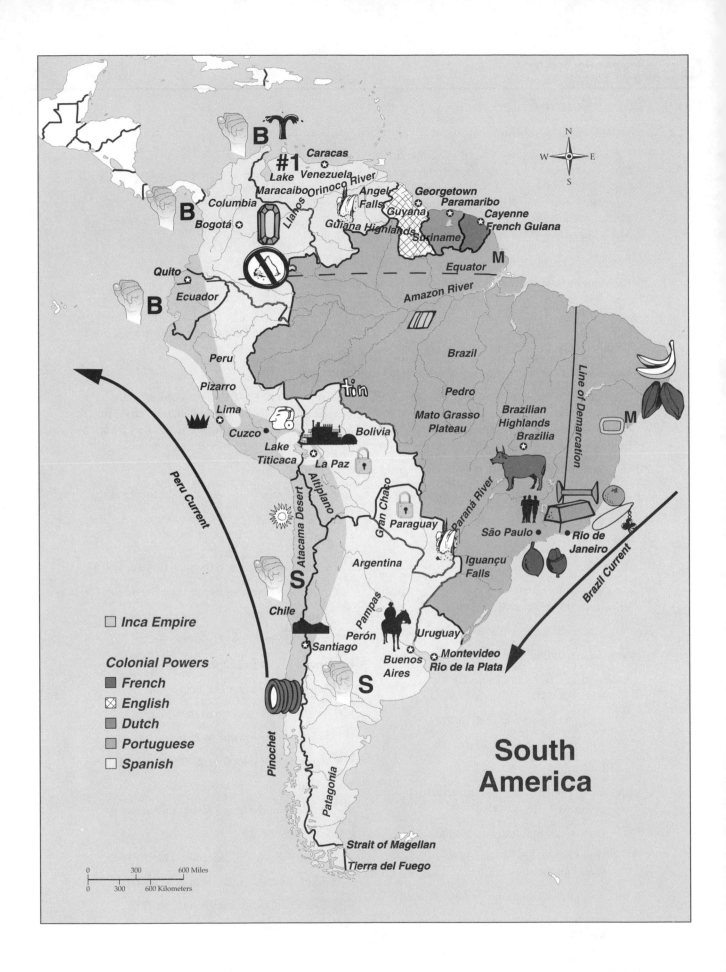

South America

Inca Empire

Colonial Powers
- French
- English
- Dutch
- Portuguese
- Spanish

B T
#1
Caracas
Venezuela
Lake Orinoco River
Maracaibo
B Columbia Angel Georgetown Paramaribo
Falls Guyana Cayenne
Bogotá Guiana Highlands Suriname French Guiana
M
Quito Equator
Ecuador Amazon River
B
Peru Brazil
Pizarro Pedro
Lima Mato Grasso Brazilian
Cuzco Plateau Highlands M
Bolivia Brazilia
Lake
Titicaca La Paz
Gran Chaco Line of Demarcation
Altiplano Paraguay Paraná River
Atacama Desert São Paulo Rio de
S Argentina Iguançu Janeiro
Falls
Chile Pampas
Perón Uruguay
S Peru Current Santiago Buenos Montevideo
Aires Rio de la Plata
Pinochet
Patagonia

Peru Current
Brazil Current

Strait of Magellan
Tierra del Fuego

| 0 | 300 | 600 Miles |
| 0 | 300 | 600 Kilometers |

Geography

Nuggets from *National Geographic*

National Geographic magazine is published by the National Geographic Society. For over one hundred years it has been a vital source of information on geography-related topics. Look up the following articles and answer the questions about them.

"Pizarro: Conqueror of the Inca" (February 1992)

1. What was the author's occupation at the time he wrote the article? What kind of research did he do for this article? (See pp. 98-99.) __*director of the Royal Geographical Society; he lived for a year in Peru,*__ __*researched archives for many years, and returned several times to visit*__

2. According to the map on page 95, what was the southernmost Peruvian city captured by Pizarro? Why was this an important conquest? __*Cuzco; Cuzco was the capital of the Inca empire*__

3. Read pages 111-12. Why was Pizarro, who had less than two hundred men, able to defeat the Inca ruler Atahualpa, who had tens of thousands of native warriors? __*Pizarro and his men had better armor*__ __*and weapons and had the advantage of fighting on horseback.*__

4. How many cities did Pizarro build? What is the meaning of the original name of Peru's present-day capital? (See pp. 95 and 116.) __*seven; "City of the Magi"*__

5. Read the final four paragraphs on page 121. What influences of the Spanish conquest are still evident in Peru today? Can you think of any other results of the conquest that are not mentioned in these paragraphs? __*One-third of all Peruvians are of mixed Indian and Spanish blood (mestizos). The Catholic*__ __*Church is the main religion in Peru. The Spanish language is an official language in Peru.*__

"Peru Begins Again" (May 1996)
Read page 15; then answer the following questions.

6. What resources are present in Peru? Look at the map on page 12. Where are most of the oil fields located? the mining areas? __*fish, copper, zinc, lead, silver, gold, oil, natural gas; northern Peru (on the*__ __*coast and in the jungle); western Peru, in the Andes*__

7. What signs of national unity and patriotism did the author see on his visit to Peru? __*many Peruvian*__ __*flags and the Peruvian colors displayed*__

8. Why did the population of Lima more than triple in less than thirty years? *During the 1960s, poor people came to the city from the mountains to look for jobs; another wave of immigrants came from the Andes to escape the Shining Path guerrillas during the 1980s.*

Beginning with the last paragraph on page 27, read through page 35. Then answer the following questions.

9. List at least two causes of road problems in Peru. Where are most of Peru's paved roads? What section of the country has almost no roads? (See map on page 12.) *The Shining Path guerrillas destroyed some roads, while other roads were neglected; most of the roads are located along the coast of Peru; the Amazon jungle.*

10. What tourist attraction is mentioned in this section? Why did tourism to this site increase during the mid-1990s? *Machu Picchu; people weren't worried about terrorists*

"The Amazon: South America's River Road" (February 1995)

11. Look at the map and charts on pages 12-13. In what country is the Amazon water black? Does any other river have even half as much discharge at its mouth? *Peru; no*

12. How long did the author spend traveling the Amazon so he could write this article? (See page 14.) *four months*

13. According to this article (page 30), how do South Americans feel about the United States' influence in their countries? Why? *They are confused. Some North Americans want the Amazon region to provide lumber and cocaine, but at the same time other North Americans want to preserve the rainforest and stop the cocaine traffic.*

14. What kept the author from traveling on the Amazon in part of Peru (page 35)? Would this still be a problem today? *Shining Path guerrillas; answers will vary, depending on how active the group is currently*

15. The title of this article describes the Amazon as a "river road." How is the river like a road? In what other ways is the Amazon the lifeblood of the Amazonian people? *Ships transport people and goods on the river; the river is also important for fishing and tourism.*

16. Read page 27. How many different Indian languages exist in Amazonian Brazil? *over 180*
Remind the students that many of these people do not have the Bible translated into their language; many have never heard the gospel. There is a great need worldwide for missionaries and Bible translators.

Geography

Lost City of the Incas

Born in Honolulu in 1875, the American explorer Hiram Bingham attended Yale, the University of California, and Harvard. Although he later became a teacher of Latin American history at Yale, the governor of Connecticut, and then a U.S. Senator, he is best remembered for his 1911 expedition to Peru. There he uncovered Machu Picchu, magnificent Inca ruins high in the Andes. Read the following excerpts from his book *Lost City of the Incas;* then answer the questions below.

People often say to me: "How did you happen to discover Machu Picchu?" The answer is, I was looking for the last Inca capital [Vilcabamba, the last refuge of the Incas who fled from Spanish adventurer Francisco Pizarro in the sixteenth century]. Its ruins were believed to be in the Cordillera Vilcabamba. . . . Those snow-capped peaks in an unknown and unexplored part of Peru fascinated me greatly. They tempted me to go and see what lay beyond. In the ever famous words of Rudyard Kipling there was "Something hidden! Go and find it! Go and look behind the ranges—Something lost behind the Ranges. Lost and waiting for you. Go! . . ."

My father had taught me to love mountain climbing. He took me for my first steep climb when I was just four years old. Later we had climbed together a number of mountains in the suburbs of Honolulu. So I knew the thrill of that great and hazardous sport. . . .

[In the winter of 1910] at a Class dinner at the Yale Club in New York, I was called upon for a "speech." Naturally I spoke of what was on my mind. To my great surprise one of my classmates, the late Herbert Scheftel, came to me offering to pay the expenses of a topographer on the expedition now fairly launched in my mind's eye! Other friends soon offered to furnish a surgeon, a naturalist and a mountain-climbing engineer. An undergraduate offered to go along as an assistant. And so the Yale Peruvian Expedition of 1911 was organized in the hope that we might climb the highest mountain in America, collect a lot of geological and biological data and above all try to find the last capital of the Incas. . . .

[The following excerpts record Bingham's first look at Machu Picchu.]

The morning of July 24 dawned in a cold drizzle. Arteaga [a local farmer] shivered and seemed inclined to stay in his hut. I offered to pay him well if he would show me the ruins. He demurred [objected] and said it was too hard a climb for such a wet day. But when he found that I was willing to pay him a *sol* (a Peruvian silver dollar, fifty cents, gold), three or four times the ordinary daily wage in this vicinity, he finally agreed to go. When asked just where the ruins were, he pointed straight up to the top of the mountain. No one supposed that they would be particularly interesting. And no one cared to go with me. The Naturalist said there were "more butterflies near the river!" and he was reasonably certain he could collect some new varieties. The Surgeon said he had to wash his clothes and mend them. Anyhow it was my job to investigate all reports of ruins and try to find the Inca capital.

So, accompanied only by Sergeant Carrasco [the party's armed escort] I left camp at ten o'clock. Arteaga took us some distance upstream. On the road we passed a snake which had only just been killed. He said the region was the favorite haunt of "vipers.". . .

[W]e now struggled up the bank through dense jungle, and in a few minutes reached the bottom of a very precipitous slope. For an hour and twenty minutes we had a hard climb. A good part of the distance we went on all fours, sometimes holding on by our fingernails. Here and there, a primitive ladder made from the roughly notched trunk of a small tree was placed in such a way as to help one over what might otherwise have proved to be an impassable cliff. In another place the slope was covered with slippery grass where it was hard to find either handholds or footholds. Arteaga groaned and said that there were lots of snakes here. Sergeant Carrasco said nothing but was glad he had good military shoes. The humidity was great. We were in the belt of maximum precipitation in Eastern Peru. The heat was excessive; and I was not in training! There were no ruins or *andenes* [terraces] of any kind in sight. I began to think my companions had chosen the better part.

Shortly after noon, just as we were completely exhausted, we reached a little grass-covered hut 2,000 feet above the river where several good-natured Indians, pleasantly surprised at our unexpected arrival, welcomed us with dripping gourds full of cool, delicious water. . . .

Through Sergeant Carrasco I learned that the ruins were "a little further along." In this country one never can tell whether such a report is worthy of credence. "He may have been lying" is a good footnote to affix to all hearsay evidence. Accordingly, I was not unduly excited, nor in a great hurry to move. . . . The view was simply enchanting. Tremendous green precipices fell away to the white rapids of the Urubamba below. Immediately in front, on the north side of the valley, was a great granite cliff rising 2,000 feet sheer. To the left was the solitary peak of Huayna Picchu, surrounded by seemingly inaccessible precipices. On all sides were rocky cliffs. Beyond them cloud-capped snow-covered mountains rose thousands of feet above us.

We continued to enjoy the wonderful view of the canyon, but all the ruins we could see from our cool shelter were a few terraces.

Without the slightest expectation of finding anything more interesting than the ruins of two or three stone houses such as we had encountered at various places on the road [already], I finally left the cool shade of the pleasant little hut and climbed farther up the ridge and around a slight promontory [a protruding crest of rock]. Melchor Arteaga had "been there once before," so he decided to rest and gossip with Richarte and Alvarez [the Indian farmers who gave the party water]. They sent a small boy with me as a "guide." The Sergeant was in duty bound to follow, but I think he may have been a little curious to see what there was to see.

Hardly had we left the hut and rounded the promontory than we were confronted with an unexpected sight, a great flight of beautifully constructed stone-faced terraces, perhaps a hundred of them, each hundreds of feet long and ten feet high. They had been recently rescued from the jungle by the Indians [Richarte and Alvarez]. A veritable forest of large trees which had been growing on them for centuries had been chopped down and partly burned to make a clearing for agricultural purposes. The task was too great for the two Indians so the tree trunks had been allowed to lie as they fell and only the smaller branches removed. But the ancient soil, carefully put in place by the Incas, was still capable of producing rich crops of maize and potatoes. . . .

[W]e patiently followed the little guide along one of the widest terraces where there had once been a small conduit [channel for transporting water] and made our way into an untouched forest beyond. Suddenly I found myself confronted with the walls of ruined houses built of the finest quality of Inca stone work. It was hard to see them for they were partly covered with trees and moss, the growth of centuries, but in the dense shadow, hiding in bamboo thickets and tangled vines, appeared here and there walls of white granite ashlars [square blocks of building stone] carefully cut and exquisitely fitted together. . . .

[Bingham then discovered a temple, which he describes in the following excerpt.]

The flowing lines, the symmetrical arrangement of the ashlars, and the gradual gradation of the courses, combined to produce a wonderful effect, softer and more pleasing than that of the marble temples of the Old World. Owing to the absence of mortar, there were not ugly spaces between the rocks. They might have grown together. On account of the beauty of the white granite this structure surpassed in attractiveness the best Inca walls in Cuzco [ancient Inca capital] which had caused visitors to marvel for four centuries. It seemed like an unbelievable dream. Dimly, I began to realize that this wall and its adjoining semicircular temple over the cave were as fine as the finest stone-work in the world.

It fairly took my breath away. What could this place be? Why had no one given us any idea of it? Even Melchor Arteaga was only moderately interested and had no appreciation of the importance of the ruins which Richarte and Alvarez had adopted for their little farm. Perhaps after all this was an isolated small place which had escaped notice because it was inaccessible.

Then the little boy urged us to climb up a steep hill over what seemed to be a flight of stone steps. Surprise followed surprise in bewildering succession. We came to a great stairway of large granite blocks. Then we walked along a path to a clearing where the Indians had planted a small vegetable garden. Suddenly we found ourselves standing in front of the ruins of two of the finest and most interesting structures in ancient America [two temples]. Made of beautiful white granite, the walls contained blocks of Cyclopean size, higher than a man. The sight held me spellbound. . . .

I could scarcely believe my senses as I examined the larger blocks in the lower course and estimated that they must weigh from ten to fifteen tons each. Would anyone believe what I had found? Fortunately, in this land where accuracy in reporting what one has seen is not a prevailing characteristic of travelers, I had a good camera and the sun was shining. . . .

In view of the probable importance of the ancient Inca city which we had found on top of the ridge between the peaks of Machu Picchu and Huayna Picchu, our first task was to make a map of the ruins. On account of the forest and the dense undergrowth this proved to be a difficult task, but it was finally accomplished. . . . After the map was completed everyone was amazed at the remarkable extent of the area which had once been the site of an important city.

1. Underline the sentence that tells the purpose of the Yale Peruvian Expedition of 1911.

2. List the hardships Bingham faced on his search for the ruins.   *heat, rain, a difficult and dangerous*
   climb, snakes

3. What descriptions show that this expedition took place in a tropical rainforest? Can you explain why
   some mountains were snow-covered?   *rain, humidity, large trees, dense jungles and vines, snakes,*
   rapids; the lapse rate (discussed on p. 51 in the text)

4. How did the locals feel about the ruins? What was Bingham's expectation of the ruins before he saw
   them?   *They were not impressed; he was not expecting to be impressed.*

5. Why did the Inca masonry at Machu Picchu impress Bingham?   *The stones were very large and were*
   cut to fit together perfectly.

6. What precaution did Bingham take to ensure that others would believe his report?   *He took a camera*
   with him and took pictures of the ruins.

Geography

Current Events in South America

The issues that you study in your text are still being discussed today. Try to find a current reference to each topic below. Write (1) the magazine or newspaper you found it in, (2) the date of the publication, (3) the title of the article, and (4) a summary of what the article said about this topic.

Drug War in Colombia

Magazine/Date _____

Title _____

Summary _____

_____

_____

Rebels in Peru

Magazine/Date _____

Title _____

Summary _____

_____

_____

Politics in Chile

Magazine/Date _____

Title _____

Summary _____

_____

_____

Economic Struggles in Argentina

Magazine/Date _____

Title _____

Summary _____

_____

_____

Deforestation of the Amazon

Magazine/Date _____

Title _____

Summary _____

_____

_____

Geography

Brazil's States

Color in the key and the map with the four cultural subregions in Brazil discussed in your text. The key also gives the number of states within each region. (Note that the interior includes the federal district around the capital, as well as three states.) Which four Brazilian states are mentioned in the text?

Using this map when discussing the four regions of Brazil will make the student text more meaningful. Pará and Rondônia are mentioned on p. 295, and Amazonas (p. 295) and Minas Gerais (p. 293) are boldface terms.

Geography

Country Grab Bag

Match each country with the descriptions below. Give *all* the countries that fit each description.

A. Argentina
B. Bolivia
C. Brazil
D. Chile

E. Colombia
F. Ecuador
G. Guyana
H. Paraguay

I. Peru
J. Suriname
K. Uruguay
L. Venezuela

A copy of the countries' chart from the Teacher's Resource Guide in the teacher's edition will help the students answer questions 10-13.

_____*E, L (p. 244)*_____	1. Caribbean cultural subregion
_____*B, D, F, I (p. 244)*_____	2. Andes cultural subregion
_____*A, H, K (p. 244)*_____	3. Río de la Plata subregion
_____*G, J (p. 244)*_____	4. Guiana Highlands subregion
_____*C (K) (p. 273)*_____	5. former Portuguese colony
_____*A, B, D, E, F, H, I, K, L (p. 273)*_____	6. former Spanish colony
_____*G (p. 296)*_____	7. former British colony
_____*J (G) (p. 296)*_____	8. former Dutch colony
_____*E, F, L (p. 273)*_____	9. former member of Bolívar's Gran Colombia
_____*D, E, F, H, L (pp. 271, 289)*_____	10. mestizo majority (five countries, including Ecuador and Chile)
_____*A, C, K (pp. 286, 288)*_____	11. white majority (three, including Brazil)
_____*B, F, I (pp. 278, 281)*_____	12. large pure-blooded Indian minority (three)
_____*G, J (p. 296)*_____	13. large Hindu minority (two)
_____*J (p. 273)*_____	14. lowest population
_____*C (p. 273)*_____	15. highest population
_____*F (p. 273)*_____	16. highest population density
_____*L (p. 273)*_____	17. highest per capita GDP
_____*G (p. 273)*_____	18. lowest per capita GDP
_____*C (p. 293)*_____	19. most iron ore
_____*D (p. 284)*_____	20. most copper
_____*L (pp. 275–76)*_____	21. most oil
_____*C (p. 276)*_____	22. most coffee
_____*C (p. 293)*_____	23. most beef
_____*A, B, D, E, F, I, L (p. 272)*_____	24. Andes Mountains (seven)
_____*A, B, C, E, F, I (p. 272)*_____	25. Amazon basin (six)
_____*C, G, J, L (p. 272)*_____	26. Guiana Highlands (four)
_____*E (p. 272)*_____	27. both Pacific and Gulf coasts

Answers given in parentheses are true but are not found in the student book. Do not penalize the students for not knowing this information.

Geography

☆ **Comparison of Latin and Northern America**

Complete the chart showing some of the similarities and differences between Latin America and North America. For national statistics, check the statistical tables on pages 138, 234, 249, and 273. Don't forget to look at the maps and statistical charts in Chapters 2-5 (including pages 20, 26, 80, 81, 87, 96, 103, and 104).

☆ *Class discussion. See page v. Remind students to check information they wrote for Activity 2 of Chapter 10 (if they did it).*

		Latin America	Northern America
Geography	Climate (pp. 48-49)	*every type of climate, with major areas of tropical rainy and humid subtropical climates*	*every type of climate, with major areas of humid continental, humid subtropical, semiarid, and cold climates*
	Main Mountain Regions	*Sierra Madre systems Andes Mountains (pp. 255, 277)*	*Appalachians, Pacific Mountain System (three parts—Rockies, Cascades and Sierra Nevada, Coastal Ranges) (pp. 147, 218-19)*
	Main Lakes	*Lake Maracaibo (largest) Lake Titicaca (pp. 275, 283)*	*Great Lakes (Superior, largest), Great Slave Lake, Great Bear Lake (pp. 169, 232, 242)*
	High Point (p. 20)	*Mt. Aconcagua (22,834 ft.)*	*Mt. McKinley (20,320 ft.)*
	Longest River (p. 26)	*Amazon (4,000 mi.)*	*Mackenzie (2,635 mi.)*
Economy	Per Capita GDP (best and worst) (See tables on pp. 80, 249, 273.)	*Venezuela ($9,300) Haiti ($290)*	*U.S. ($27,900, 1st worldwide) Canada ($24,400, 4th worldwide)*
	Major Agricultural Products	*coffee, bananas, cacao, wheat, corn, beef, oranges, cocaine (pp. 275, 276, 286, 291, 293)*	*wheat, corn, dairy, tobacco, fruit (pp. 143, 160, 170, 176, 182)*
	Major Mining Products (See table on p. 66 and map on p. 287.)	*gold, silver, iron, chromium, copper, zinc, tin, bauxite, emeralds, oil (The first six are also listed under North America.)*	*gold, silver, iron, chromium, copper, zinc, nickel, lead, phosphates, nitrates, sulfur, potash, coal, natural gas, uranium*
	Major Industry	*primary industries, manufacturing (pp. 247, 287)*	*textiles, automobiles, computers, newsprint, etc. (pp. 120, 146, 176, 210, 226-27)*
Demography	Population (p. 87)	*496,000,000*	*297,000,000*
	Population Density (p. 87)	*56 people per sq. mi.*	*40 people per sq. mi.*
	Largest City (p. 103)	*Mexico City based on UN statistics (16,562,000) [or São Paulo, p. 292, based on almanac statistics]*	*New York City (16,332,000)*
	Most Populous Country (p. 104)	*Brazil (165,000,000)*	*United States (268,000,000)*
	Least Populous Country (p. 249)	*St. Kitts and Nevis (40,992)*	*Canada (29,123,194)*

		Latin America	Northern America
History	First Settlement	*Santo Domingo (Dominican Republic, 1496, p. 267)*	*Port Royal (Nova Scotia, 1604, p. 227) or St. Augustine (Florida, 1565, pp. 159-60)*
	Main Colonial Power(s)	*Spain (and Portugal)*	*Great Britain (France) (pp. 116-17, 223)*
Government	Total Area of Region	*8,800,000 sq. mi.*	*7,500,000 sq. mi.*
	Largest Country in Size	*Brazil (3,300,171 sq. mi., 5th worldwide)*	*Canada (3,849,674 sq. mi., 2nd worldwide)*
	Smallest Country in Size	*St. Kitts and Nevis (104 sq. mi.)*	*U.S. (3,675,031 sq. mi., 4th worldwide)*
	Form of Government	*wide variety, including republics, juntas, and a Communist dictatorship*	*federated republic/parliament*
Society	Two Main Cultural Subregions	*Middle and South America*	*United States and Canada*
	Most Common Language (p. 88)	*Spanish (Indo-European language family)*	*English (Indo-European language family)*
	Ethnic Diversity	*mestizo, White, Indian, Black, mulatto (p. 261)*	*European, Black, Hispanic, Asian, Indian (pp. 153-54, 204-5, 208)*
	Main Religion (p. 94)	*Christianity (Roman Catholicism)*	*Christianity (Protestantism)*
	Popular Sports	*soccer* *bullfighting (p. 249)*	*baseball* *football* *(general knowledge)* *hockey* *rodeo*
	Famous Buildings	*Answers may vary (ruins of Chichen Itza, Tikal, Machu Picchu).*	*Sears Tower in Chicago, Empire State Building and twin towers of the World Trade Center in NYC, CN Tower in Toronto*

Geography

England's Counties

Color in the key and the map with the six subregions in England discussed in your text. Which seven English counties are mentioned in the text? *Use this map in discussing the three main regions of England; it will make the student text more meaningful. Seven counties of the Southern Lowlands are mentioned on p. 307.*

Map Work *Note: This section is optional.*

1. Write these numbers in the seven metropolitan counties of England: (1) Greater London, (2) Greater Manchester, (3) West Midlands (Birmingham), (4) West Yorkshire (Leeds), (5) Merseyside (Liverpool), (6) South Yorkshire (Sheffield), (7) Tyne and Wear (Newcastle upon Tyne)

2. Write the name of these famous regions in the appropriate place.
   "Home Counties" (Greater London, Surrey, Berkshire, Oxfordshire, and Gloucestershire)
   East Anglia (Norfolk and Suffolk)
   Black Country (counties west of Birmingham)
   Lake District (Cumbria)

3. Draw these figures in the county with which they are associated.

   Buckingham Palace (Greater London)   Shakespeare's home (Warwickshire)

   Oxford University   Hereford cow

   Cambridge University   Derby hat

   Chunnel (Kent)   Cheshire cat (from *Alice in Wonderland*)

   white cliffs of Dover (Kent)   Robin Hood (Nottingham)

   Battle of Hastings (East Sussex)   biggest port on the Irish Sea (Liverpool)

   Stonehenge (Wiltshire)

Map Questions

4. What is the largest metropolitan area in each region?

   • Southern Lowlands   *Greater London* _____

   • Midlands   *Birmingham* _____

   • Pennines   *Leeds* _____

   • Lancashire Plain   *Greater Manchester* _____

5. What two of England's six regions do not have a metropolitan area?   *Southwestern Plateau,*
   Yorkshire Plains _____

6. Which of England's six regions has *two* metropolitan areas?   *Lancashire Plain* _____

7. Which of England's six regions has *three* metropolitan areas?   *Pennines* _____

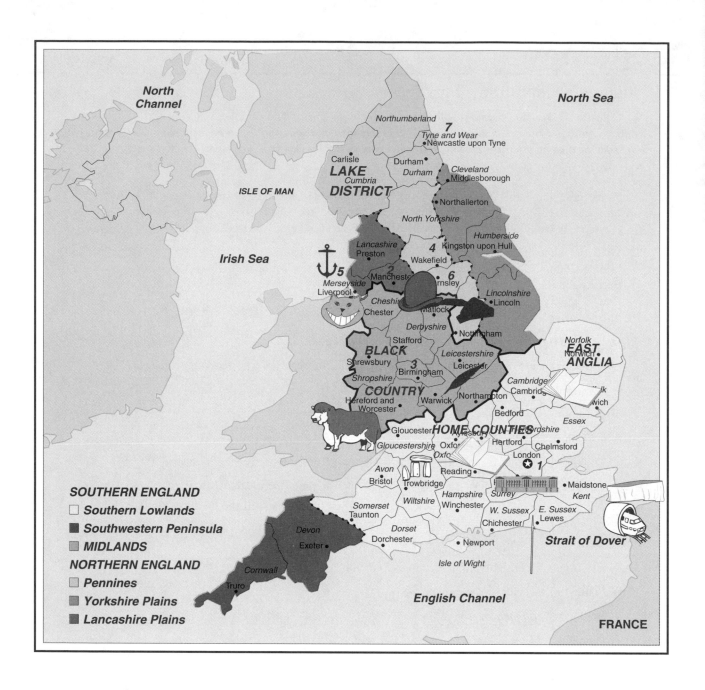

North Channel

North Sea

ISLE OF MAN

Irish Sea

Northumberland

7

Tyne and Wear
Newcastle upon Tyne

Carlisle

Durham
Durham

LAKE
Cumbria
DISTRICT

Cleveland
Middlesborough

Northallerton

North Yorkshire

Humberside

Lancashire
Preston

4
Kingston upon Hull

Wakefield

5

Merseyside
Liverpool

2
Manchester

6
Barnsley

Lincolnshire
Lincoln

Cheshire
Chester

Matlock

Derbyshire

Nottingham

Stafford

BLACK

Leicestershire
Leicester

Norfolk
Norwich

EAST
ANGLIA

Shrewsbury

3
Birmingham

Shropshire

COUNTRY

Warwick

Northampton

Cambridge
Cambridge

Suffolk
Ipswich

Hereford and
Worcester

Gloucester

HOME COUNTIES

Aylesbury

Hertfordshire

Essex

Gloucestershire

Oxford
Oxford

Hertford

Chelmsford

Avon
Bristol

Reading

London

1

Maidstone
Kent

Trowbridge

Hampshire
Winchester

Surrey

W. Sussex
Chichester

E. Sussex
Lewes

Strait of Dover

Somerset
Taunton

Wiltshire

Dorset
Dorchester

Newport

Isle of Wight

English Channel

FRANCE

SOUTHERN ENGLAND
☐ **Southern Lowlands**
■ **Southwestern Peninsula**
■ **MIDLANDS**
NORTHERN ENGLAND
☐ **Pennines**
■ **Yorkshire Plains**
■ **Lancashire Plains**

Devon
Exeter

Cornwall
Truro

Geography

A Modest Proposal by Jonathan Swift

The writer Jonathan Swift was born and educated in Ireland, although he had an English ancestry. He served as an Anglican priest in England for several years and then went to Dublin to serve as the Dean of St. Patrick's Cathedral. Swift is known for his irony and satire (sarcasm used to attack and expose evil). He wrote *A Modest Proposal* in 1729 to expose the terrible conditions of the Irish poor under the English government. The Penal Laws of 1695 ordered the confiscation of most of the Roman Catholics' land, sending many Irish people to the verge of starvation. The first few paragraphs describe his "modest proposal" for removing the cost of feeding and clothing the 120,000 children born each year to impoverished Irish families. Swift then lists six "advantages" to his proposal. Each "advantage" makes a mockery of English prejudices, which had placed the Irish into such a terrible condition. Read the following excerpts and then answer the questions below.

A Modest Proposal for Preventing the Children of the Poor People of Ireland from Being a Burden to Their Parents or Country, and for Making Them Beneficial to the Public:

. . . The number of souls in this kingdom being usually reckoned one million and a half, of these I calculate there may be about two hundred thousand couple whose wives are breeders; from which number I subtract thirty thousand couples who are able to maintain their own children . . . this being granted, there will remain an hundred and seventy thousand breeders. I again subtract fifty thousand for those women who miscarry, or whose children die by accident or disease within the year. There only remains one hundred and twenty thousand children of poor parents annually born. The question therefore is, how this number shall be reared and provided for, which, as I have already said, under the present situation of affairs, is utterly impossible by all the methods hitherto proposed. For we can neither employ them in handicraft or agriculture; we neither build houses (I mean in the country) nor cultivate land. . . .

I shall now therefore humbly propose my own thoughts, which I hope will not be liable to the least objection.

I have been assured by a very knowing American of my acquaintance in London, that a young healthy child well nursed is at a year old a most delicious, nourishing, and wholesome food, whether stewed, roasted, baked, or boiled. . . .

A child will make two dishes at an entertainment for friends; and when the family dines alone, the fore or hind quarter will make a reasonable dish, and seasoned with a little pepper or salt will be very good boiled on the fourth day, especially in winter.

I have reckoned upon a medium that a child just born will weigh 12 pounds, and in a solar year, if tolerably nursed, increaseth to 28 pounds.

I grant this food will be somewhat dear [expensive], and therefore very proper for landlords, who, as they have already devoured most of the parents, seem to have the best title to the children.

Infant's flesh will be in season throughout the year . . . and I believe no gentleman would repine [complain] to give ten shillings for the carcass of a good fat child, which, as I have said, will make four dishes of excellent nutritive meat, when he hath only some particular friend or his own family to dine with him. Thus the squire will learn to be a good landlord, and grow popular among his tenants; the mother will have eight shillings net profit, and be fit for work till she produces another child.

I think the advantages by the proposal which I have made are obvious and many, as well as of the highest importance.

For first, as I have already observed, it would greatly lessen the number of Papists [Roman Catholics], with whom we are yearly overrun, being the principal breeders of the nation as well as our most dangerous enemies; and who stay at home on purpose with a design to deliver the kingdom to the Pretender, hoping to take their advantage by the absence of so many good protestants, who have chosen rather to leave their country than stay at home and pay tithes against their conscience to an episcopal curate.

Secondly, the poorer tenants will have something valuable of their own, which by law may be made liable to distress and help to pay their landlord's rent, their corn and cattle being already seized, and money a thing unknown.

Thirdly, whereas the maintenance of an hundred thousand children, from two years old and upward, cannot be computed at less than ten shillings a-piece per annum [annually], the nation's stock will be thereby increased fifty thousand pounds per annum, beside the profit of a new dish introduced to the tables of all gentlemen of fortune in the kingdom who have any refinement in taste. And the money will circulate among ourselves, the goods being entirely of our own growth and manufacture.

Fourthly, the constant breeders, beside the gain of eight shillings sterling per annum by the sale of their children, will be rid of the charge of maintaining them after the first year.

Fifthly, this food would likewise bring great custom to taverns; where the vintners will certainly be so prudent as to procure the best receipts [recipes] for dressing it to perfection, and consequently have their houses frequented by all the fine gentlemen, who justly value themselves upon their knowledge in good eating: and a skillful cook, who understands how to oblige his guests, will contrive to make it as expensive as they please.

Sixthly, this would be a great inducement to marriage, which all wise nations have either encouraged by rewards or enforced by laws and penalties. It would increase the care and tenderness of mothers toward their children, when they were sure of a settlement for life to the poor babes, provided in some sort by the public, to their annual profit instead of expense. We should see an honest emulation [ambition to equal or surpass another] among the married women, which of them could bring the fattest child to the market. Men would become as fond of their wives during the time of their pregnancy as they are now of their mares in foal, their cows in calf, their sows when they are ready to farrow [give birth]; nor offer to beat or kick them (as is too frequent a practice) for fear of a miscarriage.

Many other advantages might be enumerated. For instance, the addition of some thousand carcasses in our exportation of barreled beef, the propagation of swine's flesh, and improvement in the art of making good bacon, so much wanted among us by the great destruction of pigs, too frequent at our tables; which are no way comparable in taste or magnificence to a well-grown, fat, yearling child, which roasted whole will make a considerable figure at a lord mayor's feast or any other public entertainment. But this and many others I omit, being studious of brevity [being brief].

1. What is Swift's "modest proposal"? _sell one-year-old children for food_

2. What effect do Swift's details have on the reader? Why do you think he went into such detail?

His descriptions are nauseating; he wanted his readers to see how their concern for money had blinded them to human suffering.

3-8. Tell in your own words the six advantages Swift gives for adopting his proposal.

- _fewer Roman Catholics_

- _the poor would have money to pay their rent_

- _more money would circulate in the nation_

- _mothers would receive money for each child instead of having to pay for each child_

- _taverns would receive more money_

- _more people would marry, and husbands would treat their wives properly_

9. Each "advantage" exposes an evil attitude among the British rulers. The first advantage deals with what kind of prejudice? _religious_

10. Which advantages concern money? What attitude towards money is Swift actually condemning?

the second, third, fourth, and fifth; greed

11. Which of Swift's advantages concerns family relations? What problem does Swift imply existed in Ireland? *the sixth; abuse of wives by their husbands*

12. Swift accused the Whigs (the English political party in control of the government at that time) of caring only about enhancing English trade. In which paragraphs does Swift suggest that the Irish should use their own goods and export more goods to England? *in the paragraph citing the third advantage and in the last paragraph*

13. Do you think the prejudices and problems that Swift alluded to are still evident in Ireland today?

    Feelings between Ireland and Britain are still tense today, though the Republic of Ireland is self-governed. Divisions between Roman Catholics and Protestants remain strong.

14. Are the prejudices and problems mentioned above evident in the world today? What are possible solutions? *Answers will vary; prejudice, greed, and abuse are problems worldwide. Even the United States continues to struggle with this perennial predicament. Solutions will vary, but the only permanent solution is the gospel.*

15. Do you think Swift's satirical writings changed the way the Irish were treated? Does satirical writing ever change things? *Answers will vary; Swift's writings did not change the treatment of the Irish by England; again, only the gospel can permanently change men's hearts.*

Geography

Map of the British Isles

Refer to the student text, page 301. Fill in each blank below with the correct location. Political divisions are uppercase letters (A, B, C), cities are lowercase letters (a, b, c), and physical features are numbers (1, 2, 3). (Note: The map does *not* give a letter for Great Britain, but instead it gives letters for the six political divisions within Great Britain.) **Encourage students to try to complete this activity without looking at the book and then to doublecheck their answers with the book.**

Political Divisions

A. _____ *Ireland* _____

B. _____ *Northern Ireland* _____

C. _____ *Scotland* _____

D. _____ *England* _____

E. _____ *Wales* _____

F. _____ *Isle of Man* _____

G. _____ *Channel Islands* _____

Cities

a. _____ *Dublin* _____

b. _____ *Belfast* _____

c. _____ *Glasgow* _____

d. _____ *Edinburgh* _____

e. _____ *Manchester* _____

f. _____ *Birmingham* _____

g. _____ *Cardiff* _____

h. _____ *London* _____

Physical Features

1. _____ *Irish Sea* _____

2. _____ *North Sea* _____

3. _____ *Pennines* _____

4. _____ *Trent River* _____

5. _____ *Thames River* _____

6. _____ *English Channel* _____

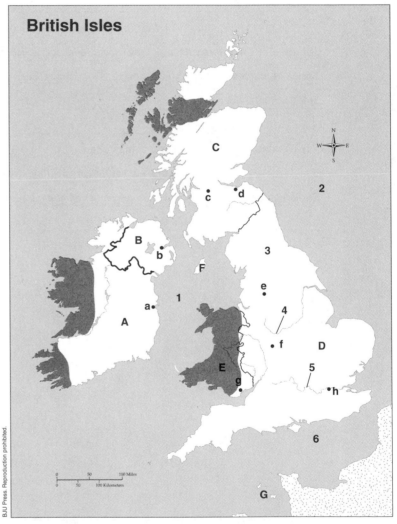

British Isles

Map Work

Look at the map on page 313, and shade red those areas in the British Isles that have a Celtic language subfamily.

Geography

Map of Scandinavia

Refer to the student text, page 317. Fill in each blank below with the correct location. Countries are uppercase letters (A, B, C), cities are lowercase letters (a, b, c), and physical features are numbers (1, 2, 3).

Encourage students to try to complete this activity without looking at the book and then to doublecheck their answers with the book.

Countries

A. _____ *Iceland* _____

B. _____ *Norway* _____

C. _____ *Sweden* _____

D. _____ *Finland* _____

E. _____ *Denmark* _____

Cities

a. _____ *Oslo* _____

b. _____ *Reykjavik* _____

c. _____ *Stockholm* _____

d. _____ *Helsinki* _____

e. _____ *Copenhagen* _____

Physical Features

1. _____ *Jutland* _____

2. _____ *Skagerrak* _____

3. _____ *Kjølen Mountains* _____

4. _____ *Lapland* _____

5. _____ *Lake Region* _____

6. _____ *Gulf of Bothnia* _____

7. _____ *Baltic Sea* _____

Map Work

1. Shade light blue those areas in Scandinavia that have a subpolar climate (map on p. 320). Shade deep blue those areas that have a polar climate.

2. Draw a dotted line across Scandinavia to represent the Arctic Circle.

Geography

Name _____

Chapter 13   **Activity 5**

Modified True/False

If the statement is true, write the word *true* in the blank. If it is false, change the underlined words to make the statement true.

true, p. 304	1. The longest-ruling monarch in English history was <u>Queen Victoria</u>.
Westminster Abbey, p. 305	2. The Anglican archbishop crowns monarchs at <u>Windsor Castle</u>.
true, p. 305	3. In 1931 Great Britain created the <u>Commonwealth of Nations</u>.
Anglican, p. 305	4. The Church of England is sometimes called the <u>Methodist</u> Church.
true, p. 306	5. In a parliamentary system, political parties sometimes join to form a <u>coalition</u> government.
true, p. 307	6. The word England means "<u>Angles</u>' Land."
true, p. 307	7. In 1066 England fell to Normans led by <u>William the Conqueror</u>.
downs, p. 307	8. South of London are a series of grassy, rolling chalk hills, called <u>fens</u>.
true, p. 308	9. The focus of the Industrial Revolution was in the western Midlands around <u>Birmingham</u>.
true, p. 308	10. The southwestern plateau in England is famous for its treeless <u>moors</u>.
factory, p. 308	11. The Industrial Revolution introduced the <u>cottage</u> system to England.
true, p. 309	12. When the government takes control of a private industry, it is called <u>nationalization</u>.
loch, p. 310	13. A <u>glen</u> is a deep lake carved by glaciers.
Celts, p. 310	14. The ancestors of the Scots, Welsh, and Irish were <u>Angles</u>.
Cheviot Hills, p. 311	15. The England/Scotland border lies in the <u>Cambrian Mountains</u>.
true, p. 314	16. The <u>North Atlantic Drift</u> explains Ireland's warm, moist climate.
Roman Catholics, p. 315	17. Most people in the Republic of Ireland are <u>Lutherans</u>.
IRA, p. 315	18. The <u>Irish Home Front</u> has waged the longest and deadliest campaign of terrorism in modern European history.
Gaelic, p. 315	19. Many Irishmen speak the Celtic language known as <u>brogue</u>.
true, p. 316	20. Both Newfoundland and Greenland were colonized by <u>Vikings</u>.
Queen Margaret, p. 316	21. At one time Scandinavia was united under <u>King Gustavus Adolphus</u>.
true, p. 316	22. Irish families sometimes burn <u>peat</u>, made up of partly decayed mosses that have been compressed.
Lutherans, pp. 316, 318	23. Most Scandinavians are <u>Roman Catholics</u>.
true, p. 318	24. Norway and Sweden lie on the <u>Scandinavian</u> Peninsula.
true, p. 318	25. A <u>fjord</u> is a long, narrow sea inlet carved by glaciers.
Finland, p. 319	26. All Scandinavian countries except <u>Denmark</u> speak similar languages.
Stockholm, p. 319	27. The largest city in Scandinavia is <u>Helsinki</u>.
Sweden, p. 319	28. During the World Wars, the Scandinavian nation <u>Norway</u> was neutral.
Greenland, p. 321	29. The largest island in the world is <u>Britain</u>.
true, p. 321	30. "Land of Fire and Ice" is a nickname for <u>Iceland</u>.

Geography

Map of Continental Europe

Complete the map on the next page, referring to the relief map on page 325 in your textbook.

1. Label these features of physical geography:
   Rivers—Danube River, Elbe River, Garonne River, Loire River, Rhine River, Rhone River, Seine River
   Mountains—Alps, Jura Mountains, Matterhorn, Mont Blanc, Pyrenees
   Forests—Black Forest, Bohemian Forest
   Miscellaneous—Ardennes, Bavarian Plateau, Massif Central

2. Label these features of human geography:
   Cities—Amsterdam, Berlin, Brussels, Cologne, Essen, Frankfurt, Geneva, The Hague, Marseille, Munich, Paris, Rotterdam, Vienna, Zurich
   Miscellaneous—Brittany, Canal du Midi, Flanders, Kiel Canal

3. Label all the countries in Continental Europe and their capitals.

4. Look at the table on page 332. Shade blue those countries that have a per capita GDP over $22,000.

5. Look at the climate map on page 320. Shade grey the only region in Continental Europe that has a mediterranean climate.

6. Look at the religion map on page 336. Shade yellow the region in Continental Europe that is predominantly Lutheran.

7. Place its rank beside each of the ten largest cities in Continental Europe. (Note that Paris has the largest metro area (9,523,000), followed by Essen (6,482,000) and Berlin (4,150,000))

Berlin, Germany	3,317,000
Paris, France	2,176,000
Hamburg, Germany	1,652,363
Vienna, Austria	1,539,848
Munich, Germany	1,229,026
Cologne, Germany	953,551
Marseille, France	874,436
Amsterdam, Netherlands	722,245
Frankfurt, Germany	659,800
Essen, Germany	626,973

Optional Activity

8. Draw these figures in the appropriate place.

   highest mountain in the Alps *(p. 329)*

   triple cirque peak *(p. 344)*

   country where the Protestant Reformation was born *(p. 336)*

   largest industrial region in Europe *(p. 339)*

   largest city in Continental Europe *(p. 336)*

   "City of Light" *(p. 326)*

   world leader in sugar beets *(p. 337)*

   world leader in oats *(p. 337)*

   Europe's leader in rye *(p. 337)*

   Europe's leader in wheat *(p. 327)*

   Europe's leader in hogs *(p. 337)*

   Europe's leader in natural gas *(p. 333)*

   Europe's leader in coal *(p. 339)*

   Europe's leader in automobiles *(p. 341)*

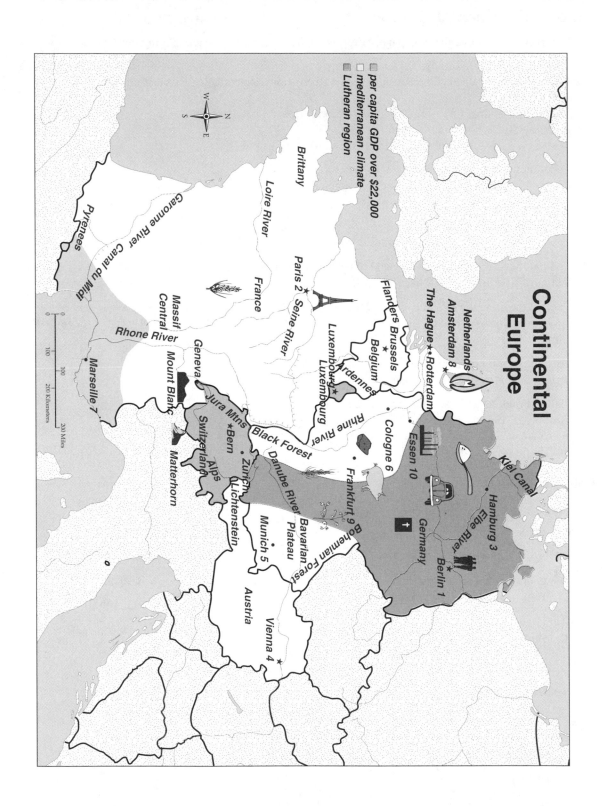

Continental Europe

per capita GDP over $22,000
mediterranean climate
Lutheran region

N W E S

Brittany
Loire River
France
Garonne River
Canal du Midi
Pyrenees
Paris 2
Seine River
Massif Central
Rhone River
Marseille 7
Mount Blanc
Geneva
Jura Mtns
Switzerland
Bern
Alps
Matterhorn
Zurich
Lichtenstein
Black Forest
Danube River
Munich 5
Bavarian Plateau
Bohemian Forest
Austria
Vienna 4
Rhine River
Frankfurt 9
Cologne 6
Luxembourg
Luxembourg
Ardennes
Belgium
Flanders
Brussels
The Hague
Amsterdam 8
Netherlands
Rotterdam
Essen 10
Germany
Berlin 1
Hamburg 3
Elbe River
Kiel Canal

0 100 200 Kilometers
0 100 200 Miles

Geography

Outlining Nations

Complete the outline for Chapter 14. Also, write beside each heading any boldfaced words that appear in that section. Then answer the questions that follow.

Introduction to Continental Europe   **Protestant Reformation** _____

I. The French Revolution   **French Revolution** _____

   A. Paris, the City of Light   **Paris** _____

      1. Palace of the Sun King   **Louis XIV** _____

      2. Capital of a World Empire   **Seine River, Napoleon Bonaparte** _____

   B.   *Northern France* _____

      1.   *Northern France Plains*   *(Loire River, Joan of Arc)* _____

      2.   *Northwest Hills of Brittany and Normandy*   *(Brittany, Normandy)* _____

      3.   *Contested Provinces on the Eastern Plateau*   *(Alsace-Lorraine, Rhine River, Jura Mountains)* _____

   C.   *Southern France* _____

      1.   *The Alps*   *(Mont Blanc)* _____

         a.   *The Rhone River*   *(Rhone River)* _____

         b.   *The Riviera*   *(French Riviera)* _____

         c.   *Corsica*   *(Corsica)* _____

      2.   *Massif Central*   *(Massif Central, Garonne River, Pyrenees Mountains)* _____

      3.   *Aquitanian Lowlands of the Southwest*   *(Aquitanian Lowlands)* _____

II.   *The Low Countries*   *(Charlemagne)* _____

   A.   *The Netherlands' Battle with the Sea*   *(William the Silent, dikes, polders)* _____

      1.   *Holland*   *(Holland, Amsterdam, The Hague, Rotterdam)* _____

      2.   *Ten Outlying Provinces* _____

   B.   *Belgium, the Capital of Europe*   *(Brussels, Flanders, Ardennes, Wallonia)* _____

   C.   *Luxembourg*   *(duchy)* _____

III.   *Germany, Birthplace of the Reformation* _____

   A.   *The Search for National Unity*   *(Thirty Years' War, Nazi Empire, Holocaust)* _____

   B.   *The Berlin Wall*   *(Berlin, Berlin Wall, reunification)* _____

   C.   *Northern Plains*   *(loess)* _____

      1.   *Eastern Germany*   *(Elbe River)* _____

      2.   *Western Germany*   *(Kiel Canal, Ruhr)* _____

D. _Central Uplands_ _(Central Uplands)_

    1. _The Upper Rhine_ _(Black Forest)_

    2. _Bavaria_ _(Bavaria, Bohemian Forest, Munich, Bavarian Alps)_

IV. _The Alps, Europe's Backbone_ _(Alps)_

  A. _Neutral Switzerland_ _(cantons)_

    1. _The Jura in the North_ _(John Calvin)_

    2. _Great Cities of the Central Swiss Plateau_ _(foehn)_

      a. _Geneva_ _(Geneva, Jean-Jacques Rousseau)_

      b. _The Capital, Bern_

      c. _Zurich_ _(Zurich)_

    3. _Cultural Diversity of the Swiss Alps_ _(Swiss Alps, Matterhorn)_

  B. _Liechtenstein_

  C. _The Austrian Empire_ _(Hapsburg)_

    1. _The Blue Danube_ _(Danube River, Vienna)_

    2. _Many Alpine Ranges_

Outline Investigation

1. How many countries are discussed in this chapter? _eight_

2. What are the three Low Countries? _the Netherlands, Belgium, Luxembourg_

3. What are the three countries under the Alps heading? _Switzerland, Liechtenstein, Austria_

4. Which two countries have their own master heading? _France, Germany_

5. How many headings include the names of natural features:

    rivers _three (Rhone, Rhine, Danube)_

    mountains _five (Alps—four times, Jura)_

    plateaus (including hills, uplands, and massifs) _five, but answers may vary (northwest hills, eastern_

    plateaus, Massif Central, Central Uplands, central Swiss plateau)

6. Outside of its capital, France is divided into two basic regions. How many subregions are these two

    regions divided into? _three apiece_

7. What are the three main regions in Switzerland? _Jura, Central Swiss Plateau, Swiss Alps_

8. What are the two main regions in Austria? _Danube River, Alpine ranges_

9. How many rivers appear as terms in the chapter? Of these, how many are discussed under France?

    seven; five

   Look at the map on page 325. What two countries include part of the Danube River? Under which

    country is it given as a term? Why is it listed under that country? _Germany and Austria; Austria; the_

    river is bigger and more important in Austria, where it flows by the capital

Geography

Name _____

Chapter 14   **Activity 3**

France's Provinces

Color in the key and the map with the six cultural subregions in France discussed in your text. The key also gives the number of provinces within each region. (Note that Ile-de-France touches all of the other six provinces in the Northern France Plains.) *Use this map in discussing the six regions of France; it will make the student text more meaningful.*

Map Work

1. Label the locations of the five minority languages spoken in France.

2. Draw the five rivers that flow through France's largest cities, and label the rivers.

3. Write their ranking beside the ten largest cities in France.

Paris	2,176,000
Marseille	874,000
Lyon	413,000
Toulouse	348,000
Nice	337,000
Strasbourg	248,000
Nantes	240,000
Bordeaux	208,000
St. Etienne	208,000
Le Havre	199,000

Map Questions

1. Which subregion has the most large cities?   *Alps (including the Rhone River valley)*

2. Which two of France's top-ten cities are not close to any major rivers? Why do you think they grew so big?   *Nice and Marseille; Nice lies on the important coastal route between Italy and France, where no major rivers flow, and Nice also offers the attractions of the French Riviera; Marseille has a great port on the Mediterranean and also lies on the overland route to Italy.*

Geography

Germany's States

Color in the key and the map with the four cultural subregions in Germany discussed in your text. (Note that East Germany includes Berlin as a sixth city-state.) *Use this map in discussing the four regions of Germany; it will make the student text more meaningful.*

Map Work

Write their ranking beside the ten largest metropolitan areas in Germany.

Essen	6,482,000
Berlin	4,150,000
Frankfurt	3,605,000
Düsseldorf	3,030,000
Cologne	2,984,000
Hamburg	2,385,000
Stuttgart	2,005,000
Munich	1,900,000
Nuremberg	1,065,000
Hanover	1,000,000

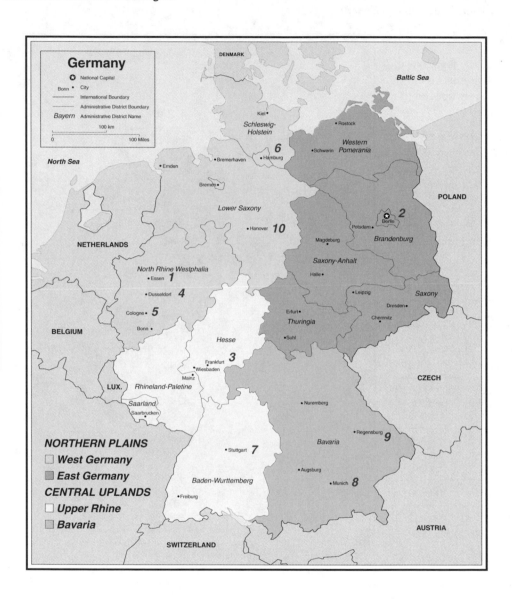

Map Questions

1. What is the largest metropolitan area in each region?

   • East German Plains ___*Berlin*___

   • West German Plains ___*Essen*___

   • Upper Rhine ___*Frankfurt*___

   • Bavaria ___*Munich*___

2. Which of Germany's four regions has the most major metropolitan areas? ___*West German Plains*___

Geography

☆ **Comparison of Two Giants**

Complete the chart showing some of the similarities and differences between France and Germany. Don't forget to look at the statistical chart and various maps of Europe. (See the map index on pages vi-vii.) Also, you may need to review the survey of world history on page 99. ☆ *Class discussion. See page v.*

		Germany	France
Geography	Area (p. 332)	*137,828 sq. mi.*	*210,026 sq. mi.*
	Climate (map on p. 320)	*predominantly marine west coast with some varied highlands (Alps)*	*predominantly marine west coast with some mediterranean and varied highlands (Alps)*
	Geographic Regions	*northern plains (Great European Plain), Central Uplands, Bavarian Alps (pp. 337-42)*	*Northern France Plains (Great European Plain), Hills of Brittany and Normandy, Central Uplands (Massif Central, Jura Mountains, Alsace-Lorraine), Alps, Pyrenees Mountains, Aquitanian Lowlands (pp. 327-31)*
	High Point	*Zugspitze (9,721 ft., p. 342)*	*Mont Blanc (15,771 ft., p. 329)*
	Main Rivers	*Seine, Loire, Rhine, Garonne, and Rhone (pp. 326, 328, 330-31)*	*Rhine, Elbe, (and Danube) (pp. 338, 340)*
Economy	Per Capita GDP (See table on p. 332.)	*$16,580*	*$18,670*
	Major Agricultural Products	*sugar beets, oats, rye, hogs (p. 337)*	*sugar beets, corn, wheat, barley, wine (pp. 327, 330, 331)*
	Major Mining Products	*not many—coal (p. 339)*	*not many—iron in the Vosges Mountains (p. 328)*
	Major Manufacturing	*crude steel, refined copper, smelted lead, smelted zinc, various synthetic materials (including rubber, rayon, nylons, and polyesters), automobiles (pp. 340-41)*	*steel (p. 328)*

		Germany	France
Demography	Population (p. 332)	83,536,000	58,040,000
	Population Density (p. 332)	606	276
	Natural Increase (p. 332)	–0.1%	0.2%
	Life Expectancy (p. 332)	76	79
	Literacy Rate (p. 332)	100%	99%
History	Early Settlement	German tribes (p. 336)	Gauls (Celtic tribes) conquered by the Franks (Germanic tribes) in A.D. 486 (p. 326)
	Creation of the United Country	German territories not united until 1871 (p. 336)	first king of France in 987 (p. 326)
	Impact of Communism	division into East and West (p. 336)	none mentioned in the text
	Famous Rulers	Adolf Hitler (p. 336)	Louis XIV, Napoleon Bonaparte (pp. 326-27)
Government	Form of Government	federated republic (pp. 336, 338)	parliamentary republic (p. 327)
	Number of Political Divisions (States/Provinces)	sixteen states (Landers, p. 338)	twenty-two provinces (p. 327)
Society	Main Minorities	none mentioned in the text (Turks, p. 338)	Flemish (Dutch), Bretons, Alsatian (German), Corsican (Italian), and Basque (pp. 328, 330-31)
	Main Religion	Lutheranism (p. 336)	Roman Catholicism (p. 325)
	Famous Buildings	much was destroyed in World War II but Neuschwanstein Castle stands (p. 342)	Notre Dame, Eiffel Tower, Arc de Triomphe, Chartres Cathedral (pp. 326, 328)

Geography

Your Best Friend's Letters from Abroad

Your best friend is on a trip to Continental Europe and begins sending you post cards. The cards describe all of the wonderful places on the trip but they also assume you know the places because you are studying geography. Read each description and tell who or what the underlined word or phrase is.

Paris, p. 326	1. We landed in "the most beautiful <u>city</u> in the world" this morning.
Eiffel Tower, p. 326	2. Strolling along the Seine River, I looked up to see what was once the tallest <u>structure</u> in the world.
Louis XIV, p. 326	3. My dad took me to the palace of the "<u>Sun King</u>."
French Revolution, p. 325	4. I was trying out my French at a local café when the conversation turned to the most pivotal <u>event</u> in modern Europe.
battle of Orléans, p. 328	5. We drove south of Paris yesterday to see the <u>battlefield</u> where Joan of Arc triumphed over the English in the Hundred Years' War.
Normandy, p. 328	6. We stopped at the historic <u>site</u> where American troops staged the largest amphibious invasion in history.
Mont Blanc, p. 329	7. We were walking in the Alps and glimpsed the highest <u>mountain</u> in the entire range, but I would never want to climb it!
Rhone River, p. 330	8. We visited Lyon and then sailed down the <u>river</u> on a small tour boat to the coast, enjoying the view of all the well-kept vineyards.
Garonne River, p. 331	9. We ate some cheese and bread for lunch at a restaurant in Toulouse, and then we drove down the <u>river</u> to Bordeaux to spend the night. I was amazed to see fields of corn.
polders, p. 332	10. We crossed the border into the Netherlands, and I saw my first dike, as well as the beautiful tulips in the <u>land</u> reclaimed by the sea.
The Hague, p. 333	11. We toured the government buildings and saw the monarch's palace at the <u>capital</u> of the Netherlands.
Rotterdam, p. 333	12. We saw ships coming and going at the busy <u>port</u> of the "New Orleans of Europe."
Brussels, p. 335	13. After our visit to the Netherlands, our next stop was at the <u>capital</u> of Belgium. I especially enjoyed a peek in the Parliament of the European Union.
Flanders, p. 335	14. I was amazed by the similarities between the <u>lowland region</u> of Belgium and the Dutch landscape.
Wallonia, p. 335	15. The contrast between the coastal region and the <u>southern district</u> of Belgium was striking—the tiny villages, the forested hills, and the relative poverty.
Grand Duke, p. 335	16. We stopped in Luxembourg just to know that we had visited the little country, and while we were there we looked at the residence of its <u>hereditary monarch</u>.
Berlin, p. 337	17. We flew into the newly unified <u>capital</u> of Germany; it was so much more modern than Paris, but I missed the historic buildings we had enjoyed in Paris.

18. We stayed in Berlin and took day trips to various cities in East Germany. The relative poverty of the people was very depressing, but I enjoyed going up the <u>river</u> from Magdeburg to the Wittenberg cathedral, where Luther nailed his ninety-five theses.

19. In West Germany I got to see some of the rich farms that have the thick, wind-born <u>soil</u> we read about in class. The farms were a big contrast to those we saw in East Germany.

20. We stayed one night in Essen, in the midst of the ugly "<u>smokestack region</u>."

21. We took a boat up the <u>most important river</u> in Germany through Cologne and Bonn.

22. From Stuttgart we drove southwest into Germany's famous dark <u>forest</u> near the border with France.

23. During our stay in Munich, we enjoyed a breathtaking view of the <u>mountains</u> near the border with Austria. I even got to ski during the afternoon.

24. While we were driving into Switzerland, I saw a huge crowd gathered. I later learned that I had witnessed a Landsgemeinde being held by that <u>self-governing district</u>.

25. We drove along the Ruhr River into Switzerland and spent the night at Basel, where the famous <u>reformer</u> wrote *Institutes of the Christian Religion.*

26. I was surprised by the <u>warm winds</u> that blew in the Alpine valley around Innsbruck.

27. While we were in the <u>Swiss mountains</u>, I wanted to see the Matterhorn, but Mom said we didn't have time.

28. When we drove through <u>the smallest country in Continental Europe</u>, it looked more like a town than a country!

29. Of course we got tickets to a concert while staying in <u>the capital of Austria</u>. They played the "Blue Danube."

30. All across the country we saw castles built by the <u>ancient ruling family</u> of Austria.

Skill: Comprehension

Geography

Map of Mediterranean Europe

Complete the map on the next page, referring to the relief map on page 349 in your textbook.

1. Label these features of physical geography:
   Bodies of Water—Mediterranean Sea, Po River, Strait of Gibraltar, Tagus River
   Mountains—Apennine Mountains, Cantabrian Mountains, Mount Vesuvius, Pindus Mountains, Sierra Morena, Sierra Nevada
   Miscellaneous—Crete, Meseta, Peloponnesus, Sicily

2. Label these cities—Athens, Barcelona, Lisbon, Madrid, Milan, Naples, Porto, Rome, Thessaloniki, Turin, Valencia

3. Label all the countries in Mediterranean Europe.

4. Look at the table on page 349. Shade green the country with the lowest per capita GDP in Mediterranean Europe.

5. Place its rank beside each of the eleven largest metropolitan areas in Mediterranean Europe.

Milan, Italy	4,300,000
Madrid, Spain	4,100,000
Athens, Greece	3,100,000
Naples, Italy	3,000,000
Barcelona, Spain	2,800,000
Rome, Italy	2,700,000
Lisbon, Portugal	2,000,000
Porto, Portugal	1,600,000
Valencia, Spain	1,300,000
Turin, Italy	1,300,000
Thessaloniki, Greece	1,000,000

Optional Activity

6. Draw these figures in the appropriate place.

   ▲ mainland Europe's only active volcano *(p. 358)*

   ◻ birthplace of the Italian Renaissance *(p. 358)*

   center of the Orthodox Church *(p. 363)*

   part of Italy that is home to the Mafia *(p. 360)*

   island that was home to the Minoan civilization *(p. 365)*

   most populous Mediterranean island *(p. 360)*

   country with the highest population density in Europe *(p. 349)*

   ⚓ Spain's key port *(p. 353)*

   ⚓ one of the world's best natural harbors *(p. 355)*

   most cultivated region in Italy *(pp. 359-60)*

   most productive agricultural area in Greece *(p. 365)*

   world's leader in olives *(p. 348)*

   Europe's leader in citrus fruits (4th worldwide) *(p. 352)*

   Mediterranean's leader in wood pulp (5th worldwide) *(p. 355)*

   Western Europe's leader in silver (10th worldwide) *(p. 352)*

Mediterranean Europe

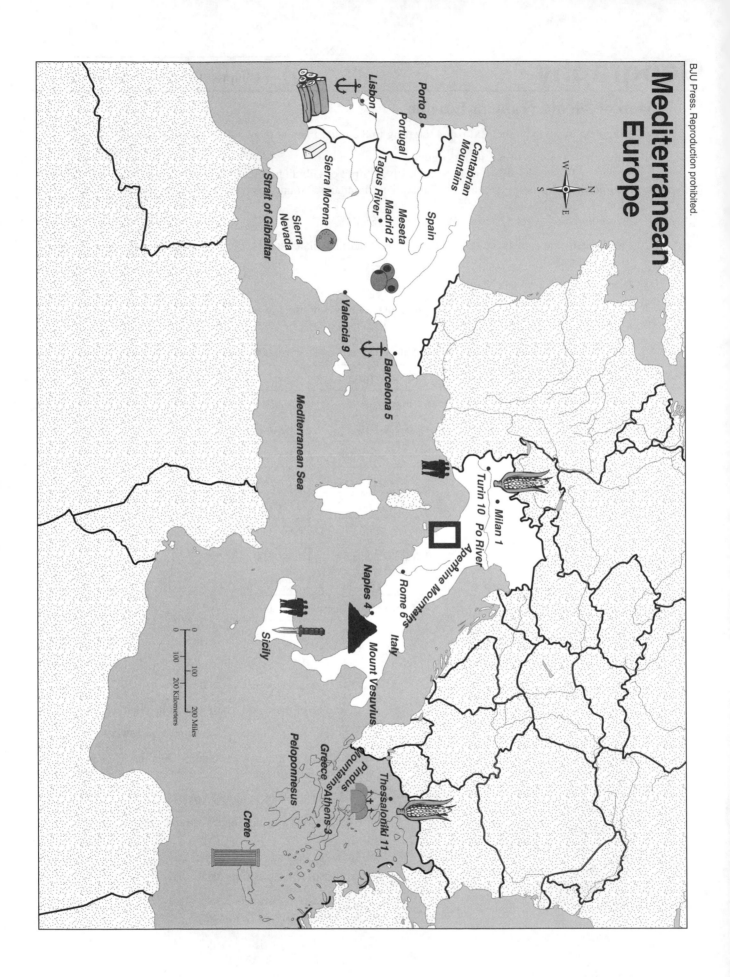

N
W — E
S

Cantabrian Mountains

Porto 8

Portugal

Spain

Lisbon 7

Tagus River

Meseta

Madrid 2

Sierra Morena

Sierra Nevada

Strait of Gibraltar

Valencia 9

Barcelona 5

Mediterranean Sea

Milan 1

Turin 10   Po River

Apennine Mountains

Rome 6

Italy

Naples 4

Mount Vesuvius

Sicily

Peloponnesus

Greece

Pindus Mountains

Athens 3

Thessaloníki 11

Crete

0
100
200 Kilometers

0
100
200 Miles

Skill: Maps

Geography

Name _____

Chapter 15   Activity 2

Famous Regions of the Mediterranean

Below and on the next page are three maps showing Spain, Italy, and Greece. Color in the keys and maps with the subregions discussed in your text.

Using these maps in discussing the regions of each country will make the student text more meaningful.

Map Work

1. Based on your reading in the textbook, label the locations of the three minority languages spoken in Spain.

2. Write their ranking beside the ten largest cities in Spain. (Note: The Canary Islands do not appear on the map.)

Madrid	3,100,000
Barcelona	1,700,000
Valencia	770,000
Seville	670,000
Sargossa	600,000
Málaga	600,000
Bilbao	380,000
Las Palmas (Canary Is.)	370,000
Palma (Balearic Is.)	320,000
Murcia	310,000

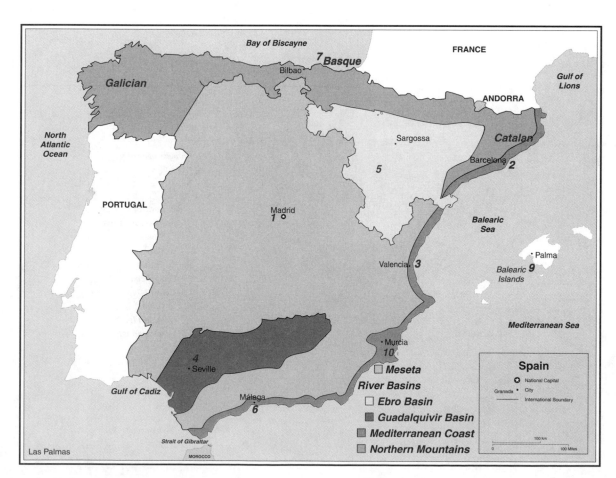

Map Work

Write their ranking beside the eleven largest cities in Italy.

Rome	2,500,000
Milan	1,600,000
Naples	1,200,000
Turin	1,000,000
Genoa	760,000
Palmero	700,000
Bologna	460,000
Florence	450,000
Catania	380,000
Bari	370,000
Venice	350,000

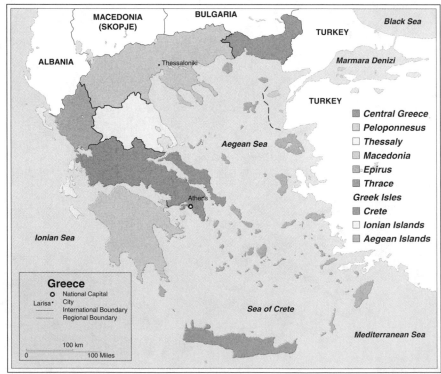

Geography

Seven Things a Roman Catholic Must Do to Be Saved

A leading controversy among Protestants today involves the status of the Roman Catholic Church. Although Evangelicals and Charismatics acknowledge serious doctrinal differences with the Catholic Church, they desire fellowship with all people who are "born again." By working together with believers in the Catholic Church, Evangelicals believe they can reach more people with the gospel.

But the Great Commission is not the only New Testament command. The New Testament epistles end with an equally forceful command: "Earnestly contend for the faith" (Jude 3). Even the Great Commission ends with a solemn command for Christians to make disciples, teaching them to observe all things Jesus has commanded (Matt. 28:20). The *Catechism of the Catholic Church* (1994)—the first in over one hundred years—shows that the church has not changed its basic doctrines. The catechism lists at least seven essentials for salvation. Study the list and answer the questions that follow.

183. Faith: "Faith is necessary for salvation. The Lord Himself affirms: 'He who believes and is baptized will be saved, but he who does not believe will be condemned' (Mark 16:16)."

846. The Church: "Basing itself on Scripture and Tradition, the Council teaches that the Church, a pilgrim now on earth, is necessary for salvation" [quoted from a church council known as Vatican II].

980. Penance: "This sacrament of Penance is necessary for salvation for those who have fallen after Baptism, just as Baptism is necessary for salvation for those who have not yet been reborn."

1129. The Mass: "The Church affirms that for believers the sacraments of the New Covenant [particularly the mass] are necessary for salvation."

1257. Baptism: "The Lord himself affirms that Baptism is necessary for salvation. . . . The Church does not know of any means other than Baptism that assures entry into eternal beatitude."

2027. Good Works: "No one can merit the initial grace which is at the origin of conversion. Moved by the Holy Spirit, we can merit for ourselves and for others all the graces needed to attain eternal life."

2068. Ten Commandments: "All men may attain salvation through faith, Baptism, and the observance of the Commandments" [quoted from Vatican II].

Discussion Questions

1. Both Roman Catholics and Evangelicals believe that people must be saved by "faith." Do they mean the same thing? *The Catholic Church means essentially the same thing by the word* faith *as do evangelicals. The word* faith *means "belief in something, or trust in a person or object." The key is not the type, amount, or sincerity of faith but rather the object of that faith. Paragraph 182 from the Catechism lists the object of a Catholic's faith: "We believe all 'that which is contained in the word of God, written or handed down, and which* the Church proposes *for belief as divinely revealed' (Paul VI, CPG, Sec 20)" [emphasis added]. The Catholic's faith extends not only to the Bible but to Church traditions ("the word of God handed down") as well as everything the Church ever declares true. When a Roman Catholic claims he "is saved by faith," he means faith in the Lord Jesus Christ, as well as faith in the Church leaders and all they teach.*

2. Both Roman Catholics and Evangelicals believe Ephesians 2:8-9. What is different about their interpretation of "grace"?   *Grace means simply "something good done for someone, whether or not it is reciprocated (a gift)." Evangelicals believe that grace encompasses everything the Lord Jesus Christ did to save sinners and to bring them back to God. God's grace is always free because people cannot earn it or deserve it. When the Bible speaks of God's grace, it can always be narrowed to a specific good thing, such as salvation or adoption.*

Roman Catholics, on the other hand, define grace in a very broad and complex manner. The Catholic Biblical Encyclopedia: New Testament devotes seven pages to "grace" (285-92). Catholics would agree with the above definition of grace but then add many other extrabiblical ideas based on Church tradition. For example, they speak of "sanctifying grace"—a virtual commodity, though immaterial and not strictly measurable, that is infused into people. Different people have different amounts of this grace, and it can be transferred from one person to another. The Catholic system sees grace as an earned commodity of righteousness.

3. Both Roman Catholics and Evangelicals quote Mark 16:16. What is different about their interpretation of baptism?   *The Catechism repeatedly and unmistakably asserts that baptism is the means of salvation, whether for infants, children, or adults. For example, paragraph 1213 states, "Through Baptism we are freed from sin and reborn as sons of God; we become members of Christ, are incorporated into the Church and made sharers in her mission."*

Baptism is so closely tied to salvation that it is understandable why readers of the Bible confuse the two. But on closer inspection, Evangelicals conclude that the New Testament commands baptism but never equates it with salvation. Water baptism is a picture and symbol of the heavenly "baptism into Jesus Christ" described in Romans 6. Mark 16:16 sometimes causes confusion, especially in the Latin Vulgate (the official translation of the Catholic Church), because it translates both verbs in the future tense. The original Greek language, however, reads, "The one having believed and been baptized will be saved," simply assuming that any believer will be baptized. The next clause in verse 16 makes the truth clear, for it omits baptism and focuses on belief.

4. Based on your knowledge of the Protestant Reformation, how do Evangelicals differ with Catholics on each of the seven "essentials of salvation"?   *Evangelicals differ from Catholics on all seven "necessities": (1) faith—Evangelicals affirm that faith is necessary to salvation when it is faith in Christ and in what He has done; (2) church—Evangelicals hold that any saved person is by definition a member of the true church of Christ and deny that the Roman Catholic Church is necessary for salvation; (3) penance—Evangelicals agree that the Bible requires repentance of sin for salvation but deny that penance, a sacrament requiring good works to regain God's favor, "restores" salvation to a sinner; (4) mass—Evangelicals obey the Lord's command to observe the Lord's Supper, but they deny that the bread or wine undergo any transformation or that quantitative grace is infused to participants or that this sacrament is necessary to salvation; (5) baptism—Evangelicals agree that symbolic water baptism is commanded but deny its necessity to salvation; (6) good works—Evangelicals maintain that regenerated people do good*

works by the power of God, but they reject the doctrine that any human work can earn favor for salvation;

(7) Ten Commandments—Evangelicals believe the Ten Commandments summarize God's perfect moral law,

which no man but Jesus Christ kept perfectly, earning the righteousness that is fully and freely accounted

to a believer at salvation.

5. Can a Roman Catholic who believes the Catechism fit the definition of an Evangelical? Why or why not?   *Because of the large number of diametrically opposed doctrines, it is impossible for anyone who*

subscribes completely to the Catechism to fit the historic definition of an Evangelical.

6. Should a believer stay in the Roman Catholic Church even if he disagrees with its teachings about salvation?   *This question hinges on the definition of a false teacher (see II Peter 2). True Christians must*

separate themselves from teachers of doctrinal error; that is, they must avoid any relation that recognizes a

false teacher as authoritative. Therefore, a believer who disagrees with the fundamental doctrines of the

Roman Catholic Church should separate from that church.

7. Should your presentation of the gospel to a nonbelieving Catholic be different from your presentation to a nonbelieving Evangelical? If so, how?   *Answers will vary. The gospel message is the same for all*

people, but it is wise to adapt your presentation to the special hindrances of each hearer. When presenting

the gospel to Catholics, one effective approach is to get them to study a key passage of the New Testament

in its entirety. For example, you could set up a time together to study Galatians at length. Catholics know all

the terminology, such as "saved by faith," "believe in Christ," and "born again," but they are trusting many

things besides Christ for salvation. Because they claim to believe the Bible, point them to the Bible and let

the Word of God speak for itself. Soon enough, they will see that the New Testament contradicts Church

tradition. Evangelicals often know the right doctrines but fail to see that they have not applied them to their

own lives.

It might be wise to preface the answers by reading from the 1994 Catechism or the Council of Trent on the Church's exclusive authority and infallibility. This information educates non-Catholics who do not realize the Church's claims of absolutism, and it challenges Catholics to realize how difficult it is for their Church's claims to withstand close scrutiny. Furthermore, readers should consider that the Roman Church defines itself as the Christian Church. Catholics give equal weight to Church tradition and councils as to the Bible. The Catechism slides from a Bible verse to a Church Father to a Church council or unsupported claims, often in the same paragraph!

Geography

Brain Drain

Without looking at your textbook, answer as many questions as you can. Then, with the help of your teacher or your textbook, check your answers and note your total score on the chart below.

Use this activity as a pretest for the chapter. Students will be surprised at what they already know about the Mediterranean.

Physical Geography

1. What is the name of the peninsula that includes Portugal and Spain (pp. 348-49)? *Iberian Peninsula*

2. What narrow strait separates Spain from Africa (p. 352)? *Strait of Gibraltar*

3. What river flows by Rome (p. 356)? *Tiber*

4. What mountain range separates Italy from the European continent (p. 359)? *Alps*

5. What large island lies near Italy's "boot" (p. 360)? *Sicily*

History

6. What do we call Spain's brutal effort to eliminate non-Catholic teachings through torture and execution (pp. 349-50)? *Spanish Inquisition*

7. Name one Roman emperor (p. 356). *Answers include Julius Caesar.*

8. Name one famous building in the Mediterranean region (pp. 356, 358, 360, 362). *Answers include the Colosseum and Parthenon.*

9. Name one famous general in Greek history (p. 363). *Alexander the Great*

10. What city is considered the birthplace of democracy (pp. 363-64)? *Athens*

11. What country is famous for the Mafia (p. 360)? *Italy*

12. What country held the first Olympics (p. 364)? *Greece*

13. What period of "rebirth" of art in Italy followed the Middle Ages (p. 358)? *Renaissance*

Modern Culture

14. Name a product for which the Mediterranean region is famous (p. 348). *olives or wine*

15. Identify a popular sport in Spain (p. 350). *bullfighting or soccer*

16. What religion dominates Spain and Italy (p. 350)? *Roman Catholicism*

17. Name the capital of Spain (p. 350). *Madrid*

18. Name the capital of Italy (p. 356). *Rome*

19. Name the capital of Greece (p. 363). *Athens*

20. What is unique about Venice (p. 359)? *gondolas or canals*

Score	Rating
0–4	Not so fair (You're starting from scratch.)
5–9	Fair (You should find this chapter very helpful.)
10–14	Good (This chapter should be a piece of cake.)
15–17	Excellent (Congratulations! You don't have much more to learn.)
18–20	Outstanding (You're a brain. But you can still learn some things from this chapter.)

Geography

Who Am I?

Read each phrase and decide the person it describes. Write the correct answer in the blank.

Philip II, p. 350	1. I moved my capital to Madrid and built the Spanish Armada.
Prince Henry, p. 355	2. I started a school of navigation in Portugal and financed voyages of discovery in Africa.
Julius Caesar, p. 356	3. I conquered Gaul and became Rome's first emperor.
Garibaldi, p. 357	4. My "Red Shirts" united Italy by 1870.
Alexander the Great, p. 363	5. I built the largest empire in the ancient world.
Basques, p. 354	6. I am an ancient people living in the Pyrenees.

Where Am I?

Read each phrase and decide the place it describes. Write the correct answer in the blank.

Apulia, p. 358	7. I am the "boot heel" of Italy.
Iberian Peninsula, p. 348	8. I am a large peninsula shared by Spain and Portugal.
Meseta, p. 351	9. I am a high plateau that covers most of Spain.
Ionian Islands, p. 365	10. I am a group of fertile islands that Britain gave to Greece in 1864.
Rhodes, p. 366	11. I am a large Aegean island that displayed the Colossus, an ancient wonder of the world.
Madrid, p. 350	12. I am the highest capital in Europe.
Escorial, p. 352	13. I am the royal residence of Spanish monarchs.
Andorra, p. 354	14. I am a small country in the Pyrenees.
San Marino, p. 361	15. I am a small country in the Apennines.
Vatican City, p. 361	16. I am the smallest country in the world.
Malta, p. 362	17. I am an island country in the Mediterranean once controlled by Britain.
Sparta, p. 364	18. I am a city-state on the Peloponnesus that conquered ancient Athens.

What Am I?

Read each phrase and decide the thing it describes. Write the correct answer in the blank.

Reconquista, p. 349	19. I am the Spanish campaign to retake the Iberian Peninsula from the Moors.
Spanish Inquisition, pp. 349-50	20. I am the Spanish campaign to stop doctrines contrary to the Roman Catholic Church.
French, p. 361	21. I am the official language of Monaco.
Castilian, p. 350	22. I am the official language of Spain.
mediterranean, pp. 50, 348	23. I am the main climate on the Mediterranean Sea—hot, dry summers and mild, wet winters.
Parthenon, p. 364	24. I am a temple to Athena built on the Acropolis.
Liguria, p. 358	25. I am sometimes called the Italian Riviera.
icon, p. 363	26. I am a painted image of Christ used by the Orthodox Church as an aid in worship.

Geography

A Second Look at Western Europe

Fill in each blank with the best answer.

C (p. 324) 1. most common climate in Continental Europe

    A. humid continental   C. marine west coast
    B. humid subtropical   D. mediterranean

A (p. 342) 2. greatest mountain system in Europe

    A. Alpine   C. Atlantic
    B. Andes   D. Himalayan

C (p. 329) 3. highest mountain in the Alps

    A. Glittertinden   C. Mont Blanc
    B. Matterhorn   D. Montserrat

D (p. 308) 4. birthplace of the Industrial Revolution

    A. France   C. Italy
    B. Germany   D. United Kingdom

B (p. 336) 5. birthplace of the Protestant Reformation

    A. France   C. Italy
    B. Germany   D. United Kingdom

B (pp. 339, 341) 6. Europe's leading source of coal and automobiles

    A. France   C. Italy
    B. Germany   D. United Kingdom

B (p. 332) 7. most populous country in Western Europe

    A. France   C. Italy
    B. Germany   D. United Kingdom

A (p. 325) 8. largest area in Western Europe

    A. France   C. Spain
    B. Germany   D. Sweden

B (p. 302) 9. biggest city in Western Europe

    A. Berlin   C. Madrid
    B. London   D. Paris

B (p. 313) 10. most-spoken language family in Western Europe

    A. Caucasian   C. Semitic
    B. Indo-European   D. Ural-Altaic

A (p. 336) 11. most common religion in Western Europe

    A. Christianity   C. Islam
    B. Eastern religions   D. Jewish

Geography

Chapter 16   **Activity 1**

Map of Eastern Europe

Refer to the relief map on page 372. Using the letters and numbers given below, label the following features on the map.

Countries

A. Albania	J. Lithuania
B. Belarus	K. Macedonia
C. Bosnia-Herzegovina	L. Moldova
D. Bulgaria	M. Poland
E. Croatia	N. Romania
F. Czech Republic	O. Slovakia
G. Estonia	P. Slovenia
H. Hungary	Q. Ukraine
I. Latvia	R. Yugoslavia

Cities

a. Belgrade	f. Kraków
b. Bucharest	g. Minsk
c. Budapest	h. Prague
d. Chernobyl	i. Warsaw
e. Kiev	

Regions

aa. Bohemia	dd. Silesia
bb. Crimea	ee. Walachia
cc. Moravia	

Physical Features

1. Balkan Mountains	6. Hungarian Basin
2. Carpathian Mountains	7. Oder River
3. Dinaric Alps	8. Pinsk Marshes
4. Dnieper River	9. Rhodope Mountains
5. Donets Basin	10. Transylvanian Alps
	11. Vistula River

Map Work *This section is optional.*

1. Look at the map on page 369. Label and draw borders around the four cultural subregions of Eastern Europe: Balkans, Baltic Rim, Carpathian Divide, and Eastern Plain. Use a different color for each region.

2. Place its rank beside each of the ten largest cities in Eastern Europe.

Kiev, Ukraine	2,640,000	Minsk, Belarus	1,630,000
Bucharest, Romania	2,060,000	Dnipropetrovsk, Ukraine	1,230,000
Budapest, Hungary	1,900,000	Plovdiv, Bulgaria	1,220,000
Kharkov, Ukraine	1,680,000	Prague, Czech Rep.	1,210,000
Warsaw, Poland	1,660,000	Belgrade, Yugoslavia	1,140,000

3. Draw these figures in the appropriate place.

🔺 headquarters of the Commonwealth of Independent States *(p. 388)*

☪ only country in Europe with a Muslim majority *(p. 385)*

👥 most populous city in Eastern Europe *(p. 389)*

🕊 Velvet Revolution (capital) *(pp. 377-78)*

$ most prosperous country in the Balkans *(p. 382)*

WWII city in the Crimea where a major conference was held in 1945 *(p. 391)*

⬛ Europe's leader in coal (outside German Ruhr) *(p. 374)*

▬ Europe's leader in lead *(p. 383)*

▬ Europe's leader in pig iron, steel, and

🄽 synthetic nitrogen *(p. 390)*

M world's leader in manganese *(p. 390)*

Jigsaw Puzzle

The eighteen countries in Eastern Europe have become jumbled up. Identify the pieces and label them with the correct country name.

Geography

Interview a Foreign Student

Pretend you are a student from one of the countries in this chapter and that you have come to live in the United States for a year as an exchange student. How would you answer the following questions about your country? You'll need to check outside resources. **You can save this assignment for a later chapter.**

1. Do you live in the country or in the city? _____

2. If you live in the city,

   • Which city? _____

   • How many people live there? _____

   • What are some popular spots in your city? _____

3. What is the climate where you live? _____

   _____

4. Can you describe the terrain and vegetation near your home? _____

   _____

5. Where do you like to go for vacation? _____

6. What religion does your family follow? _____

7. What language do you speak? _____

8. How big is your family? _____

9. How big is your house? What does your house look like? _____

   _____

10. What kind of work do your parents do? _____

11. What is your favorite traditional food? _____

    _____

12. What sports do you play? Do you have any other recreation? _____

    _____

13. What kind of government do you have? _____

14. Does your country have any enemies? _____

15. What do you think about Russia? _____

    _____

16. Do people back home like Americans? _____

17. Do you remember what life was like under Communism, or have your parents said anything about

    what life was like then? _____

    _____

18. What is considered the "golden age" in your nation's history? _____

    _____

19. What is the saddest period in your nation's history? _____

    _____

Geography

Tying Threads (Looking Ahead, Looking Behind)

Your textbook constantly refers to information that should now be familiar to you. Eastern Europe, for example, shares much in common with the things you learned about Western Europe. Look up each of the bold topics below. Then answer the questions about what you have learned in past chapters and what you learned in this chapter. *Use the map of Europe on page 381 to tie together the students' knowledge of European geography.*

1. What famous city in France lies in the **Great European Plain?** What is produced near the city?

   (p. 327)   *Paris; wheat, barley, sugar beets*

   The Great European Plain is the dominant land feature in what four countries on the Baltic Rim?

   (p. 370)   *Poland, Lithuania, Latvia, Estonia*

   How wide is the Great European Plain? What product of the plains makes up 90 percent of the

   world's supply? (p. 388)   *over one thousand miles; rye*

2. According to page 340, what large plateau in France is included in the **Central Uplands?** According

   to page 331, how is this plateau used for agriculture?   *Massif Central; good only for grazing*

   livestock

   What two famous forests lie in Germany's portion of the Central Uplands? What agricultural products

   are grown there? (pp. 341-42)   *Black Forest and Bohemian (Bavarian) Forest; dairy cattle and hops*

3. What are the three main divisions of the **Alps?** Which division spreads into Eastern Europe?

   (pp. 342-43)   *Western, Central, and Eastern Alps; Eastern Alps*

   What is the highest mountain in the Alps? What country is it in? (p. 329)   *Mont Blanc; France*

   What subrange of the Alps runs along Germany's southern border? (p. 342)   *Bavarian Alps*

   What subrange of the Alps runs down the western edge of the Balkan Peninsula? (p. 380)

   Dinaric Alps

4. Where are the headwaters of the **Danube River?** (p. 341)   *the Black Forest in Germany's Central*

   Uplands

   What important city in Austria is located on the Danube River? Who composed a famous waltz

   entitled "The Blue Danube"? (p. 345)   *Vienna; Johann Strauss*

   Compared to the length of other European rivers, what is the rank of the Danube River? What capital

   in the Hungarian Basin lies on two sides of the Danube River? (pp. 379-80)   *second (first is Russia's*

   Volga R.); Budapest, Hungary

   What is the name of the famous break in the Carpathian Mountains where the Danube drops to a plain

   in Romania? (p. 387)   *Iron Gate*

Extra Challenge: Several topics in this chapter were discussed in previous chapters on Europe: Adriatic Sea, Baltic Sea, Balkan Peninsula, Macedonia, and Scandinavia. Find a page reference to these topics in previous chapters and find a page reference in this chapter. Then give one fact you learned about each topic.

Geography

☆ **Ethnic Cleansing and Human Rights**

The term **ethnic cleansing** was first used in the Balkans during World War II. Draža Mihajlovic', the leader of a resistance army in Yugoslavia, proposed in 1942 that Serbs create "a great Serbia which is to be *ethnically clean . . .* of all national minorities and non-national elements." Over a million people died during the bitter war between countrymen in Yugoslavia. The United Nations, founded after World War II, adopted the "Universal Declaration of Human Rights" on December 10, 1948, to guarantee a long list of human rights for all people. The term **human rights** refers to the right of each individual to life, liberty, and property. In spite of these guarantees, civil war again tore Yugoslavia apart during the early 1990s. One-quarter million people died, towns and cities were laid waste, and over two million people were left homeless. How could such horror take place in modern Europe?

The failure of the UN to stop the bloodshed has awakened old questions about the best way to protect the rights of people around the world. Can foreigners stop bloodshed in the Balkans? What profitable role can the United States play? Christians must ask themselves what they believe about human rights. Below are excerpts from the "UN Declaration of Human Rights." Read the excerpts and then answer the questions that follow.

The complete UN Declaration, which is not very long, is available in many books and on the Internet.

☆ *Class discussion (or allow students more than one day to complete the assignment)*

Preamble

Whereas recognition of the inherent dignity and of the equal and inalienable rights of all members of the human family is the foundation of freedom, justice and peace in the world, . . . Now, therefore, the General Assembly, proclaims this Universal Declaration of Human Rights as a common standard of achievement for all peoples and all nations.

Article 1: All human beings are born free and equal in dignity and rights. They are endowed with reason and conscience and should act towards one another in a spirit of brotherhood.

Article 3: Everyone has the right to life, liberty and security of person.

Article 5: No one shall be subjected to torture or to cruel, inhuman or degrading treatment or punishment.

Article 9: No one shall be subjected to arbitrary arrest, detention or exile.

Article 17: Everyone has the right to own property alone as well as in association with others. No one shall be arbitrarily deprived of his property.

Article 18: Everyone has the right to freedom of thought, conscience and religion; this right includes freedom to change his religion or belief, and freedom, either alone or in community with others and in public or private, to manifest his religion or belief in teaching, practice, worship and observance.

Article 19: Everyone has the right to freedom of opinion and expression; this right includes freedom to hold opinions without interference and to seek, receive and impart information and ideas through any media and regardless of frontiers.

Article 20: Everyone has the right to freedom of peaceful assembly and association.

No one may be compelled to belong to an association.

Article 21: Everyone has the right to take part in the government of his country, directly or through freely chosen representatives. . . .

The will of the people shall be the basis of the authority of government; this will shall be expressed in periodic and genuine elections which shall be by universal and equal suffrage and shall be held by secret vote or by equivalent free voting procedures.

Article 22: Everyone, as a member of society, has the right to social security and is entitled to realization, through national effort and international co-operation and in accordance with the organization and resources of each State, of the economic, social and cultural rights indispensable for his dignity and the free development of his personality.

Article 23: Everyone has the right to work, to free choice of employment, to just and favourable conditions of work and to protection against unemployment.

Everyone, without any discrimination, has the right to equal pay for equal work.

Everyone who works has the right to just and favourable remuneration ensuring for himself and his family an existence worthy of human dignity, and supplemented, if necessary, by other means of social protection.

Everyone has the right to form and to join trade unions for the protection of his interests.

Article 24: Everyone has the right to rest and leisure, including reasonable limitation of working hours and periodic holidays with pay.

Article 25: Everyone has the right to a standard of living adequate for the health and well-being of himself and of his family, including food, clothing, housing and medical care and necessary social services, and the right to security in the event of unemployment, sickness, disability, widowhood, old age or other lack of livelihood in circumstances beyond his control.

Motherhood and childhood are entitled to special care and assistance. All children, whether born in or out of wedlock, shall enjoy the same social protection.

Article 26: Everyone has the right to education. Education shall be free, at least in the elementary and fundamental stages. Elementary education shall be compulsory. . . .

Education shall be directed to the full development of the human personality and to the strengthening of respect for human rights and fundamental freedoms.

It shall promote understanding, tolerance and friendship among all nations, racial or religious groups, and shall further the activities of the United Nations for the maintenance of peace.

Parents have a prior right to choose the kind of education that shall be given to their children.

Article 28: Everyone is entitled to a social and international order in which the rights and freedoms set forth in this Declaration can be fully realized.

Article 29: Everyone has duties to the community in which alone the free and full development of his personality is possible.

In the exercise of his rights and freedoms, everyone shall be subject only to such limitations as are determined by law solely for the purpose of securing due recognition and respect for the rights and freedoms of others and of meeting the just requirements of morality, public order and the general welfare in a democratic society.

These rights and freedoms may in no case be exercised contrary to the purposes and principles of the United Nations.

Biblical Foundation

1. The Bible has several words translated "right."

   - Look up Lamentations 3:33-36. What right will God not allow to be "turned aside" (v. 35)?

     "the right of a man" (based on a Hebrew word usually translated "judgment")

   - Look up these verses: Psalm 140:12, Isaiah 10:2, Jeremiah 5:28-29. What right will God defend?

     He will defend the "right of the poor" against oppressors. (See verses on unjust gain, such as Proverbs 16:8 and Jeremiah 17:11.)

2. God established a complex legal system in the Old Testament to protect the rights of citizens. What were some of those rights?

   - Deuteronomy 1:16-17   *right to be heard by a judge*

   - Leviticus 24:22   *impartiality of the law, whether for a foreigner or for a citizen*

   - Deuteronomy 25:1-3   *no excessive punishment*

   - Deuteronomy 24:14-15   *right to receive wages on time*

3. If people are oppressed by wicked rulers and employers, where should they turn for safety, according to Psalm 12:5?   *the Lord*

4. The apostle Paul was well aware of the rights and obligations of citizens.

   - As a Roman citizen, Paul demanded his rights at least three times, in Acts 16:35-40; 22:24-29; 25:10-12. What were some of these rights?   *freedom from being bound, beaten, and jailed unless a citizen is formally condemned in court; right to appeal a case to Caesar*

- But when the Corinthians brought cases to court, what did Paul warn them about their legal rights (I Cor. 6:7)?   *Christians should allow themselves to be defrauded rather than take fellow believers to court.*

5. In I Corinthians 8-10 the apostle Paul gives the most lengthy discussion of "rights" in the New Testament. He is discussing the "freedom" of Christians in their choices about daily living.

   - What rights (or "power") did Paul claim, as an apostle, in I Corinthians 9:4-6?   *to receive financial support and to have a wife and to travel with her*

   - Why did he choose not to use his rights (I Cor. 9:12, 18-19)?   *He did not want anything to hinder the gospel, so he willingly gave up his freedom of choice and became a slave to others.*

Rights in the U.S. Constitution

6. Which of the UN articles are parallel to the U.S. Bill of Rights (the first ten amendments to the U.S. Constitution)?   *Articles 18-20 are parallel to Amendment I (freedom of religion, speech, and assembly); Articles 3 and 17 roughly parallel Amendment V (rights of the accused); and Article 5 parallels Amendment VIII (cruel and unusual punishment).*

7. Which of the UN articles have no parallel to any portion of the U.S. Constitution? Why do you think our American forefathers did not include these provisions?   *The UN articles after 21 have no parallel in the U.S. Constitution. Answers will vary on the second question, but Amendment IX guarantees that the American people will retain rights not enumerated in the Constitution. The Founding Fathers believed that the Constitution's duty was to limit the powers of the government, not to increase government power. The UN, on the other hand, supports a socialistic vision that governments should take money from the rich and redistribute it among the poor to make sure that everyone enjoys social security, a decent standard of living, and "free" education.*

Evaluation of the UN Declaration

8. How does the preamble to the UN declaration contradict Christ's statements in John 8:36 and 14:27?   *Christ, not international cooperation and recognition of human rights, is the foundation of freedom and peace.*

9. According to Article 21, what is the basis of the authority of government? According to the Bible in Romans 13:1, what is the source of the authority (or "power") of rulers?   *"will of the people" (see discussion of the Enlightenment in the student text on pp. 98-99); God*

10. Contrast Article 23b with the rights of the businessman in Christ's parable of the laborers in the vineyard (Matthew 20:1-15).   *The UN says everyone has a right to equal pay, but the parable in Matthew implies that a business owner has the right to dispose of his money and property as he chooses.*

11. Article 24 claims that people have a right to leisure and limited work hours (typically 40 hours in 5 days), but what do the Ten Commandments say (Exod. 20:9)?   *Man was to labor six days and take a break only on the sabbath in order to honor God (not for play).*

12. Contrast Article 25 with what John the Baptist told soldiers in Luke 3:14.   *The UN says everyone has a right to a decent standard of living, but John the Baptist stressed contentment with wages.*

13. Articles 22 and 25 assert the right to social security.

    - But according to Matthew 6:31-33, who supplies people's needs?   *God*
    - What does the Bible say about those who look to government for assistance (Jer. 17:5-8)?   *It is wrong to focus on our personal needs and the assistance of man, rather than to look to God.*

14. Look up the word *compulsory* in a dictionary. Is it possible for people to have a "right" to "compulsory" education, as Article 26 states?   *True freedom includes the right to say "no" to using that freedom; true freedom allows people to teach the truths they believe (not the liberal doctrines of "tolerance and friendship" commanded by the UN).*

15. What type of world government does Article 28 claim as every man's right? Why did God oppose the unity of all people in Genesis 11:6-8?   *The UN demands a world order that enables everyone to enjoy his rights, including the "full development of the human personality" (Article 26), but God wants to restrain man's desires, which naturally lead to evil.*

16. The UN claims a long list of human rights, but what if these rights contradict each other? For example, the UN claims that people have a right to freedom of religion (Article 18) and freedom of expression (Article 19), and parents have a right to direct the education of their children. But the UN also says that we must exercise these rights in line with other fundamental doctrines: "These rights and freedoms may in no case be exercised contrary to the purposes and principles of the United Nations" (Article 29). Can you think of an example of how the UN could use its declaration on human rights to attack churches, private schools, and Christian homes?   *Answers will vary. It is impossible to have religious freedom without the freedom to disagree, but the UN could use its declaration on human rights to justify shutting down all church schools and home schools that expose false religions.*

💡 Do countries have a responsibility to protect people of other countries? Does the United States share that responsibility? If so, how far should that responsibility be carried? What is the best way to promote human rights worldwide?   *Answers will vary. God holds leaders accountable for their mistreatment of the poor and needy, but nowhere does He specifically authorize one country to interfere in another country.*

Geography

The Next War

To be ready for the next war, military leaders must look far into the future and make educated guesses. At the National War College in Washington, D.C., American generals debate hypothetical wars thirty years from now, not just skirmishes today. Describe at least one serious issue that might spark a war in Eastern Europe between the countries listed below. Then rank the likelihood of the war, with *1* being the most likely. (Hint: In most cases war is sparked over disputed land.) *Rankings will vary. Note: There are many other possible sparks for war in Eastern Europe. A financial collapse, for example, could encourage a war of aggression.*

_____ 1. Germany attacks Poland.   *The Soviets give Silesia to Poland in return for land it took from eastern Poland, and the Germans want it back (p. 375).*

_____ 2. Russia attacks Latvia.   *Russia demands equal rights for Russians living in Latvia (pp. 376-77).*

_____ 3. Germany attacks the Czech Republic.   *Bitterness explodes into war as Germans demand retribution for the Czech takeover of German homes in the Sudetenland (p. 379).*

_____ 4. Yugoslavia attacks Croatia.   *Possible reasons include disagreements about the future of Bosnia and disputes over the takeover of Serb homes in Slavonia (p. 383).*

_____ 5. Hungary attacks Yugoslavia.   *Hungary is concerned about the welfare of the large Hungarian minority living in the region of Vojvodina (p. 383). It lost this region after World War I.*

_____ 6. Yugoslavia attacks Bosnia-Herzegovina.   *The Serbs desire to "protect" the Serb minorities or to recreate a "Greater Serbia" (pp. 383-84).*

_____ 7. Croatia attacks Bosnia-Herzegovina.   *The Croats desire to "protect" the Serb minorities or to recreate a "Greater Croatia" (pp. 383-84).*

_____ 8. Albania attacks Yugoslavia.   *The Albanians try to defend the oppressed minority living in Yugoslavia's southern territory of Kosovo (p. 383).*

_____ 9. Greece attacks Macedonia.   *Greece accuses Macedonia of supporting rebels in the Greek province of the same name (p. 385).*

_____ 10. Hungary attacks Romania.   *Hungary is concerned about the welfare of the large Hungarian minority living in Transylvania (p. 387). It lost this region after World War I.*

_____ 11. Romania attacks Moldova.   *Romania owned Moldova until the Soviets snatched it away in World War II (p. 388).*

_____ 12. Russia attacks Ukraine.   *Russia wants to protect the Russians living in the Crimean Peninsula (and it would like the territory back); it also wants the Black Sea fleet (pp. 390-91).*

_____ 13. Russia attacks Moldova.   *Russia wants to protect the Russian majority living in the Trans-Dniester region (p. 391).*

Extra Challenge: In 1997 the NATO military alliance was expanded to include three countries in Eastern Europe—Poland, the Czech Republic, and Hungary. Based on what you know about NATO's presence in Eastern Europe, is it likely that the United States will enter a war there in the next thirty years? If so, what is the most likely site of the war? *Answers will vary.*

Geography

The Kaleidoscope of Eastern Europe

Beside each country write the letter(s) and number(s) of the places, people, and events associated with that country. If not otherwise indicated, each item will be used once.

Places

A. Baltic Rim (four)
B. Carpathian Divide (three)
C. the Balkans (eight)
D. Oder River
E. Kraków
F. Donets Basin
G. Karst
H. "Russian Riviera"
 I. highest mountain in Eastern Europe
J. most populous city in Eastern Europe
K. Bohemia
L. Moravia
M. Kievan Rus
N. Serbia
O. Silesia
P. Slavonia
Q. Trans-Dniester
R. Transylvania
S. Walachia

People and Events

a. Western Slavs (three)
b. Southern Slavs (six, map on p. 385)
c. Eastern Slavs (two)
d. language that developed from Latin
e. most Gypsies in the world
 f. Nicolae Ceausescu
g. John Huss
h. Cyril and Methodius (two)
 i. Marshal Tito
j. Lech Walesa
k. Battle of Kosovo
l. "Velvet Revolution" (two)
m. invasion of the Magyars
n. invasion of the Teutonic Knights
o. largest Nazi concentration camp
p. first atheist nation
q. mass privatization
r. Dayton Peace Accords

Statistics

1. per capita GDP greater than $10,000 (two)
2. per capita GDP less than $1,000 (two)
3. largest land area in Europe
4. most densely populated country in Eastern Europe
5. Muslim majority
6. Lutheran majority (two)
7. Roman Catholic majority (seven)
8. Orthodox majority (seven, map on p. 336)

C p 5	1. Albania		C b 2 8	11. Macedonia
c 8	2. Belarus		Q 4 8	12. Moldova
C b 2	3. Bosnia-Herzegovina		A D E O a j o 7	13. Poland
C l b h 8	4. Bulgaria		C R S d e f 8	14. Romania
C P b 7	5. Croatia		B a l 7	15. Slovakia
B K L a g h l q 1 7	6. Czech Republic		C G b 1 7	16. Slovenia
A 6	7. Estonia		F H J M c 3 8	17. Ukraine
B m 7	8. Hungary		C N b i k r 8	18. Yugoslavia
A n 6	9. Latvia			
A 7	10. Lithuania			

Page 385 mentions that Cyril and Methodius also worked in Moravia.

Skill: Recognition

Geography

Map of Russia

Refer to the relief map on pages 394-95 to complete the map on the next page.

1. Label these features of physical geography:
   Rivers—Don River, Lena River, Ob River, Volga River, Yenisey River
   Mountains—Altai (Altay) Mountains, Mount Elbrus, Ural Mountains
   Peninsulas—Kamchatka Peninsula, Taymyr Peninsula
   Islands—Kuril Islands, Sakhalin Island
   Miscellaneous—Lake Baykal, Siberia

2. Label these cities—Moscow, Nizhniy Novgorod, Novosibirsk, Rostov, St. Petersburg, Vladivostok, Volgograd, Yekaterinburg.

3. Label the two largest European lakes east of St. Petersburg. *(p. 402)*

4. Trace red along the longest river in Europe. *(p. 404)*

5. Trace blue along the longest river system in Eurasia. *(p. 410)*

6. Look at the map on page 378. Shade blue those areas in Russia that are tundra.

7. Draw these figures in the appropriate place. *Note: This section is optional.*

   ✴ northernmost mainland area in the world *(p. 411)*

   #1 largest plain in the world *(p. 410)*

   ⬇ deepest lake in the world *(p. 411)*

   largest city in Europe *(p. 396)*

   ♔ Russia's "second capital" built after the Great Northern War *(p. 402)*

   first ruling dynasty of Russia *(p. 403)*

   tallest statue in the world *(p. 406)*

   ⚓ Russia's main Pacific port *(p. 412)*

   ◎ peninsula where nickel is mined *(pp. 403-4)*

   ☢ peninsula where uranium is mined *(pp. 403-4)*

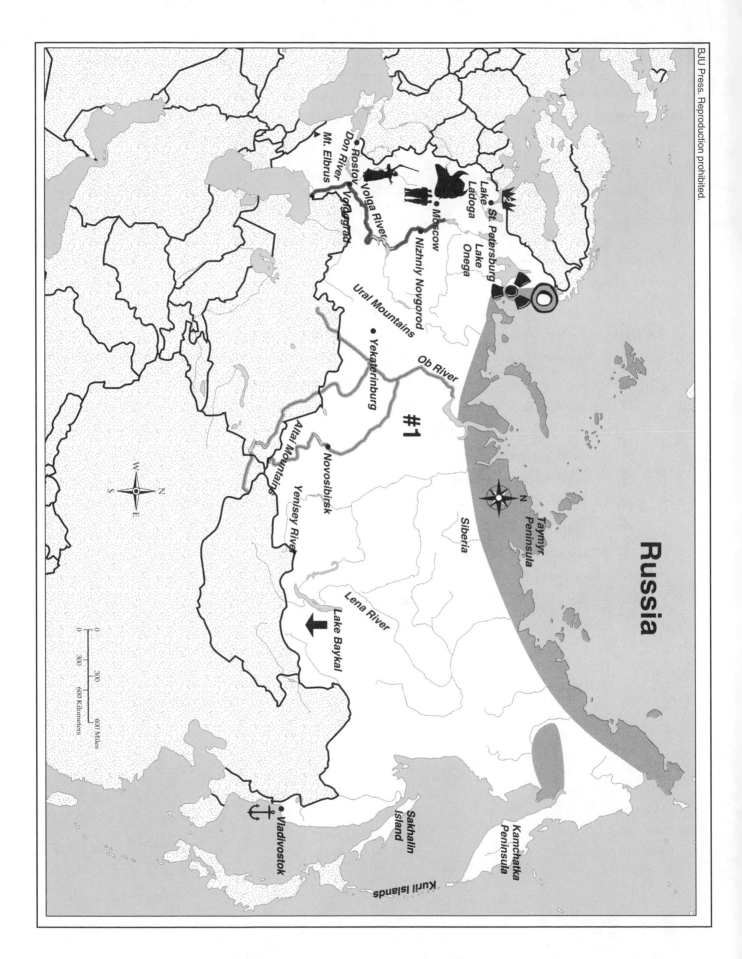

Russia

Rostov
Don River
Mt. Elbrus
Volga River
Volgograd
Moscow
Nizhniy Novgorod
Lake Ladoga
Lake Onega
St. Petersburg
Ural Mountains
Yekaterinburg
Ob River
#1
Altai Mountains
Novosibirsk
Yenisey River
Siberia
Taymyr Peninsula
Lena River
Lake Baykal
Vladivostok
Sakhalin Island
Kuril Islands
Kamchatka Peninsula

0   300   600 Kilometers
0   300   600 Miles

Geography

Russia's Regions

The map on the next page divides Russia into nine cultural subregions, from Greater Moscow (described on pages 400-401) to the Easter Siberian Uplands (described on pages 411-12). Carefully examine the headings in the student textbook to find these nine subregions. Then color the key and the subregions on the map.

Using this map in discussing the various subregions of Russia will make the student text more meaningful.

Map Work *Note: This section is optional.*

1. Draw these figures in the appropriate region or near the appropriate city.

   ● "Detroit of Russia" *(p. 405)*

   ▰ "Pittsburgh of Russia" *(p. 405)*

   #1 largest Russian republic *(p. 411)*

   ✊ small Russian republic that seceded in 1991 *(p. 408)*

   ☪ Volga republic with the largest ethnic minority in Russia *(p. 405)*

   🌾 "Breadbasket of Russia" *(p. 406)*

   ◖ world's leader in potatoes *(p. 406)*

   ⊤ republic with the most accessible oil fields in Russia *(p. 405)*

   ⊨ iron ore (world's largest reserves) *(p. 409)*

   ▪ coal *(p. 410)*

   ▱ platinum *(p. 411)*

   ▰ gold-mining region that has grown rapidly *(p. 411)*

2. Draw the main route of the Trans-Siberian Railroad between Samara and Vladivostok, and label it.

3. Write their ranking beside the ten largest cities in Russia.

Moscow	8,800,000	Samara	1,260,000
St. Petersburg	4,470,000	Omsk	1,160,000
Nizhniy Novgorod	1,480,000	Chelyabinsk	1,150,000
Novosibirsk	1,440,000	Kazan	1,110,000
Yekaterinburg	1,370,000	Ufa	1,100,000

Map Questions *Be sure to discuss the relative sizes and locations of Russia's major cities.*

1. What is the largest city in each region?

   • Greater Moscow   *Moscow (1st, pp. 400-401)*

   • Northwest   *St. Petersburg (2nd, p. 402)*

   • Volga   *Nizhniy Novgorod (3rd, p. 405)*

   • Don River Basin   *Yekaterinburg (5th, p. 409)*

   • West Siberian Lowland   *Novosibirsk (4th, p. 410)*

2. Which of Russia's nine regions has the most major cities?   *The Volga has three.*

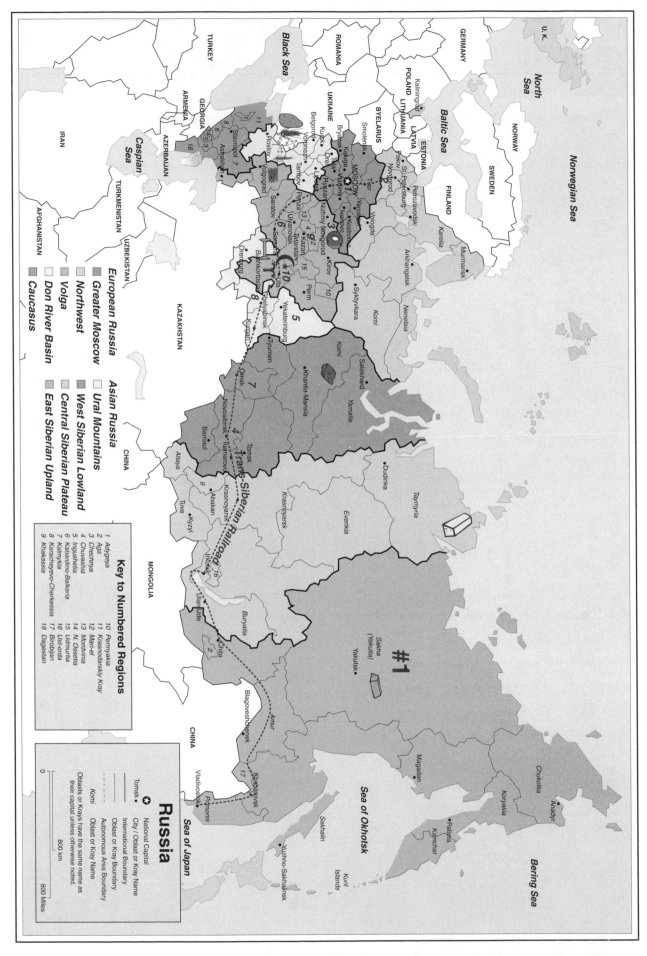

Russia

National Capital ⊛
City / Oblast Name • Tomsk

International Boundary — — —
Autonomous Area Boundary - - -
Oblast or Kray Name *Komi*
Oblast or Kray Name *Tomsk*
Oblasts or Krays have the same name as
their capital unless otherwise noted.

0   800 km
0   800 Miles

Key to Numbered Regions

1 Adygeya	10 Permyakia
2 Aga	11 Krasnodarskiy Kray
3 Chechnya	12 Mari-el
4 Chuvashia	13 Mordvinia
5 Ingushetia	14 N. Ossetia
6 Kabardino-Balkaria	15 Udmurtia
7 Kalmykia	16 Ust-orda
8 Karachayevo-Cherkessia	17 Birobidjan
9 Khakassia	18 Dagestan

European Russia
■ Greater Moscow
□ Northwest
□ Volga
■ Don River Basin
■ Caucasus

Asian Russia
□ Ural Mountains
■ West Siberian Lowland
□ Central Siberian Plateau
■ East Siberian Upland

Geography

☆ **Comparison of Russia and the United States**

One way to understand the viewpoint of a foreign nation is to consider what it is *not* rather than what it is. In the blanks below, write as many similarities and differences as you can between Russia and the United States. Don't forget to look at the statistical charts in the student book. ☆ *Class discussion. Students already have the information to complete most of the U.S. column if they did the activity comparing Canada and the United States (Chapter 10, Activity 2) or the activity comparing Northern and Latin America (Chapter 12, Cumulative Review).*

Physical Geography (Compare maps on pages 147, 218, 394-95.)

Main Mountain Ranges   *Both have north-south systems (Appalachians and Pacific Mountain System versus the Urals and the Eastern Siberian Upland) and both have scattered systems (Ozark-Ouachitas versus Caucasus).*

High Point   *Both have the highest points on their respective continents—Mt. McKinley (20,320 ft.) and Mt. Elbrus (18,510 ft.).*

Plains   *Both countries have large plains (Central and Great Plains versus the Great European Plain and the West Siberian Lowland). Russia has the largest plain in the world, but unlike the U.S. plains, much of it is unproductive.*

Plateaus   *Both countries have major interior plateaus (Appalachian, Colorado, and Columbia Plateaus versus the Central Siberian Plateau). Russia's plateau is rich in minerals.*

Main Lakes   *The United States has the largest system of freshwater lakes in the world (Great Lakes), while Russia has the deepest lake with the most water (Baykal).*

Rivers   *Both have long river systems—the Mississippi-Missouri and the Ob-Irtysh. Russia has more long rivers than the United States, but their locations are bad for trade.*

Climate (maps on pp. 184, 378)   *Both have polar, subpolar, humid continental, and semiarid climates. The United States has all the other climates, but not Russia.*

Economy

Per Capita GDP (tables on pp. 138, 396)   *The U.S. has five times the income of Russia ($27,607 versus $5,300).*

Agricultural Products   *Both are major producers. The United States is a world leader in wheat, corn, dairy products, tobacco, and fruit (pp. 143, 160, 170, 176, 182); Russia is a world leader in wheat, sheep, swine, sugar beets, and beef cattle, and it is number one in rye, barley, and potatoes, but Russians still struggle with poverty and starvation (p. 406).*

Major Mining Products (See chart on p. 66.)   *Both have large mineral reserves—including natural gas. The U.S. is a leader in gold, copper, lead, phosphates, nitrates, sulfur, and coal; while Russia produces all of these metals and coal, it also is a leader in platinum, nickel, tungsten, uranium, and petroleum.*

Major Manufacturing   *Both are major manufacturing countries. The quality of American manufactured goods far surpasses the quality in Russia (p. 398).*

Major Ports   *Both countries have ports with access to the Atlantic and Pacific. The United States has many ports, but Russia's ports are few and inaccessible (especially in winter).*

Demography (Compare tables on pages 138 and 396.)

Total Population   *Both are among the ten largest populations. The U.S. population (267,954,767) is nearly double Russia's population (147,987,101).*

Population Density   *Both countries have a low population density compared to other countries. Russia's population density (22) is less than a third of the U.S. density (72).*

Natural Increase   *A high death rate gives Russia a negative increase (–0.5%), but the U.S. increase is high (0.6%).*

Life Expectancy   *Russia has a shockingly low life expectancy (64) compared to the United States (76).*

Literacy Rate   *Both countries have a high literacy rate (96% in the United States, 99% in Russia).*

Largest City   *New York (7 million) and Moscow (9 million) have large populations. They are located at key junctures for trade. New York is part of a great megalopolis that includes 19.5 million people. (Although not stated in the student text, Russia's metro area is minimal.)*

History

First Settlement   *The earliest settlements were overshadowed by later cities. Novgorod was established in 862, long before Jamestown (1607) or St. Augustine (1565) (pp. 144-45, 159-60, 403)*

Creation of the Country   *Both countries overthrew an "oppressive" ruler (the British and the Mongols). Russia has nothing similar to the American War for Independence (1775-83). In the Bolshevik Revolution (1917), Lenin overthrew the czar (p. 397).*

Manifest Destiny   *Both peoples believed it was their destiny to overspread their respective continents. Russia fought constant wars against many foes, but it has not yet reached the Indian Ocean; by contrast, the United States fought few wars and has spread far from its shores (p. 393).*

Famous Leaders   *Both countries had both weak and strong leaders who helped determine the direction of their countries. Answers will vary about which leaders might be compared to the leading men in United States history. American leaders were elected, but the czars or Communist dictators were not. The Russian leaders have treated the people with contempt, but American leaders usually bow to public opinion (pp. 393, 397, 402).*

Government

Area (See tables on pp. 138, 396.)   *Both are among the largest countries in the world: Russia is first, and the U.S. is fourth. Russia's area (6,592,800 sq. mi.) far surpasses the area of the U.S. (3,675,031 sq. mi.)—or of any other country.*

Form of Government   *Both are federated governments with a strong president. Both legislatures are divided, with one for the general population and one to represent the states/okrugs/ethnic republics. Russia has a parliament and a short history of "freedom" (pp. 138, 404-5).*

Political Divisions   *The United States has fifty states, while Russia has many parts that include about 50 oblasts, 21 autonomous republics, 6 krais (territories), and 11 okrugs (areas). U.S. states historically have held great power, but power is only now devolving to the local governments in Russia (pp. 138, 404).*

Military Strength (See table on p. 110.)   *Both are military powers that spend much more than other countries on defense. [The text does not mention it, but both are the leading nuclear powers too.] The U.S. is the only superpower, spending nearly three times more than Russia on defense ($270 billion versus $98 billion). Russia is a dangerous militarized state that spends a much larger percentage of its GDP and manpower on the military than the United States does.*

Society

Cultural Subregions   *The United States is divided between the Northeast (population center and historic cities), South (regionalism), Midwest (breadbasket), and West (frontier). Somewhat parallel to the United States is (1) the populous region of Greater Moscow and the historic cities of the Northwest; (2) the independent-minded peoples of the Volga; (3) the plains and farms of the Black Earth region; and (4) the frontier of Siberia. Obviously these similarities cannot be stretched too far. Southern Americans speak the same language as the rest of America, and Siberia has no equivalent to America's rich valleys and big ports in the Pacific West.*

Main Minorities   *Both countries have a large ethnic majority—Whites in the U.S. and Russians in Russia. Both have many minorities. The main minorities in the U.S. are Blacks, Hispanics, Asians, and Indians (pp. 153, 204, 208-9, 216), but the Russian minorities are quite varied. Most U.S. citizens learn English, but minority languages are still widespread in Russia (pp. 396, 404-5).*

Main Religion   *Both countries consist mostly of "Christians." The U.S. is divided among Roman Catholics and a wide range of Protestant denominations (p. 174). But most Russians belong to the Orthodox Church (p. 397).*

Compared to other nations that you have studied so far, would you expect Russians to be more similar or less similar to Americans?   *Answers will vary. Russians have a hard time understanding Americans, and vice versa. While our fundamental concerns as major nations are often similar, we often draw different conclusions about the best course of action.*

Geography

Cultures of the World: Russia

Your textbook includes a series of feature boxes on famous cultures of the world, from Mexico to Japan. You have been assigned to write the box for Russia. Reread the box on Latin culture, pages 252-53, to get ideas for how to write the box. (Other culture boxes are found in later chapters on pages 433, 483, 494, 519, and 578.) Be sure to include common terms in italics. You will need to consult outside resources to complete this activity.

1. How do you say hello in Russian? *zdrazstzuyte or trivet* _____

2. How do you say goodbye in Russian? *do svidania* _____

3. Describe the struggle to buy food and necessities in a corrupt society. *Daily life can be frustrating for Russians. City residents regularly wait in long lines. Goods and money may be in short supply.*

_____

4. Describe a typical apartment home. *Housing is crowded in cities, so many live in small apartments in high-rise buildings. Apartment dwellers may have to share kitchen and bathroom facilities with other families. Telephone service to a new apartment building may not be available for years.*

5. Describe Russian winters, traditional Russian clothes, and Russian entertainment. *Russia's climate can be harsh. Winters are long and cold. Moscow has snow about five months each year, but farther north the snow may last for eight or nine months. Russian clothes reflect more Western influence today than they did in earlier days of Soviet rule, but they must still be designed for cold weather. Traditional festive clothing, rarely worn today, includes colorfully embroidered shirts, blouses, and headgear and shoes of bast, a tough tree fiber. Sports are very popular in Russia. Russians ski and skate throughout the long winter months. The favorite team sport is soccer. Gymnastics and basketball are also popular. On the intellectual side, Russians like to play chess and visit museums. In the summer wealthy families travel to seaside resorts or vacation at dachas, cottages in the countryside.*

6. Describe traditional foods and eating habits. *Russians eat hearty meals. Thick soups with lots of vegetables are popular. Borscht (beet soup) is a favorite. Bread is served with almost every meal, and a variety of meats are served, most of them fried. The main meal of the day is eaten at noon. Children and adults meet at home for this meal, which may include a salad or appetizer, soup, meat and potatoes or kasha (cooked buckwheat), and a dessert. Tea is a standard beverage, but mineral water and soft drinks are becoming more popular. A meal at a nice restaurant might offer ikra zernistaia (caviar) for an appetizer and kotleta po kievski ("Chicken Kiev") for a main dish. The traditional vodka and other drinks contribute to problems of alcohol abuse.*

7. Describe religious rituals and festivals. *Religious activity was severely limited in the days of strong Communist rule, but the government began to ease up in the late 1980s. The major denomination in Russia today is the Russian Orthodox Church. The Russian Orthodox Christmas, celebrated on January 7, was made a national holiday. Other national, though nonreligious, celebrations are held on New Year's Eve and May Day, a time for large fireworks displays.*

Geography

Russians Abroad

Below is a list of the fifteen countries that were once republics in the Soviet Union. The conditions of Russians living in these countries is a top concern of Russia today. Study the map of Russia on pages 394-95 and the charts below; then answer the questions that follow.

Russia and the "Near Abroad"	Percentage of Ethnic Russians
Russia	82%
Baltic Rim	
Estonia	30%
Latvia	34%
Lithuania	9%
Eastern Plain	
Belarus	13%
Moldova	13%
Ukraine	22%

Russia and the "Near Abroad"	Percentage of Ethnic Russians
Caucasus	
Armenia	2%
Azerbaijan	2.5%
Georgia	6%
Central Asia	
Kazakhstan	37%
Kyrgyzstan	22%
Tajikistan	3.5%
Turkmenistan	10%
Uzbekistan	8%

1. Which of the four regions (outside Russia) appears to have the largest percentage of Russians?

   Baltic Rim

2. Which of the four regions (outside Russia) appears to have the smallest percentage of Russians?

   Caucasus

3. Which country (outside Russia) has the largest percentage of Russians?   *Kazakhstan*

4. Which country (outside Russia) has the smallest percentage of Russians?   *Armenia*

5. Which countries share *no* borders with Russia? What is the highest percentage of Russians among any of these countries?   *Moldova, Armenia, Kyrgyzstan, Tajikistan, Turkmenistan, Uzbekistan; 22% in*

   Kyrgyzstan

Geography

Alert! Terrorists Are Developing a Nuclear Bomb

You belong to an anti-terrorist division of the Russian secret police. A spy has just discovered a vast underground network of terrorists secretly assembling a nuclear bomb at various sites around the country. Your job is to find the pieces of the bomb and apprehend the terrorists. To accomplish your task, identify the terms that correspond to the italicized definitions.

Profile on the Terrorists

_____pogrom, p. 393_____   1. The name of the terrorist network is *a Russian term for the massacre of a local minority.*

_____Chechnya, p. 408_____   2. The headquarters of the terrorists is located in *a tiny republic that tried to secede from Russia in 1991.*

_____dissidents, p. 398_____   3. The objective of the terrorists is unclear, except that many of them support *those who openly disagree with the government.*

_____Duma, p. 405_____   4. The terrorists have political allies in the Russian *legislature* who belong to the Communist party.

Profile of the Terrorist Leader

_____czar, p. 397_____   5. The head of the terrorists goes by an alias name meaning *caesar* in Russian.

_____St. Basil's Cathedral, p. 398_____   6. Although the person's identity is not yet certain, the head of the terrorists has an unusual hobby, building models of *Russia's most famous cathedral, located in Red Square.*

_____Ivan the Terrible, p. 397_____   7. The leader's hero is *Russia's first czar, the cruel leader who built this cathedral.*

_____St. Petersburg, p. 402_____   8. The leader was last sighted at *the city known for white nights.*

_____Catherine the Great, p. 408_____   9. Rumors say that the leader is a woman who has the same name as *the Russian czarina who conquered the Cossacks and parts of the Caucasus.*

Location of the Bomb

_____Kola Peninsula, p. 403_____   10. Most of the plutonium is stored at one of the villages in the *mineral-rich peninsula on the Barents Sea.*

_____Volga-Baltic Waterway, p. 402_____   11. The terrorists will soon be shipping the plutonium on the *canal that links the Arctic waters to Moscow.*

_____Rostov, p. 406_____   12. The detonator was manufactured in China and it has been shipped through the Black Sea to *Russia's vital port at the mouth of the Don River.*

_____Volga-Don Canal, p. 407_____   13. If we cannot uncover the detonator at the port, we know it will soon be shipped up the *canal that links the Black Sea and Moscow.*

_____Vladivostok, p. 412_____   14. The metal container for the bomb was manufactured in Japan and is now somewhere in *Russia's main Pacific port.*

_____Trans-Siberian Railway, p. 410_____   15. We have discovered that the terrorists plan to ship the container in a concealed crate on the *rail system that links the Pacific port to Moscow.*

Geography

Chapter 18   **Activity 1**

Map of the Caucasus and Central Asia

Refer to the student text, page 415. Fill in each blank below with the correct location. Countries are uppercase letters (A, B, C), cities are lowercase letters (a, b, c), and physical features are numbers (1, 2, 3).

Encourage students to try to complete this activity without looking at the book and then to double-check their answers in the book.

Countries

A. Georgia
B. Armenia
C. Azerbaijan
D. Turkmenistan
E. Uzbekistan
F. Afghanistan
G. Tajikistan
H. Kyrgyzstan
I. Kazakhstan

Cities

a. Tbilisi
b. Yerevan
c. Baku
d. Ashkhabad
e. Bukhara
f. Tashkent
g. Kabul
h. Dushanbe
i. Bishkek
j. Almaty
k. Aqmola

Physical Features

1. Caucasus Mountains
2. Caspian Sea
3. Caspian Depression
4. Aral Sea
5. Kara Kum Desert
6. Kyzyl-Kum Desert
7. Hindu Kush
8. Pamir Mountains
9. Tien Shan

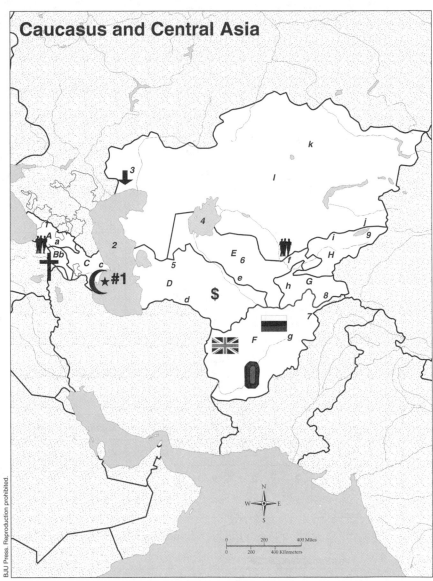

Caucasus and Central Asia

Map Work *Note: This section is optional.*

Draw these figures in the appropriate place.

$ richest nation in Central Asia *(p. 420)*

† first nation to adopt Christianity officially *(p. 416)*

👫 largest city in the Caucasus and Central Asia *(p. 421)*

👫 most densely populated nation in the Caucasus and Central Asia *(p. 416)*

nation fought over by Britain and Russia *(pp. 422-23)*

☪ Muslim country in the Caucasus influenced by Iran *(p. 417)*

#1 largest lake in the world *(p. 417)*

⬇ lowest region in Central Asia *(p. 419)*

world's leading miner of lapis lazuli *(p. 424)*

Geography

Chart of the Nations

Complete the chart and then use the chart to answer the questions. (The first four columns should give rankings, from 1 to 9, based on the statistical table. The language families are shown on the map on page 419.)

Nations	Area	Pop.	Per Capita GDP	Pop. Density	Religion	Main Language Family	Major Resources/Industry
Caucasus							
Georgia	8	6	7	3	Orthodox	Caucasian	citrus fruit, grapes, tobacco, wheat, copper, manganese [8th worldwide]
Armenia	9	9	3	1	Orthodox	Armenian	barley, wheat, potatoes, copper, bauxite
Azerbaijan	7	4	5	2	Muslim	Turkic	cotton, grain, tea, silk, textiles, chemicals, fish, salt, petroleum
Central Asia							
Kazakhstan	1	3	2	9	Muslim	Turkic	lead and chromite [2nd worldwide], fruit, copper, uranium
Turkmenistan	3	8	1	8	Muslim	Turkic	cotton, petroleum, natural gas
Uzbekistan	4	1	4	4	Muslim	Turkic	cotton [5th worldwide], uranium
Kyrgyzstan	5	7	6	7	Muslim	Turkic	cotton
Tajikistan	6	5	8	5	Muslim	Iranian	hydroelectricity
Afghanistan	2	2	9	6	Muslim	Iranian	afghans, rugs, jewelry [1st in lapis lazuli], wheat, barley, corn, cotton, sheep, goats

1. Find the country with the highest population density. Where does it rank in area and population?

    Armenia; last place

2. Find the two countries with the most population. Where do they rank in population density?

    Uzbekistan is fourth in density; Afghanistan is sixth.

3. Find the country with the highest per capita GDP. What unique product does it produce?

    Turkmenistan; petroleum

4. Find the two countries with the lowest per capita GDP. What other characteristics on the table do they share in common?   *Afghanistan and Tajikistan are both Muslim, and the people speak Iranian languages.*

Geography

Nuggets from *National Geographic*

Look up the following articles in *National Geographic* and answer the questions about them.

"In Focus: The Fractured Caucasus" (February 1996)

1. Explain why Caucasia is so splintered.   *The region contains over fifty ethnic groups who want their own nations.*

2. Look at the map on pages 130-31 of the article. What autonomous republic has the most languages? What Indo-European language family is found in all three Caucasian nations?   *Dagestan; Iranian*

3. Why would mountain regions be especially resistant to outside powers?   *The mountains isolate the ethnic groups, helping them retain their language and customs; also, the mountains provide protection for the groups when attacked.*

4. Why does Russia want to keep its southern border secure?   *to protect itself against Turkey and Iran and to have access to oil and gas from the Caspian Sea basin*

"A Soviet Sea Lies Dying" (February 1990)
Point out to the students that this article was written before the breakup of the Soviet Union.

5. Look at the map on pages 74-75 of the article. What two cities did the Aral Sea reach in 1960 (one in the northeast, one in the southwest)?   *Aralsk and Muynak*

6. Look at the map on page 80. What two new desert lakes have been created by irrigation runoff?
   Aydarkul and Sarykamysh

7. Describe the problems brought about by the shrinking of the Aral Sea.   *Many fishermen have lost their jobs because there are no fish in the sea; once booming fishing towns now have small populations struggling for work; cases of throat cancer, respiratory problems, and eye diseases have dramatically increased; the quality of the region's water supply is poor; salt and dust storms are frequent; climatic changes have produced extreme temperatures.*

8. Why are some people against cutting cotton irrigation? (See page 92.)   *The cotton industry provides jobs for many people; many government officials believe that the Aral Sea could never be what it once was, even if the entire cotton industry were cut.*

Geography

Journey Through the Caucasus and Central Asia

If you took a trip to this region of the world, where would you go? See how many answers you can give without looking in your book.

Georgia, p. 415	1. Journey to an independent-minded country that was the first Soviet republic to declare independence in the Caucasus or Central Asia.
Armenia, p. 417	2. Pass out gospel tracts in the small country that has not fully recovered from a massive earthquake in 1988.
Azerbaijan, p. 417	3. Visit the oil-rich Muslim country in the Caucasus, where the people speak a Persian tongue.
Caspian Sea, p. 417	4. Cross the sea filled with oil wells.
Nagorno-Karabakh, p. 418	5. Be careful in the territory in Azerbaijan where Armenians live.
Kazakhstan, p. 418	6. Next, look at the farms on the steppes of the Central Asian country that borders Russia and has many Russians.
Turkmenistan, pp. 420-21	7. Take a detour to a country with natural gas fields in the Kara Kum.
Uzbekistan, p. 420	8. Journey to the most populous country in Central Asia, which would like to unite the region into Turkistan.
Turkmenistan, p. 420	9. Drive along the Kara Kum Canal, located in the Central Asian country that borders Iran.
Aral Sea, p. 420	10. Witness the devastation at the sea that has lost 40 percent of its surface area since 1960.
foothills, p. 421	11. Journey to the crowded region in Uzbekistan where most of the people live.
Kyzyl-Kum, p. 421	12. Take in the sun at the main desert of Uzbekistan, where cotton is the main crop.
Bukhara, p. 421	13. Visit the old center of learning where the philosopher Avicenna lived and translated Aristotle.
Bukhara, p. 421	14. Sleep at the oasis that was a major stop on the old Silk Road and became the capital of the Samanid empire.
Samarkand, p. 421	15. Tour the former capital of the Mongol Empire and burying place of the Mongol conqueror Tamerlane.
Tien Shan, p. 422	16. Climb the arduous mountain range on the border between Kyrgyzstan and China.
Pamirs, p. 422	17. View the "knot" of mountains in Tajikistan that ties together the world's highest ranges.
Khyber Pass, p. 424	18. Wind through the pass that cuts through the Hindu Kush.
Afghanistan, p. 423	19. Explore the country that was once a buffer state fought over by Russia and Britain.
Wakhan Corridor, p. 424	20. Glimpse the mountainous region of Afghanistan where more than thirty seven-thousand-meter peaks are found.

Geography

Foremost Facts About Each Country

For each country, give what you think is the most important single fact for you to remember, especially a fact that will likely appear in the news. Then give the most interesting, "memorable" fact.

Answers will vary.

1. Georgia's Foremost Fact _*Georgia is an Orthodox country with two regions of Muslim minorities—Abkhazia and South Ossetia—that would like independence.*_

   Most Memorable Fact _*Though a Caucasus nation, Georgia enjoys a mild climate in its Rioni river valley and Black Sea coast, where it has grown grapes since ancient times.*_

2. Armenia's Foremost Fact _*Armenia is engaged in war with Muslims in Azerbaijan.*_

   Most Memorable Fact _*Armenia was the first nation to adopt Christianity officially.*_

3. Azerbaijan's Foremost Fact _*Azerbaijan claims rights to massive petroleum reserves in the Caspian Sea; also, it has fought Armenia over control of Nagorno-Karabakh.*_

   Most Memorable Fact _*The Caspian Sea is the largest lake in the world.*_

4. Kazakhstan's Foremost Fact _*Kazakhstan is a vast country [ninth largest in the world] split between Russian farmers on the northern steppes and Kazakhs elsewhere.*_

   Most Memorable Fact _*The Caspian Depression is lower than any point in the Western Hemisphere; also, the Aral Sea on the border with Turkmenistan has lost over 40 percent of its surface area since 1960.*_

5. Turkmenistan's Foremost Fact _*Turkmenistan is the richest nation in the region because it shares rights to petroleum in the Caspian; drainage of the Amu Darya for cotton irrigation led to the Aral Sea disaster.*_

   Most Memorable Fact _*See above; also, the Kara Kum covers 80 percent of the country.*_

6. Uzbekistan's Foremost Fact _*Uzbekistan wants to unite the region into Turkistan so that it can share the wealth and trade of its neighbors.*_

   Most Memorable Fact _*It has three famous cities—the Bukhara oasis on the old Silk Road (home of Avicenna), Tashkent (most populous city in the region), and Samarkand (central city on the Silk Route).*_

7. Kyrgyzstan's Foremost Fact _*It is located on the border with China; also, the Russian minority has the best jobs.*_

   Most Memorable Fact _*Its landscape is dominated by the "Celestial Mountains" (Tien Shan).*_

8. Tajikistan's Foremost Fact _*Tajikistan has a volatile border with China and Afghanistan, patrolled by Russian soldiers.*_

   Most Memorable Fact _*The mountainous country of Tajikistan has the tallest dam in the world; the Pamir Knot is the hub of the world's highest ranges.*_

9. Afghanistan's Foremost Fact _*The country is divided between warring tribes that have never formed a strong union; the Taliban has made the latest attempt at union, hoping to form a rigid Islamic state.*_

   Most Memorable Fact _*The Khyber Pass through the Hindu Kush was a route for great conquerors of India; also, Afghanistan was a buffer state between the British and Russians.*_

Geography

A Second Look at Central Eurasia

Fill in each blank with the best answer.

A (p. 408)   1. Which mountain system does not reach seven thousand meters (twenty-three thousand feet)?
- A. Caucasus
- B. Hindu Kush
- C. Pamirs
- D. Tien Shan

C (p. 408)   2. highest mountain in Europe
- A. Communism Peak
- B. Lenin Peak
- C. Mount Elbrus
- D. Mount Musala

B (p. 417)   3. largest lake in the world
- A. Aral Sea
- B. Caspian Sea
- C. Lake Baykal
- D. Lake Ladoga

D (p. 404)   4. longest river in Europe
- A. Danube
- B. Lena
- C. Rhine
- D. Volga

A (p. 369)   5. Which culture region does not border Central Eurasia?
- A. Africa
- B. Asia
- C. Middle East
- D. Western Europe

D (pp. 110, 388)   6. country with the greatest "sphere of influence" in Central Eurasia
- A. China
- B. Germany
- C. Iran
- D. Russia

C (pp. 66, 404-6, 409)   7. world's leading producer of nickel, petroleum, potatoes, and rye; world's largest reserves of natural gas, coal, iron ore, chromium, and manganese
- A. Azerbaijan
- B. Kazakhstan
- C. Russia
- D. Ukraine

C (p. 393)   8. largest country in the world, spanning two continents
- A. Afghanistan
- B. Kazakhstan
- C. Russia
- D. Ukraine

B (p. 393)   9. biggest city on the continent of Europe
- A. Kiev
- B. Moscow
- C. Tashkent
- D. Warsaw

C (p. 385)   10. most-spoken language subfamily in Central Eurasia
- A. Caucasian
- B. Germanic
- C. Slavic
- D. Turkic

C (p. 95)   11. most common religion in Eastern Europe
- A. Islam
- B. Judaism
- C. Eastern Orthodoxy
- D. Roman Catholicism

Geography

Map of South Asia

Fill in each blank with the correct letter or number from the map given here. Countries are uppercase letters (A, B, C), cities are lowercase letters (a, b, c), and physical features are numbers (1, 2, 3). Refer to the relief map on page 430 to complete this activity. *Encourage students to try to complete the activity without looking at the book and then to double-check their answers in the book.*

Countries

_E_	1.	Bangladesh
_F_	2.	Bhutan
_B_	3.	India
_C_	4.	Maldives
_G_	5.	Nepal
_A_	6.	Pakistan
_D_	7.	Sri Lanka

Cities

_b_	8.	Bombay (Mumbai)
_g_	9.	Calcutta
_f_	10.	Colombo
_c_	11.	Delhi
_h_	12.	Dhaka
_a_	13.	Islamabad
_j_	14.	Kathmandu
_e_	15.	Male
_d_	16.	New Delhi
_i_	17.	Thimphu

Physical Features

_5_	18.	Brahmaputra River
_3_	19.	Deccan Plateau
_4_	20.	Ganges River
_6_	21.	Himalayas
_1_	22.	Indus River
_7_	23.	Karakoram Range
_2_	24.	Thar (Great Indian Desert)

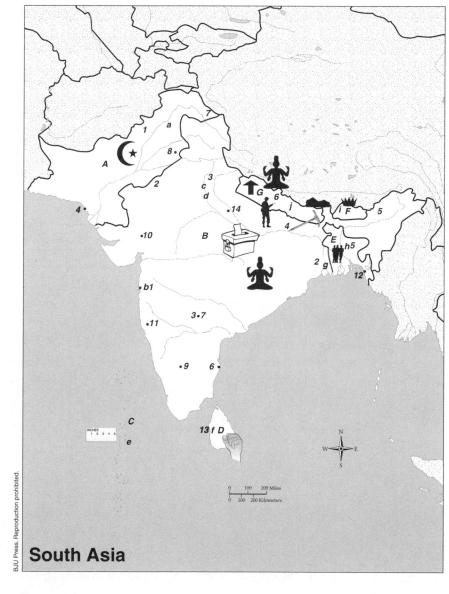

South Asia

BJU Press. Reproduction prohibited.

25. Place its rank beside each of the metropolitan areas in South Asia that have a population above two million. *Point students to the population map on p. 443.*

Bombay (Mumbai), India	15,138,000
Calcutta, India	11,923,000
Delhi, India	9,948,000
Karachi, Pakistan	9,733,000
Dhaka, Bangladesh	8,545,000
Madras (Chennai), India	6,002,000
Hyderabad, India	5,477,000
Lahore, Pakistan	5,012,000
Bangalore, India	4,799,000
Ahmadabad, India	3,312,216
Pune, India	2,493,987
Chittagong, Bangladesh	2,477,000
Colombo, Sri Lanka	2,050,000
Kanpur, India	2,029,889
Faisalabad, Pakistan	1,845,000

26. Draw these figures in the appropriate place.

 highest nation in the world *(p. 441)*

smallest nation in Asia *(p. 445)*

country with an absolute monarchy *(p. 444)*

highest mountain in the world *(p. 441)*

country with one of the highest population densities *(p. 440)*

 world's largest democracy *(p. 429)*

 Muslim nation separated from India by the British *(p. 439)*

 Hindu nation (two) *(pp. 429, 443)*

 Sherpa mountain-climbers *(p. 442)*

 Gurkha soldiers *(pp. 443-44)*

 Tamil terrorists *(p. 445)*

Geography

India's States

Color in the key and the map with the five cultural subregions in India discussed in your text. Your textbook gives you enough information to complete the map. How many states are mentioned by name in the text? Which two are boldfaced terms?

Using this map in discussing the various subregions of India will make the student text more meaningful.

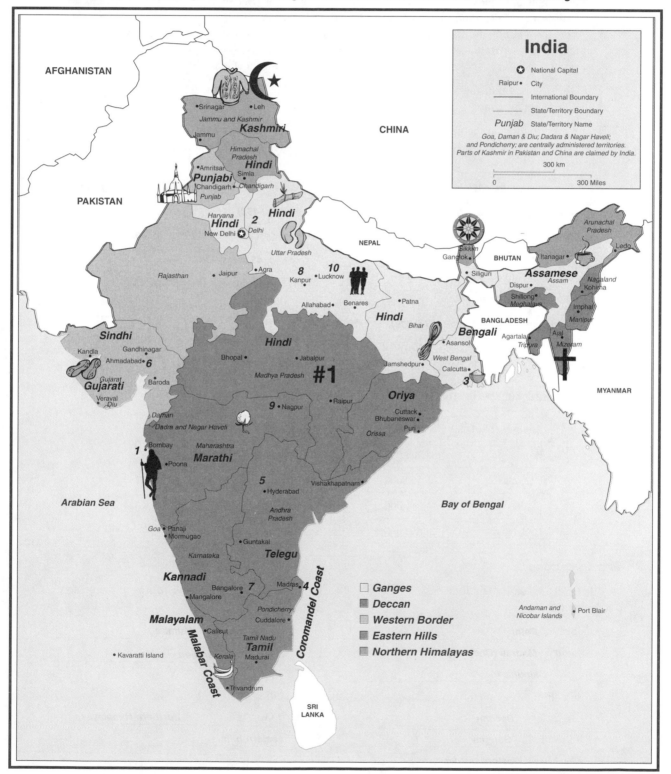

Map Work *Note: This section is optional.*

1. Hindi is the official language of India, and English is an "associate" language used in government and commerce. The government also recognizes fourteen other official languages: the ancient language of Sanskrit and thirteen regional languages. Write the names of these languages in the states where they are spoken. ***The other states have such small populations that their languages, such as Rajasthani, are not considered national languages.***
   - *Hindi* is spoken in five states (Uttar Pradesh, Madhya Pradesh, Himachal Pradesh, Bihar, and Haryana). (*Urdu,* a similar language, is also spoken in these regions and need not be shown.)
   - Four languages belong to the **Dravidian** family in the south (*Telegu* in Andhra Pradesh, *Tamil* in Tamil Nadu, *Malayalam* in Kerala, and *Kannadi* in Karnataka).
   - Apart from Hindi and Urdu, there are eight official **Indo-Aryan** languages in the north. Six of them have a separate state named for them: *Assamese, Bengali, Gujarati, Kashmiri, Oriya,* and *Punjabi.* (*Sindhi* is spoken in northwestern Gujarat; *Marathi* in Maharashtra.)

2. Find the discussion of the Malabar Coast and the Coromandel Coast in the text on pages 434-35. Label them on the map.

3. Draw these figures in the appropriate state or city. Put the symbol for products in the state where they are mentioned in the text. Note that India is the world's leader in these products, unless shown otherwise.

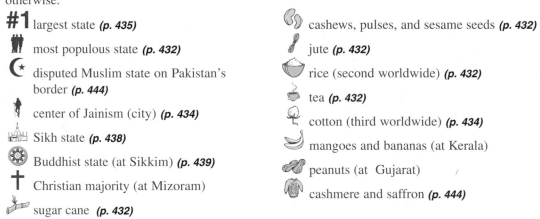

#1 largest state *(p. 435)*

most populous state *(p. 432)*

disputed Muslim state on Pakistan's border *(p. 444)*

center of Jainism (city) *(p. 434)*

Sikh state *(p. 438)*

Buddhist state (at Sikkim) *(p. 439)*

Christian majority (at Mizoram)

sugar cane *(p. 432)*

cashews, pulses, and sesame seeds *(p. 432)*

jute *(p. 432)*

rice (second worldwide) *(p. 432)*

tea *(p. 432)*

cotton (third worldwide) *(p. 434)*

mangoes and bananas (at Kerala)

peanuts (at Gujarat)

cashmere and saffron *(p. 444)*

4. Write their ranking beside the ten largest cities in India.

Bombay (Mumbai)	9,926,000
Delhi	7,207,000
Calcutta	4,400,000
Madras (Chennai)	3,841,000
Hyderabad	3,058,000

Ahmadabad	2,877,000
Bangalore	2,660,000
Kanpur	1,874,000
Nagpur	1,625,000
Lucknow	1,619,000

Map Questions

1. Generally speaking, the four largest cities are at each "corner" of India, and the fifth is in the center. Name these cities.

   - north   *Delhi*
   - south   *Madras (Chennai)*
   - east   *Calcutta*
   - west   *Bombay (Mumbai)*
   - center   *Hyderabad*

2. Which culture regions in India include some of the top ten cities?

   - five cities   *Deccan*
   - four cities   *Ganges*
   - one city   *Western border*
   - no top-ten cities   *northern Himalayas, eastern hills*

Geography

☆ **Hinduism** ☆ *Class discussion*

Hinduism has many followers and many forms. Recent interest in the New Age movement has brought a renewed interest in Hinduism, and many Westerners have tried to find peace through Hinduism. In this activity, you will read Hindu religious writings that present the key beliefs of Hinduism. Then you will compare the Hindu beliefs to the Bible.

When witnessing to a Hindu, keep in mind that the best witness you can give is the gospel. Don't be caught up in arguments, and don't be surprised or frustrated if the Hindu does not immediately turn to Christ. Many Hindus believe that all religions lead to God. A Hindu will likely tell you that it is okay for you to be a Christian, but that it is also okay for him to be a Hindu, because both paths lead to the same end. You will need to show that Christ is the only God, and the only way to salvation. Memorize verses that address these issues, and ask the Lord to give you a humble spirit as you talk with Hindus.

Hinduism has several books of scripture, which fall under two general headings. The earliest documents, the *Vedas* (meaning "knowledge") are also known as *Sruti* (which means "what is heard or revealed"). The *Vedas*, considered revelation from God, give the fundamental teachings of Hinduism. All other scriptures are called *Smriti*, or "what is

remembered." These secondary scriptures are recorded traditions that explain and illustrate the teachings of the *Sruti*. Many Hindus do not know their scriptures well because their religion is based on oral tradition, personal feelings and works, and the teachings of their prophets, priests, and gurus.

The readings in this activity come from the *Upanishads* and the *Bhagavad Gita*. The *Upanishads*, part of the *Vedas*, are philosophical essays that explain the teachings of the *Vedas*. Some of the *Upanishads* are single chapters within a *Veda;* other *Upanishads* are divided into parts, chapters, and sections (verses). For example, the reference II. v. 4 would indicate part two, chapter five, and verse four.

Though written much later than the *Vedas,* the *Bhagavad Gita* is usually included in the *Sruti* by modern Hindus. This small book, consisting of eighteen chapters, is the most popular of all Hindu scriptures. While the *Upanishads* are philosophical, the *Gita* is practical. The Gita presents a dialogue between Krishna (an incarnation of Vishnu, one of the three most important Hindu gods) and the Hindu warrior Arjuna while they are on a battlefield, about to engage in war with Arjuna's relatives.

Read the questions below before you read the following excerpts. Go back and answer the questions after reading each section.

Brahman

1. What is Brahman? the Atman?   <u>Brahman is a soul who is over all and in all; Atman is Brahman in the individual man. [Hinduism varies on its belief in God. Some Hindus believe in one single god, while others believe in many gods; the Hindu scriptures are just as contradictory.]</u>

2. According to this passage, what is the highest goal and reward? How does this compare to biblical salvation?   <u>Becoming one with Brahman and escaping the cycle of reincarnation; biblical salvation allows man to enter heaven (instead of making man a god), saves man from hell (not multiple rebirths), and comes through faith in Christ (not works).</u>

3. What does Scripture say about death? (Hebrews 9:27)   <u>Man will live and die only once; then he will face judgment.</u>

4. What is karma?   <u>fruitive actions (actions of material bodies)</u>

[Arjuna said:] "O my Lord, O supreme Person, what is Brahman? What are fruitive activities? What is the Atman, and what is the creative energy of Brahman? Explain the nature of this relative world, and of the individual man. Who is God who presides

over action in this body, and how does He dwell here? How are you revealed at the hour of death to those whose consciousness is united with you?"

[Krishna said:] "Brahman is the indestructible, the Supreme, which is imperishable, and independent

Enrichment: Section 1

Skill: Original Sources   173

of any cause but Itself. When we consider Brahman as lodged within the individual being, we call Him the Atman ["Self"]. And action pertaining to the development of these material bodies is called *karma,* or fruitive activities.

The basis of all created things is the perishable nature: the basis of the divine elements is the cosmic spirit. I alone am God who presides over action, here in this body.

And whoever, at the time of death, gives up his body and departs, thinking of me alone, then he will be united with me; of that there is no doubt. Whatever a man remembers at the last, when he is leaving the body, will be realized by him in the hereafter; because that will be what his mind has most constantly dwelt on, during this life.

Therefore remember me at all times, and do your duty and fight. If your mind and understanding are set on me, you will come to me without a doubt.

He who meditates on the Supreme Person with his thought attuned by constant practice and not wandering after anything else, he reaches the Person, Supreme and Divine.

Great souls who find me have found the highest perfection. They are no longer reborn into this condition of transience and pain." *Bhagavad-Gītā* 8:1-8, 21

Karma

5. How does man become free from bad karma? _by working with a spirit of devotion, not for rewards_

6. According to Hindu scripture, how is man freed from impurities? How is a Christian freed from impurities (I John 1:9)? _by meditating on gods and practicing penance; by confessing his sin to God (A Christian knows that he will never be perfect on this earth.)_

"Let not the wise disrupt the minds of the ignorant who are attached to fruitive action. They should be encouraged not to refrain from work, but to engage in work in the spirit of devotion.

One who executes his duties according to my injunctions and who follows this teaching faithfully becomes free from the bondage of fruitive actions.

But those who, out of envy, disregard these teachings and do not practice them regularly, are to be considered bereft of all knowledge, befooled, and doomed to ignorance and bondage." *Bhagavad-Gita* 3:26, 31-32

"Children, immersed in ignorance in various ways, flatter themselves, saying: We have accomplished life's purpose. Because these performers of karma do not know the Truth owing to their attachment, they fall from heaven, misery-stricken, when the fruit of their work is exhausted.

Ignorant fools, regarding sacrifices and humanitarian works as the highest, do not know any higher good. Having enjoyed their reward on the heights of heaven, gained by good works, they enter again this world or a lower one.

But those wise men of tranquil minds who live in the forest on alms, practicing penances appropriate to their stations of life and contemplating such deities as Brahman, depart, freed from impurities, by the Path of the Sun, to the place where that immortal Person dwells whose nature is imperishable." *Mundaka Upanishad* I. ii. 9-11

Reincarnation

7. According to the excerpts below, why does man experience reincarnation? How does he escape it?
   because his desires are not centered in Self (Atman, Brahman) but in worldly objects; by seeking the Atman

8. How does the Bible refute the notion that it is essential to perform good works over many lives in order to attain immortality (see Heb. 10:10)?   *Jesus died for our sins once for all time; we cannot atone for our sins through our works. We do not need reincarnation to give us several chances to work our way to heaven; we have a way through Christ.*

9. Hinduism is becoming more popular in the Western world, which has already accepted humanism. Describe the connection between Hinduism and humanism. How does the Bible contradict these beliefs (Ephesians 2:8-9)?   *Both Hinduism and humanism are man-centered. In Hinduism, man can achieve godhood through his works and devotion; humanists believe that man can solve problems on his own by working together. The Bible shows that salvation is centered on Jesus Christ's work, not on anything man can do.*

"Never was there a time when I [Krishna] was not, nor thou, nor these lords of men, nor will there ever be a time hereafter when we shall cease to be.

As the soul passes in this body through childhood, youth and age, even so is its taking on of another body. The sage is not perplexed by this.

That which pervades the entire body is indestructible. No one is able to destroy the imperishable soul.

Just as a person casts off worn-out garments and puts on others that are new, even so does the embodied soul cast off worn-out bodies and take on others that are new." *Bhagavad-Gita* 2:12-13, 17, 22

"He, the knower of the Self, knows that supreme Abode of Brahman, which shines brightly and in which the universe rests. Those wise men who, free from desires, worship such a person transcend the seed of birth.

He who, cherishing objects, desires them, is born again here or there through his desires. But for him whose desires are satisfied and who is established in the Self, all desires vanish even here on earth.

This Atman cannot be attained through study of the Vedas, nor through intelligence, nor through much learning. He who chooses Atman—by him alone is Atman attained. It is Atman that reveals to the seeker its true nature.

He who knows the Supreme Brahman verily becomes Brahman. In his family no one is born ignorant of Brahman. He overcomes grief; he overcomes evil; free from the fetters of the heart, he becomes immortal." *Mundaka Upanishad* III. ii. 1-4, 9

Geography

You're the Teacher: Report on South Asia

This student report on South Asia has twenty-five mistakes! Some mistakes are misspellings; others are simply the wrong word. Write the correct word above each underlined mistake.

           subcontinent   ***Himalayas***
South Asia is a <u>minicontinent</u>, separated from the rest of Asia by the <u>Tian Shan</u> in the north and the
                                              monsoon
Indian Ocean in the south. Life revolves around the cycle of the <u>moncoon</u> winds, which are stronger here
                                                                    typhoons
than anywhere else in the world. Besides these winds, South Asia often suffers from cyclones called <u>nirvana</u>
                       tsunamis
and destructive tidal waves called <u>sunamis</u>.
                        second
    India, whose population is <u>first</u> in the world, is the dominant country in the region. Hindu society is
                            castes
broken down into different <u>karmas</u>, which determine whom you can marry and what work you can do. Some
                                        gurus   ***Britain***
of the most respected men in India are the holy men, or <u>rajas</u>. Life in India changed under the rule of <u>China</u>,
                                      Hindi
which took over in 1858. The national language is <u>Urdu</u>, but the people speak hundreds of languages. The
            Mahatma Gandhi   ***satyagraha***
famous leader <u>Mahatima Ghandi</u>, the Father of the Nation, introduced <u>satagraha</u>, a policy of nonviolent

protests that helped bring an end to foreign rule.

    The typical person in South Asia is a farmer who lives in a small town or village. The most productive
                                Ganges
plain in India is the <u>Indus</u> river valley, where most people live. India's most valuable mineral resources,
                              Deccan
however, are located on the <u>Thar</u> Plateau in the south.
                                                        Muslims
    Apart from India, Pakistan is the most important country in South Asia. Most people here are <u>Sikhs</u>
                                                         Indus
who broke away from India in 1947 after bitter religious fighting. The key river in this country is the <u>Ganges</u>.
                                        Mahenjo-Daro
This ancient center of civilization includes the famous ruins of <u>Mahenjo-Dari</u>. Pakistan has a few other
                                    Baluchistan
isolated regions. The largest and least populated province, <u>Punjab</u>, is located on a large plateau west of the river.

    South Asia has several other interesting countries and features. In the north are several mountain ranges
                                    Himalayan Range
with peaks that exceed seven thousand meters. The <u>Karakoram</u> includes most of the world's highest
                                    Karakoram   ***Nepal***
mountains, but the most rugged range in the world is the <u>Western Ghats</u>. <u>Bangladesh</u> and Bhutan are two

mountain countries of South Asia. The monks living in the mountains of Bhutan have built beautiful
                           dzongs
monasteries called <u>tzongs</u>. South Asia also has two island countries in the south. The "Resplendent Isle,"
  Sri Lanka   ***the Maldives***
<u>Shri Lanka</u>, is known for rubies, sapphires, and tea. The other island nation is <u>Moldavia</u>, the smallest

country in Asia, which is relatively prosperous, with a normal life expectancy and high literacy rates.

The Conquest of Everest by Sir John Hunt

In the spring of 1953, an expedition led by the Englishman Sir John Hunt set out to conquer Mount Everest, the highest mountain in the world. Though organized by the British, the 1953 party included members from several nations, including Sherpas from Nepal who carried the party's equipment. The group met in India and traveled from there through Nepal to Mount Everest. It took them over two months to climb Everest. Finally, Sir Edmund Hillary of New Zealand and a Sherpa guide, Tenzing Norgay, reached the summit on May 29, 1953.

In the first three paragraphs, Hunt discusses the reasons for climbing Everest. The next section is written by Hillary and describes the last leg of the climb. The final paragraphs are reflections by Hunt. Read the excerpts, and then answer the questions below.

Reasons for Climbing Mount Everest

To those looking for a material objective, there is no satisfactory answer, for there was indeed no desire for, nor expectation of, any material reward.

Nor is the question answered simply by a passion for climbing mountains. To those who do so the sport is, or should be, a source of happiness. . . . But I doubt whether any one of our party went to Everest this year expecting to enjoy the climb as much as in the mountains nearer home. . . .

Yet to solve a problem which has long resisted the skill and persistence of others is an irresistible magnet in every sphere of human activity. . . . The possibility of entering the unknown; the simple fact that it was the highest point on the world's surface—these things goaded us on.

May 29th—Hillary's Account (included in Hunt's book)

At 4 A.M. it was very still. . . . We started up our cooker and in a determined effort to prevent the weaknesses arising from dehydration we drank large quantities of lemon juice and sugar, and followed this with our last can of sardines on biscuits. I dragged our oxygen sets into the tent, cleaned the ice off them and then completely rechecked and tested them. I had removed my boots, which had become a little wet the day before, and they were now frozen solid. Drastic measures were called for, so I cooked them over the fierce flame of the Primus [cooking stove] and despite the very strong smell of burning leather managed to soften them up. Over our down clothing we donned our windproofs and onto our hands we pulled three pairs of gloves— silk, woolen, and windproof.

At 6:30 A.M. we crawled out of our tent into the snow, hoisted our thirty pounds of oxygen gear onto our backs, connected up our masks and turned on the valves to bring life-giving oxygen into our lungs. A few good deep breaths and we were ready to go. . . . The ridge was now all bathed in sunlight and we could see our first objective, the south summit, far above us. . . .

The soft unstable snow made a route on top of the ridge both difficult and dangerous, so I moved a little down on the steep left side where the wind had produced a thin crust which sometimes held my weight but more often than not gave way with a sudden knock that was disastrous to both balance and morale. After several hundred feet of this rather trying ridge, we came to a tiny hollow and found there the oxygen bottles left on the earlier attempt by Evans and Bourdillon [members of the expedition who had tried to reach the summit a few days before]. I scraped the ice off the gauges and was greatly relieved to find that they still contained several hundred liters of oxygen—sufficient to get us down to the South Col [camp at the South "Pass"] if used very sparingly. With the comforting thought of these oxygen bottles behind us, I continued making the trail on up the ridge, which soon steepened and broadened into the very formidable snow face leading up for the last 400 feet to the southern summit. The snow conditions on this face were, we felt, distinctly dangerous, but as no alternative route seemed available, we persisted in our strenuous and uncomfortable efforts to beat a trail up it. We made frequent changes of lead on this very trying section and on one occasion as I was stamping a trail in the deep snow a section around me gave way and I slipped back through three or four of my steps. I discussed with Tenzing the advisability of going on and he, although admitting that he felt very unhappy about the snow conditions, finished with his familiar phrase, "Just as you wish." I decided to go on. . . .

The weather for Everest seemed practically perfect. Insulated as we were in all our down clothing and windproofs, we suffered no discomfort from cold or wind. However, on one occasion I removed my sunglasses to examine more closely a difficult section of the ridge but was very soon blinded by the fine snow driven by the bitter wind and hastily replaced them. . . . To my surprise I was enjoying the climb as much as I had ever enjoyed a fine ridge in my own New Zealand Alps.

After an hour's steady going we reached the foot of the most formidable looking problem on the ridge—a rock step some forty feet high. . . . On its east side was another great cornice [overhanging mass of snow or ice along a ridge, formed by wind] and running up the full forty feet of the step was a narrow crack between the cornice and the rock. Leaving Tenzing to belay [secure to a projection with a rope] me as best he could, I jammed my way into this crack, then kicking backwards with my crampons [spikes attached to boots for use on hard snow or ice] I sank their spikes deep into the frozen snow behind me and levered myself off the ground. Taking advantage of every little rock hold and all the force of knee, shoulder, and arms I could muster, I literally cramponed backwards up the crack, with a fervent prayer that the cornice would remain attached to the rock. Despite the considerable effort involved, my progress although slow was steady, and as Tenzing paid out the rope I inched my way upward until I could finally reach over the top of the rock and drag myself out of the crack onto a wide ledge. For a few moments I lay regaining my breath and for the first time really felt the fierce determination that nothing now could stop our reaching the top. I took a firm stance on the ledge and signaled to Tenzing to come on up. As I heaved hard on the rope Tenzing wriggled his way up the crack and finally collapsed exhausted at the top like a giant fish when it has just been hauled from the sea after the terrible struggle. . . .

The ridge continued as before. Giant cornices on the right, steep rock slopes on the left. I went on cutting steps [using an ice ax to cut holes in the snow to step into] on the narrow strip of snow. The ridge curved away to the right and we had no idea where the top was. As I cut around the back of one hump, another higher one would swing into view. Time was passing and the ridge seemed never-ending. In one place where the angle of the ridge had eased off, I tried cramponing without cutting steps, hoping this would save time, but I quickly realized that our margin of safety on these steep slopes at this altitude was too small, so I went on step cutting. I was beginning to tire a little now. I had been cutting steps continuously for two hours, and Tenzing, too, was moving very slowly. As I chipped steps around still another corner, I wondered rather dully just how long we could keep it up. Our original zest had now quite gone and it was turning more into a grim struggle. I then realized that the ridge ahead, instead of still monotonously rising, now dropped sharply away,

and far below I could see the North Col and the Rongbuk Glacier [in China, on the far side of Mt. Everest]. I looked upward to see a narrow snow ridge running up to a snowy summit. A few more whacks of the ice ax in the firm snow and we stood on top.

My initial feelings were of relief—relief that there were no more steps to cut—no more ridges to traverse and no more humps to tantalize us with hopes of success. I looked at Tenzing and in spite of the balaclava [hood], goggles, and oxygen mask all encrusted with long icicles that concealed his face, there was no disguising his infectious grin of pure delight as he looked all around him. We shook hands and then Tenzing threw his arm around my shoulders and we thumped each other on the back until we were almost breathless. It was 11:30 A.M. The ridge had taken us two and a half hours, but it seemed like a lifetime. I turned off the oxygen and removed my set. I had carried my camera, loaded with color film, inside my shirt to keep it warm, so I now produced it and got Tenzing to pose on top for me, waving his ax on which was a string of flags—British, Nepalese, United Nations, and Indian. Then I turned my attention to the great stretch of country lying below us in every direction. . . . Tenzing had made a little hole in the snow and in it he placed various small articles of food—a bar of chocolate, a packet of biscuits, and a handful of candies. Small offerings, indeed, but at least a token gift to the gods that all devout Buddhists believe have their home on this lofty summit. While we were together on the South Col two days before, Hunt had given me a small crucifix which he had asked me to take to the top. I, too, made a hole in the snow and placed the crucifix beside Tenzing's gifts.

I checked our oxygen once again and worked out our endurance. We would have to move fast in order to reach our life-saving reserve below the south summit. After fifteen minutes we turned to go. . . . We both felt a little tired, for the reaction was setting in and we must get off the mountain quickly.

Reflections by Hunt

What were the reasons for our success? How was it that we succeeded in getting to the top when so many others before us had failed to do so? I am adding the second question only to give what, in my mind, is the one reason transcending all others which explains the first. For I wish once again to pay tribute to the work of earlier expeditions. . . . We of the 1953 Everest Expedition are proud to share the glory with our predecessors. . . .

Next in order of events I would place sound, thorough, meticulously detailed planning. On Everest, the problems of organization assume the proportions of a military campaign; I make no apology for this comparison, or for the fact that we planned the ascent of Everest on these lines. It was thanks to this that we were able not only to foresee our needs in every detail—guided by previous experience provided by others, we judged aright—but to have constantly before us a clear program to carry out at every stage. . . .

Above all else, I should like to stress our unity as a party. This was undoubtedly the biggest single factor in the final result, for the ascent of Everest, perhaps more than most human ventures, demanded a very high degree of selfless co-operation; no amount of equipment or food could have compensated for any weakness in this respect. It would be difficult to find a more close-knit team than ours.

Was it worthwhile? For us who took part in the venture, it was so beyond doubt. We have shared a high endeavor; we have witnessed scenes of beauty and grandeur; we have built up a lasting comradeship among ourselves, and we have seen the fruits of that comradeship ripen into achievement. We shall not forget those moments of great living upon that mountain.

The story of the ascent of Everest is one of teamwork. If there is a deeper and more lasting message behind our venture than the mere ephemeral sensation of a physical feat, I believe this to be the value of comradeship and the many virtues which combine to create it. Comradeship, regardless of race or creed, is forged among high mountains, through the difficulties and dangers to which they expose those who aspire to climb them, the need to combine their efforts to attain their goal, the thrills of a great adventure shared together.

1. What reasons does Hunt give for climbing Mount Everest?   *to do something no one had been able to do, to explore the unknown, and to conquer the highest point in the world*

2. What hardships did the expedition face?   *snowstorms, cold, extreme wind, lack of oxygen, carrying heavy oxygen tanks, exhaustion from the difficult climb*

3. Why was the very last leg of the climb especially hard?   *Hillary was tired from cutting steps for over two hours, and the excitement was wearing off; they didn't know how far it was to the summit.*

4. What was Hillary's first feeling at the summit? Why?   *relief; he was extremely tired from the hard climb and not knowing when it would end*

5. Explain the significance of each flag Tenzing placed at the top of Mt. Everest.   *The expedition was organized by the British and led by an Englishman; Mt. Everest is on the border of Nepal and China, and the Sherpas who carried the party's equipment were from Nepal; the United Nations flag represents the expedition's members who came from nations other than Britain, Nepal, or India; the expedition met and traveled through India on the way to the mountain.*

6. How long were Hillary and Tenzing at the top of Mt. Everest? Why weren't they there longer?

only fifteen minutes; they had to get to their oxygen supply

_____

_____

7. What reasons does Hunt give for his team's success in reaching the top? *Previous expeditions had*

paved the way; the organization was done well; and the team had great unity.

_____

_____

8. Did Hunt think the climb was worth taking? What did he cite as a more lasting message of the

expedition? Do you agree? *yes; the value of teamwork and comradeship forged through difficult times;*

answers will vary

_____

_____

9. It has been said that the conquest of Mt. Everest was the "greatest single adventure of the twentieth

century." Would you agree or disagree? *Answers will vary. Reaching the South Pole was another feat*

of planning and endurance, but Hunt had to go up as well as go far. Reaching the moon was an even

greater triumph, but it is not an "adventure" in the same sense of the word.

_____

_____

Geography

Map of Southeast Asia

Fill in each blank with the correct letter or number from the map on the next page. Regions are upper-case letters (A, B, C), cities are lowercase letters (a, b, c), islands are double lowercase letters (aa, bb, cc), and physical features are numbers (1, 2, 3). Refer to the maps on pages 448 and 454. *Encourage students to try to complete this activity without looking at the book and then to double-check their answers in the book.*

Countries

I	1. Brunei	*F*	5. Malaysia	*B*	9. Thailand
E	2. Cambodia	*A*	6. Myanmar	*D*	10. Vietnam
H	3. Indonesia	*J*	7. Philippines		
C	4. Laos	*G*	8. Singapore		

Cities

j	11. Bandar Seri Begawan	*i*	15. Jakarta	*h*	20. Singapore
		g	16. Kuala Lumpur	*b*	21. Vientiane
f	12. Bangkok	*k*	17. Manila		
c	13. Hanoi	*e*	18. Phnom Penh		
d	14. Ho Chi Minh City	*a*	19. Rangoon		

Islands

cc	22. Bali	*jj*	26. Luzon	*aa*	30. Sumatra
gg	23. Borneo	*ii*	27. Mindanao	*dd*	31. Timor
ff	24. Celebes	*ee*	28. Moluccas		
bb	25. Java	*hh*	29. Spratly Islands		

Physical Features

3	32. Annamese Mountains	5	34. Malay Peninsula	4	36. South China Sea
1	33. Irrawaddy River	2	35. Mekong River		

Map Work   *This section is optional.*

37. Shade yellow the three countries that formerly made up French Indochina. *(pp. 450-52)*

38. Shade green the four countries that are considered to be "Little Dragons." *(pp. 454, 456-58)*

39. Draw these figures in the appropriate place.

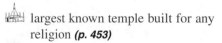

🌹 country that produces 60% of world's heroin *(p. 450)*

$ richest country in Southeast Asia *(p. 457)*

⏳ oldest country in Southeast Asia *(p. 453)*

✕ lowest literacy rate in Southeast Asia *(p. 452)*

🚶 highest population density in world *(p. 457)*

💲 lowest life expectancy/per capita GDP in Southeast Asia *(p. 452)*

🛕 largest known temple built for any religion *(p. 453)*

🚶 Indochina's largest city *(p. 454)*

🚶 Southeast Asia's largest city *(p. 458)*

☪ largest Islamic country in the world *(p. 458)*

⚫ world's leader in natural rubber *(p. 458)*

🌰 world's leader in coconuts and coconut oil *(p. 461)*

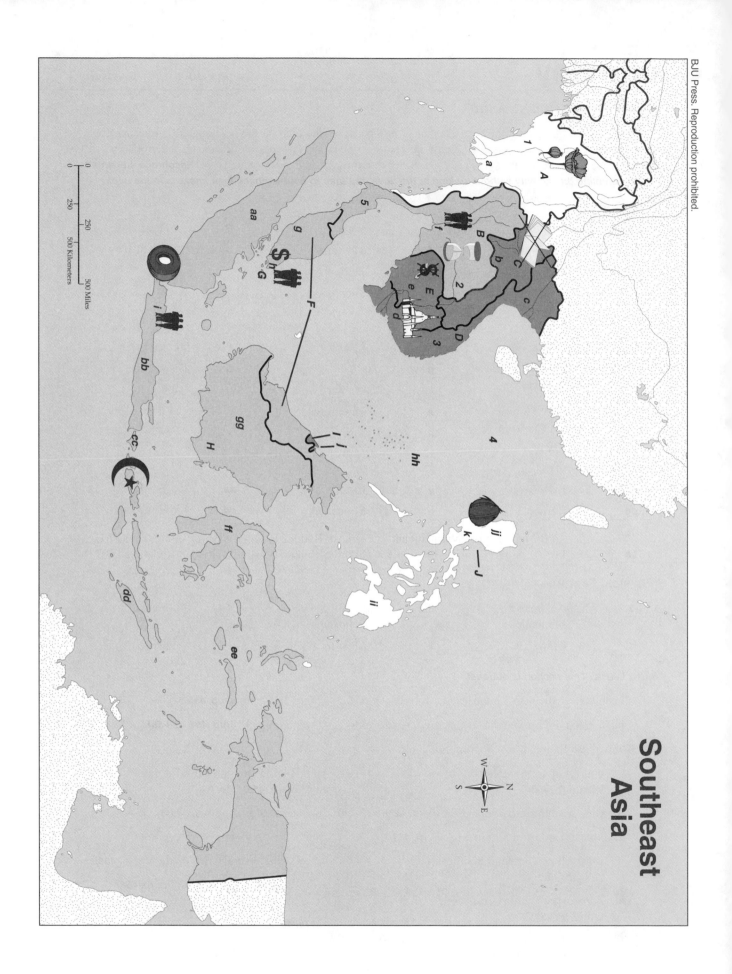

Southeast Asia

Geography

Buddhism

Buddhism began as a Hindu sect around 500 B.C. Siddhartha Gautama, the founder of Buddhism, was a rich young man. One day, after recently seeing old, sick, and dying people, he became disenchanted with his wealth and left his wife and child to become a poor wanderer, searching for an end to man's suffering. Eventually he decided that extreme self-affliction was no more righteous than worldly living. He turned to meditation, where he sought enlightenment and release from the suffering of the physical world. After long meditation, he experienced "enlightenment" and believed he had found the true way to salvation. Gautama became known as Buddha ("the enlightened one") and spent the rest of his life traveling through the land telling others of his way, which he termed "the Middle Way."

Buddha's immediate aim was to eliminate the cause of suffering; his sermons focus on the work of man to solve his own problems. The highest goal of Buddhism is to escape the cycle of death and rebirth and to reach nirvana, a state of nothingness which brings complete rest and happiness. The only way to reach nirvana is to stop desiring anything in this world; then man becomes free from attachment to the physical self and becomes enlightened. The state of nirvana comes at the moment of enlightenment.

Buddha's sayings ("suttas") were not written down for several hundred years. The Pali *Tipitaka*, over two times larger than the Bible, is the canon of scripture used by the Theravada school of Buddhism (the oldest school still practiced). The name of these scriptures comes from two parts: Pali, which is the dead language (related to Sanskrit) used in the writings, and *Tipitaka*, which means

"Three Baskets." The three "baskets" are the Basket of Discipline (rules for monks), the Basket of Discourses (Buddha's sermons), and the Basket of Further Dhamma (philosophical teachings). Other Buddhist schools add other scriptures to the Pali Canon.

Knowing the basic Buddhist beliefs will enable you to defend your faith better and witness to Buddhists. It may take several attempts before you can clearly present the gospel to a Buddhist because he has a completely different perspective from that of a Christian. For example, a Buddhist is not interested in eternal life because his ultimate goal is to stop the cycle of rebirth. Buddhists do not believe in a personal God, but in an impersonal Nirvana, or Emptiness. Also, a Buddhist may respond that Jesus was just a good teacher, like Buddha. Verses such as John 3:16 and 10:30 show that Jesus is God and has a special relationship with Him. Buddha never made claims to have a relationship with God. Whatever objections a Buddhist may have to the gospel, be patient and humble as you seek to show him the true way. Use a conversational manner rather than a preaching style.

Some Buddhists focus on the teachings of Buddha, while others worship Buddha as a god. Still, most Buddhists share several common doctrines. These common beliefs are included in Buddha's first sermon, the first selection given below. In this message, Buddha lists "The Four Noble Truths" and the "Eightfold Path."

Read the questions, and then read the excerpts from the Pali Canon. Go back and answer the questions after reading each section.

1. Read Matthew 5:6. Is all desire wrong? What did Jesus teach about desire? *No; we should desire righteousness.*

2. What are the four noble truths? *1. Life is full of pain. 2. Pain is caused by desire for things of the physical world. 3. Pain can be eliminated by destroying desire. 4. Desire can be eliminated by following the Eightfold Path.*

3. Why won't the Eightfold Path bring salvation (Isaiah 64:6)? *It is based completely on man's work; God is left out of the plan.*

Dhammacakkapavattana ["Setting the Wheel of Dhamma in Motion"]

[This excerpt relays the first sermon of Buddha, given shortly after he became "enlightened."] Thus have I heard: at one time the Lord [Buddha] dwelt

at Benares [modern-day Varanasi, India—see map on page 430 of the text] . . . in the Deer Park. There the Lord addressed the five monks:

"These two extremes, monks, are not to be practiced by a holy man . . . self-indulgence and luxury, which is vulgar, common, ignoble, and use-less; and self-torture, which is painful, ignoble, and useless. Avoiding these two extremes, the Tathagata [Buddha] has gained the enlightenment of the Middle Path, which produces insight and knowledge, and leads to calm, to higher knowledge, enlightenment, and Nirvana. And what, monks, is the Middle Path? . . . This is the noble Eightfold Way: namely, right view, right intention, right speech, right action, right livelihood, right effort, right mindfulness, right concentration. This, monks, is the Middle Path, of which the Tathagata has gained enlightenment, which produces insight and knowledge, and tends to calm, to higher knowledge, enlightenment, and Nirvana.

Now this, monks, is the noble truth of pain: birth is painful, old age is painful, sickness is painful, death is painful, sorrow, lamentation, dejection, and despair are painful. Contact with unpleasant things is painful, not getting what one wishes is painful. . . .

Now this, monks, is the noble truth of the origin of pain: the desire, which tends to rebirth, combined with pleasure and lust, seeking satisfaction now here, now there; namely, the desire for the gratification of the passions, the desire for a future life, or the desire for success in this present life.

Now this, monks, is the noble truth of the destruction of pain. It is the destruction, in which no passion remains, of this very desire; the abandonment of, forsaking of, release of, and non-attachment to this desire.

Now this, monks, is the noble truth of the way that leads to the destruction of pain: this is the noble Eightfold Way; namely, right views, right intention, right speech, right action, right livelihood, right effort, right mindfulness, right concentration. . . .

Now this knowledge and insight has arisen within me. The release of my mind is unshakable: this is my last existence; now there is no rebirth." *Sutta Pitaka, Samyutta Nikaya* 56:11 [Basket of Discourses, Grouped Collection 56, sutta 11]

4. What is wrong with being a lamp unto yourself? (See Romans 3:23.) How do Jesus' words in John 14:6 contradict the teaching of Buddha? __*Man is sinful and cannot save himself; salvation is found only*__

    __*in Jesus.*__

5. Compare Hinduism and Buddhism. __*Hinduism doesn't have a founder; Hindus want to escape*__

    __*reincarnation and join the world soul, Brahman. Buddhism has a founder; Buddhists want to escape desire*__

    __*and suffering by reaching enlightenment and Nirvana. Both religions have many scriptures and several*__

    __*schools of thought; both are man-centered, not God-centered, and both are based on works.*__

Mahaparinibbana Sutta ["The Last Days of Buddha"]

[In this sutta, the dying Buddha addresses his cousin and closest disciple, Ananda.] "Therefore, O Ananda, be ye lamps unto yourselves. Rely on yourselves, and do not rely on external help. Hold fast to the truth as a lamp. Seek salvation alone in the truth. Look not for assistance to any one besides yourselves.

And how, Ananda, can a brother be a lamp unto himself, rely on himself only and not on any external help, holding fast to the truth as his lamp and seeking salvation in the truth alone, looking not for assistance to any one besides himself?

Herein, O Ananda, let a brother, as he dwells in the body, so regard the body that he, being strenuous, thoughtful, and mindful, may, whilst in the world, overcome the grief which arises from the body's desires. . . .

And so, also, when he thinks, or reasons, or feels, let him so regard his thought that being strenuous, thoughtful, and mindful he may, whilst in the world, overcome the grief which arises from the desire due to ideas, or to reasoning, or to feeling.

Those who, either now or after I am dead, shall be a lamp unto themselves, relying upon themselves only and not relying upon any external help, but holding fast to the truth as their lamp, and seeking their salvation in the truth alone, shall not look for assistance to any one besides themselves, it is they, Ananda, among my monks, who shall reach the very topmost height! But they must be anxious to learn." *Sutta Pitaka, Digha Nikaya* ["Long Collection"] 16 [sutta number], 2:33-35 [part two, verses 33-35]

Geography

☆ **Why Do Countries Differ?**

Sometimes neighboring countries can be very different, despite their similar location and climate. Compare Thailand and Vietnam to find out just how many characteristics they share in common. Then look for the contrasts between the two countries that help to explain their differences. Based on your knowledge of geography, could you have predicted the current state of affairs? ☆ *Class discussion*

Similarities Between Thailand and Vietnam

1. Physical Shape (map on p. 448)   *Both have a compact core of land where the capital lies and a narrow strip that stretches southward.*

2. Main River and Location of the Capital   *Both have major rivers that start in China, and both have built their capitals near the mouths of these rivers.*

3. Location Relative to the Ocean and Other Countries   *Both lie on Indochina between their two large neighbors.*

4. Climate (map on p. 436)   *Both have humid subtropical climate in the north, tropical wet on the coast, and tropical wet and dry (savanna) in the interior.*

5. Religion (map on p. 438)   *The majority of people in both countries are Buddhists, while tribal religions are common in the mountains.*

6. Products and Industry (see maps on pp. 451 and 474, as well as the chart on p. 451)   *Both are major producers of rice in intensive subsistence farming. The mountain groups follow shifting agriculture.*

Why Are Thailand and Vietnam So Different?

7. Total Area and Location of the Capital (map on p. 448)   *Thailand is much larger than Vietnam and its capital more centrally located.*

8. Location Relative to the Ocean and Other Countries   *Vietnam borders China and is easily accessible to it, but Thailand requires a much longer trip by sea.*

9. Climate (map on p. 436)   *Vietnam has a broad area in the north with a humid subtropical climate that supports a large population separate from the capital in the south.*

10. Religion (map on p. 438)   *Most of the people in Thailand are Southern Buddhists, but Vietnam is divided between Southern Buddhists and Chinese religion in the north.*

11. Products and Industry (see maps on pp. 451 and 474, as well as the chart on p. 451)   *Vietnam just feeds its own large population, while Thailand produces plenty of extra rice and exports more than any other country; Thailand has diversified its economy and has become a Little Dragon. Thailand's products include tin, rubber, and teak; but Vietnam is more limited to farming.*

12. Early History (Relations with ancient China and Cambodia, see map on p. 452)   *Northern Vietnam was once in the grasp of the Han, and the South was controlled by Funan empire, but not Thailand, which is separated from these two countries by mountains.*

13. History of the Expansion of Communism   *Vietnam shared its border with Communist China and fell under its influence, but Thailand turned to the West.*

Geography

Name _____

Chapter 20   Activity 4

Playing with Shapes

Countries come in all shapes and sizes. There are five major classifications of countries by shape, and Southeast Asia has four of them. Beside each classification below, list all of the countries in this chapter that best fit the definition. For the classification that does not appear in this region, name any other country in the world that fits the description.

1. Compact (Most of the country is a single mass of land with fairly smooth borders.) *Cambodia, Brunei*

2. Elongated (Most of the country is a long, narrow mass of land.) *Myanmar (Burma), Vietnam, Laos*

3. Fragmented (The country is broken up into several pieces of separate land of varying sizes.)
   Malaysia, Singapore, Indonesia, Philippines

4. Perforated (The country has other small countries located entirely within its borders.) *Examples of this rare shape include Italy and South Africa.*

5. Prorupt (The country is mostly compact but has an elongated tail.) *Thailand*

Thought Questions

1. Which type of border would appear to be the easiest to defend? *Answers will vary. But military experts would generally agree that compact countries, such as Germany and France, with a good network of "interior lines," are the easiest to defend.*

2. What is the only country in Southeast Asia to avoid European colonization? Do you think its shape had anything to do with its ability to defend itself? *Thailand has a prorupt shape. Its central location in Indochina created a buffer between it and outside powers pushing from China, India, and the Malay Archipelago.*

3. Among the fifty U.S. states, what do you think is the best example of each shape? [Note: One of the classifications will not apply to any states.]

   • Compact *Answers will vary. Wyoming is nearly square with no odd twists.*

   • Elongated *Answers will vary—perhaps New Hampshire, Vermont, Florida, or California.*

   • Fragmented *Answers will vary. Michigan is clearly broken up, along with Hawaii and Alaska.*

   • Perforated *No states, but recall the odd boundaries on the Mississippi River and northern Minnesota.*

   • Prorupt *Answers will vary—perhaps West Virginia, Oklahoma, or Alaska.*

Geography

Chapter 20   **Activity 5**

Country Grab Bag

Match each country with the descriptions below. Give all the countries that fit each description.

A. Brunei
B. Cambodia
C. Indonesia
D. Laos

E. Malaysia
F. Myanmar
G. Philippines

H. Singapore
I. Thailand
J. Vietnam

B, D, F, I, J (pp. 447-53)	1.	Indochina cultural subregion
A, C, E, G, H (pp. 456-60)	2.	Malay Archipelago cultural subregion
F (p. 338)	3.	Irrawaddy is the main river
A, E, F, H (pp. 454, 457)	4.	former British colony
B, D, J (p. 454)	5.	former French Indochina
E (p. 454)	6.	former colony of the Netherlands (Holland)
G (p. 460)	7.	former Spanish colony
G (p. 454)	8.	former U.S. territory
I (p. 453)	9.	monarchy never under European control
all (p. 454)	10.	member of ASEAN
B, D, J (pp. 451-52)	11.	Communist control at some time in history
J (p. 451)	12.	led by Ho Chi Minh
C (p. 458)	13.	Golden Age under the Madjapahit Kingdom
H (p. 457)	14.	Chinese majority (one)
B, D, F, I, J (p. 449)	15.	Buddhist majority
A, C, E (pp. 456-58)	16.	Muslim majority
G (p. 460)	17.	Roman Catholic majority
F, J (pp. 450-52)	18.	persecuted Christian tribes living in the highlands
E (p. 456)	19.	large, rich Chinese minority
A (p. 449)	20.	lowest population
C (p. 449)	21.	highest population
H (p. 449)	22.	highest population density
H (p. 449)	23.	highest per capita GDP
B (p. 449)	24.	lowest per capita GDP
C, E, H, I (pp. 454, 456-58)	25.	"Little Dragon"
C (p. 451)	26.	most rice in Southeast Asia, total production
I (p. 455)	27.	most rice, exports worldwide
C (p. 458)	28.	most natural rubber
G (p. 461)	29.	most coconuts
F (p. 450)	30.	borders the Golden Triangle
C, E, G, J (p. 452)	31.	claims the Spratly Islands

Chapter Review   **Skill: Recognition**   **187**

Islands of Southeast Asia

Match each island with its description.

A. Bali
B. Borneo
C. Celebes
D. Java

E. Luzon
F. Mindanao
G. Moluccas

H. New Guinea
I. Sumatra
J. Timor

__H (p. 459)__	1. second largest island in the world, includes Irian Jaya
__B (p. 459)__	2. third largest island in the world, divided between Indonesia and Malaysia
__I (p. 459)__	3. sixth largest island in the world, second most populous in Indonesia
__C (p. 459)__	4. oddly shaped island, eleventh largest in the world, with four peninsulas and six ethnic groups
__D (p. 458)__	5. most populous island in Indonesia
__A (p. 460)__	6. Indonesian island famous for its version of Hinduism
__E (pp. 460-61)__	7. largest island in the Philippines, produces most of nation's products
__F (p. 461)__	8. large island in the southern Philippines
__G (p. 460)__	9. Spice Islands
__J (p. 460)__	10. illegally annexed by Indonesia in 1975

Geography

Map of China and Mongolia

Refer to the map on page 464 to complete the map on the next page.

1. Label these features of physical geography:
   Bodies of Water—Chang River, Huang He, Xi River
   Mountains—Kunlun, Qin Ling
   Deserts—Gobi Desert, Taklimakan Desert
   Miscellaneous—North China Plain, Sichuan Basin, Taiwan, Xizang (Tibet)

2. Label these features of human geography:
   Cities—Guangzhou, Hong Kong, Lhasa, Shanghai, Xi'an
   Regions—Inner Mongolia, Xinjiang

3. Label all the countries and their capitals for this part of East Asia.

4. Label the ten largest cities on the map, and beside each city place its rank.

Shanghai, China	8,214,400
Beijing, China	7,362,000
Tianjin, China	5,855,000
Shenyang, China	4,130,000
Wuhan, China	3,570,000
Guangzhou, China	3,100,000
Chongqing, China	2,730,000
Taipei, Taiwan	2,706,500
Harbin, China	2,590,000
Xi'an, China	2,210,000

5. Draw these figures in the appropriate place. ***This section is optional.***

   #2 second largest desert in the world

    "China's Sorrow" *(p. 466)*

    Forbidden City *(p. 469)*

    oldest European colony in Asia *(p. 473)*

   '49 island that Chiang Kai-shek and Chinese Nationalists fled to in 1949 *(p. 477)*

China and Mongolia

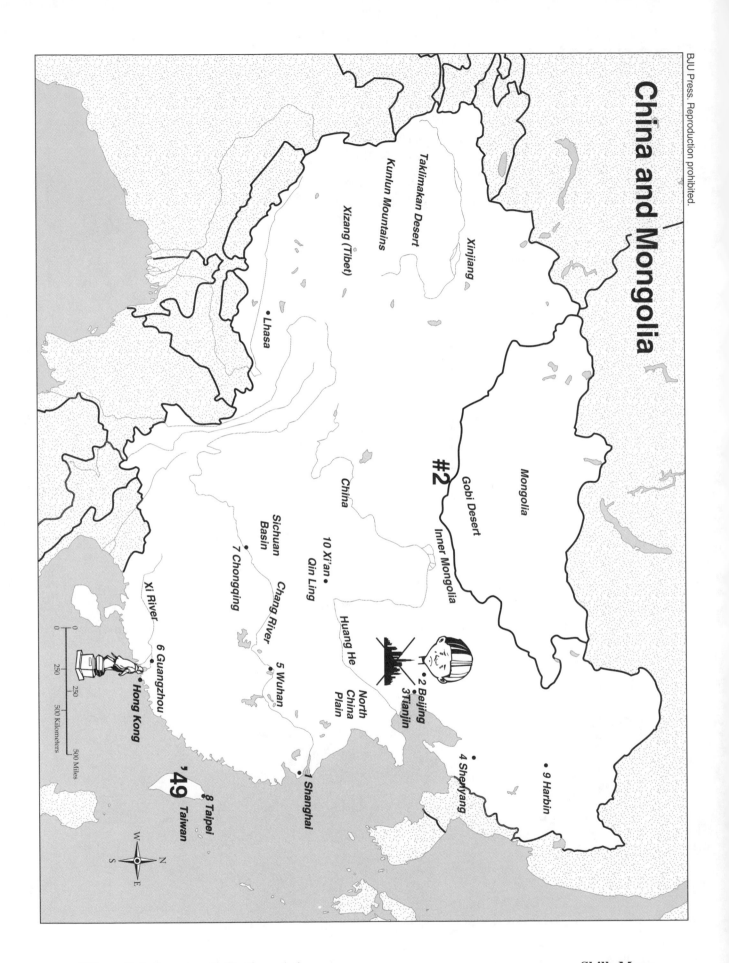

Xinjiang

Taklimakan Desert

Kunlun Mountains

Xizang (Tibet)

• Lhasa

Mongolia

Gobi Desert

#2

Inner Mongolia

China

Sichuan
Basin

7 Chongqing

Chang River

5 Wuhan

10 Xi'an •
Qin Ling

Huang He

North
China
Plain

• 2 Beijing
3 Tianjin

• 4 Shenyang

• 9 Harbin

Xi River

• 6 Guangzhou

Hong Kong

• 1 Shanghai

8 Taipei
'49 Taiwan

0
250
250
500 Kilometers
0
250
500 Miles

N
W · E
S

Geography

China's Provinces

Color in the key and the map with the six cultural subregions in China discussed in your text.
Using this map to discuss the various subregions of China will make the student text more meaningful.

Map Work *Note: This section is optional. If used, icons should be drawn before students color the subregions.*

1. Draw these figures in the appropriate state or region. Note that China is the world's leader in these products, unless shown otherwise.

   - most populous province *(p. 467)*
   - Muslim region (two) *(pp. 475-76)*
   - lowest elevation in the Far East *(p. 475)*
   - "The Roof of the World" *(p. 473)*
   - capital of many early dynasties *(p. 466)*

   - largest square in the world *(p. 469)*
   - most powerful dam in the world (under construction east of Chongqing) *(p. 467)*
   - **DL** region where Dalai Lama is leader *(p. 474)*
   - coal *(p. 465)*
   - wheat *(p. 465)*

   - rice *(p. 465)*
   - tobacco *(p. 465)*
   - swine *(p. 465)*
   - sweet potatoes *(p. 471)*
   - fish *(p. 468)*
   - silk *(p. 472)*
   - cotton *(p. 465)*
   - tin *(pp. 471-72)*

2. In the North China Plain, draw a black line on the border beween the states of the Huang and the Chang Rivers.

3. Connect the city dots from Xi'an to Kashgar, bypassing Tibet, and label this route the "Old Silk Road." Now look at the population map on page 443. What do you see?

4. Write their ranking beside the metropolitan areas in China that have at least 2 million people. (Look at the population map on page 443, if necesssary.) *Remind students of the difference between metro area and city proper. Obviously the figures for metro area are always much larger than those for city proper.*

Shanghai	13,500,000
Beijing	12,000,000
Tianjin	9,400,000
Shenyang	5,100,000
Hong Kong	4,588,000
Guangzhou	4,500,000
Chongquin	3,000,000
Harbin	2,700,000
Chengdu	2,500,000
Nanjing	2,400,000
Xi'an	2,300,000
Dalian (Luda)	2,300,000
Zibo	2,200,000
Taiyuan	2,100,000
Changchun	2,000,000
Zhengzhou	2,000,000

Map Questions

1. How many metro areas with more than two million people lie in each region of China? Give the largest city in each region.

   - North China Plain (northern portion, including the Huang He basin) *six, Beijing*

   - North China Plain (southern portion, including the Chang river basin) *five, Shanghai*

   - Manchuria *three, Shenyang*

   - Southern Uplands *two, Hong Kong*

2. Which three culture regions in China have none of the top metro areas? *Tibet, Xinjiang, Inner Mongolia*

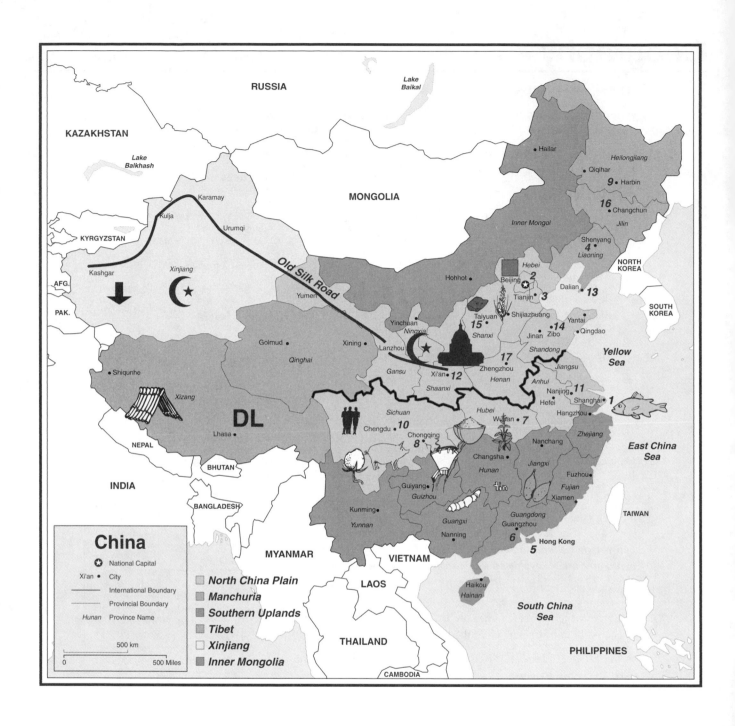

China

- ✪ National Capital
- Xi'an • City
- International Boundary
- Provincial Boundary
- *Hunan* Province Name

500 km

0   500 Miles

- North China Plain
- Manchuria
- Southern Uplands
- Tibet
- Xinjiang
- Inner Mongolia

Geography

Map of Japan and Korea

Refer to the map on page 479 to complete the map on the next page.

1. Label these features of physical geography:
   Bodies of Water—Inland Sea
   Islands—Hokkaido, Honshu, Kyushu, Shikoku
   Mountains—Mount Fuji
   Plains—Kanto Plain

2. Label all the countries and their capitals for this part of East Asia.

3. Beside each of the ten largest metropolitan areas in Japan and Korea place its rank.

Tokyo-Yokohama, Japan	26,960,000
Seoul, S. Korea	11,600,000
Osaka, Japan	10,600,000
Nagoya, Japan	4,800,000
Pusan, S. Korea	4,000,000
Pyongyang, N. Korea	2,600,000
Taegu, S. Korea	2,400,000
Sapporo, Japan	1,900,000
Fukuoka, Japan	1,750,000
Hiroshima, Japan	1,575,000

4. Draw these figures in the appropriate place. *Note: This section is optional.*

   peninsula controlled by many foreign powers over the years *(p. 478)*

   80% island that houses over 80% of Japanese *(p. 481)*

   largest megalopolis in world *(p. 481)*

   Mount Fuji *(p. 482)*

   site of second atomic bombing *(p. 485)*

   island home of Japan's first cities *(p. 485)*

   island that is similar to the American West *(p. 485)*

   world's leader in fish processing and tuna catch *(p. 485)*

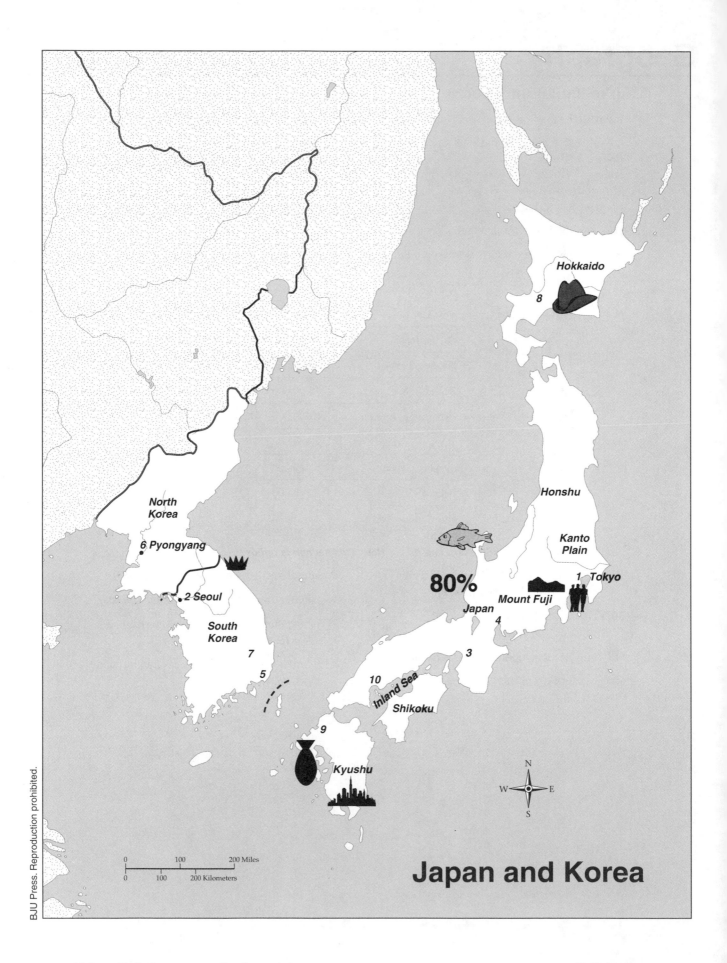

Hokkaido

8

North
Korea

6 Pyongyang

2 Seoul

South
Korea

7

5

9

Kyushu

10

Inland Sea

Shikoku

3

Honshu

Kanto
Plain

1 Tokyo

Japan

80%

Mount Fuji

4

N
W   E
S

Japan and Korea

0   100   200 Miles
0   100   200 Kilometers

Geography

☆ ## East Meets West: Comparing the United States, China, and Japan

Under each category below, decide which country is more similar to the United States—China or Japan. If you think it is China, write *C* in the first blank; if Japan, write *J;* if both are very similar to the United States, write *B,* and if neither has any similarity to the United States, write *N.* Then in the blank, support your answer with pertinent information about China and Japan. Don't forget to look at the statistical charts and the maps of Asia in your textbook. ***Answers will vary.*** ☆ ***Class discussion.***

Physical Geography

___C___ 1. Climate   *China has a much greater variety of climate than Japan (which is divided between*

humid continental and humid subtropical).

___N___ 2. Mountain Ranges   *Japan does not have the complex variety of ranges found in the United*

States, and though China has several ranges, they tend to run east-to-west.

___N___ 3. High Point   *Japan's high point (Mt. Fuji, 12,389) is much lower and more easily climbed than*

Mt. McKinley (20,320 ft.); like the United States, China has the highest point on its respective

continent—Mt. Everest (29,028 ft.), but this high point, located in the southwest, is in a class by

itself.

___C___ 4. Plains   *Japan has only one "major" plain, the Kanto Plain, whereas China has the large, well-*

watered North China Plain and the Manchurian Plain.

___N___ 5. Lakes   *Neither China nor Japan has any large lakes or lake systems to match any in*

the United States.

___C___ 6. Rivers   *Both the U.S. and China have long river systems (Huang He and Chang Rivers), but*

China's main rivers empty in the east, not south. Japan's rivers are all short.

Economy

___J___ 7. Per Capita GDP   *The Japanese income is comparable to that in the U.S. ($21,300 versus*

$27,607), but Chinese income is less than a tenth of that in the U.S. (only $2,500).

___C___ 8. Agricultural Products   *Like the U.S., China is a major agricultural producer, including wheat,*

tobacco, swine, cotton, rice, and silk. Farmland is limited in Japan, and rice is the main crop.

___C___ 9. Mining Products (See chart on p. 66.)   *Both the U.S. and China are major producers of coal,*

and China has several other deposits (tin, tungsten, and petroleum). Japan has no major resources.

___B___ 10. Manufacturing   *Both China and Japan are major manufacturing countries. (But Japan, like the*

U.S., has a large high-tech industry.)

___B___ 11. Ports   *Both China and Japan have valuable ports. Japan's capital is also a major port, unlike the*

capitals of the U.S. and China.

Demography

___N___ 12. Total Population (See chart on p. 104.)   *All three are among the ten most populous countries,*

but China's population (1,210,000,000) is over four times as large as the U.S. population

(267,954,767), whereas Japan's is less than half of that of the U.S.

_N_ 13. Population Density   *Both China and Japan have over four times the population density of the United States (327 and 389 versus 72).*

_C_ 14. Natural Increase   *China's increase is a bit higher than the U.S. increase (1.0% versus 0.6%), but Japan's rate (0.2%) is three times smaller.*

_B_ 15. Life Expectancy   *The Japanese live a bit longer than Americans (80 versus 76 years), but the Chinese have a shorter expectancy (70).*

_J_ 16. Literacy Rate   *Japan and the United States have a high literacy rate typical of developed countries (96% in the United States, 100% in Japan), but China's rate (80%) reflects a developing country.*

_B_ 17. Largest City   *All three countries have huge cities—New York (7 million), Shanghai (8 million—not in the text) and Tokyo (8 million). [Note: The metro area of Tokyo (27 million) is larger than the New York metro (20 million), while the Shanghai metro is smaller (13.5 million).]*

History

_N_ 18. History of Settlement   *Both Asian civilizations are much older than the United States, though China is even older than Japan.*

_N_ 19. Creation of the Modern Country   *Both Asian countries went through a revolution of sorts—Mao's Communists and the Meiji Restoration, but the nature of these revolutions has little in common with the American Revolution.*

Government

_C_ 20. Area   *China is only slightly larger than the U.S. (3,696,100 versus 3,675,031 sq. mi.), and both belong among the top ten in area. Japan is less than one-twentieth the size of the U.S. (145,850 sq. mi.)*

_J_ 21. Form of Government   *Both Japan and the U.S. are republics, though Japan has a figurehead emperor and its traditions are weaker. China is Communist.*

_J_ 22. Political Divisions   *The United States has fifty states, while Japan has forty-seven prefectures. China has twenty-two provinces and six autonomous regions.*

Society

_B_ 23. Cultural Subregions   *Both China and Japan have regions somewhat similar to the divisions of the United States: eastern plains similar to the U.S. population and historic center in the U.S. Northeast; a separate regional identity in the south (Cantonese in China's Southern Uplands and Japan's rural island of Shikoku) similar to the U.S. South. Neither country has anything quite like the U.S. Midwest.*

_C_ 24. Minorities   *Japan is homogeneous, not diverse like the United States. China has a large majority of Han (98%) but fifty-five ethnic minorities, including five with their own autonomous regions.*

_N_ 25. Religion   *The United States is mostly "Christian," but China is secular (or Chinese folk religion) and Japan has a mix of Eastern religions.*

Which is more similar to the United States, Japan or China?   *Answers will vary. While China is more similar in size and population, the Japanese people have more thoroughly adopted a Western lifestyle. Japan's success obviously was not hindered by the limits of its natural geography.*

Geography

Name _____

Chapter 21   Activity 5

Seven Great Ranges of the World

You have now studied the seven great ranges of Asia that have peaks above seven thousand meters. Look back at the maps on pages 415, 430, and 464 and label these seven ranges on the map on the next page. (The location of the Trans-Himalaya range is not shown in the text, but its location is discussed on page 441.) Also label these important features between the ranges: Taklimakan Desert and Tibet. Next, review the information you studied on pages 422-24, 441, and 473 to complete the chart and answer the questions.

Some student texts mistakenly give Nyenchentanglha as the highest peak in the Trans-Himalaya.

Name	Location	Length (mi.)	Number of 7000-Meter Peaks	Highest Peak	Elev. (ft.)	Interesting Fact
1. Himalayas	India-China-Nepal-Bhutan	*1200*	*150*	*Mt. Everest*	*29,028*	highest mountain in the world
2. Karakoram	Pakistan-India-China	*300*	113	*K2*	*28,250*	*most rugged range in the world*
3. Kunlun	*China*	1675	*6*	*Kongur*	*25,325*	*northern edge of the Plateau of Tibet*
4. Hindu Kush	*Afghanistan*	1000	*34*	Tirich Mir	25,282	*Persian for "Hindu Death"; forms the Wakhan Corridor buffer between Russia and Pakistan*
5. Pamirs	*Tajikistan-China*	150	*3*	*Communism Peak*	*24,457*	called the Pamir Knot because it ties other ranges together
6. Tien Shan	*Kyrgyzstan-China*	1800	2	Pobeda Peak	24,406	*northernmost great range; means "Celestial Mountains"*
7. Trans-Himalaya	China	600	*3*	Ningchin Kangsha	23,697	*southern edge of the Plateau of Tibet, north of the Brahmaputra River*

The book mentions 314 peaks over 7000 meters. The total on this chart is 311 because three isolated peaks do not appear in a range.

1. How many Asian countries share part of the seven great ranges? **eight**

2. Which country touches six ranges? What is the only range outside this country? **China; Hindu Kush**

3. What river separates the Himalayas and the Trans-Himalaya? **Brahmaputra River**

4. What is the longest range? **Tien Shan**

5. What is the shortest range? Why is it still considered one of the great ranges? **Pamirs; height above 7000 meters and central location**

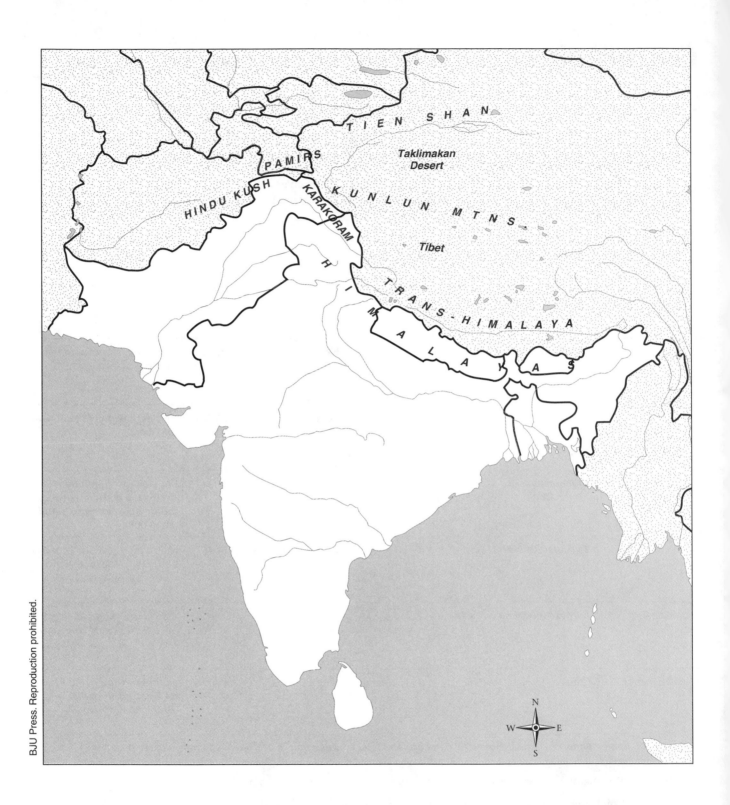

Taklimakan
Desert

TIEN SHAN

PAMIRS

HINDU KUSH

KARAKORAM

KUNLUN MTNS

Tibet

TRANS-HIMALAYA

H
I
M
A
L
A
Y
A
S

N
W   E
S

Geography

Write Your Own Test

Matching

In random order, write a phrase describing each term in the list. Then close your textbook and try to write the letter of the correct term in each blank. **Answers will vary.**

Terms

A. aquaculture
B. commune
C. demilitarized zone

D. dynasty
E. open city
F. prefecture

G. special municipality
H. theocrat
I. yurt

H	1.	one who rules by religious or divine authority (p. 474)
A	2.	fish farming (p. 468)
D	3.	series of rulers who come from the same family (p. 465)
I	4.	collapsible round tent that protects from extreme temperatures (p. 476)
B	5.	huge government farm under Communism (p. 470)
C	6.	strip of land in which no troops or weapons are allowed (p. 478)
G	7.	political unit set aside to govern each of China's leading industrial centers (p. 471)
E	8.	region in China that has the privilege of foreign trade (p. 468)
F	9.	basic political division in Japan (p. 480)

People

A. Ainu
B. Chiang Kai-shek
C. Dalai Lama
D. Genghis Khan

E. Han
F. Mao Zedong
G. Manchu

H. Meiji
I. Mongol
J. Zhuang

D	10.	Mongol conqueror who helped create the largest empire in history (p. 476)
F	11.	leader who turned China into a Communist country (p. 469)
C	12.	spiritual and political leader of Tibetans; claims to be Buddha's reincarnation (p. 474)
B	13.	Nationalist leader of China defeated by the Communists (p. 468)
H	14.	"enlightened rule" under Emperor Mutsuhito, who converted Japan to a modern state (p. 482)
E	15.	main ethnic group in China (p. 464)
G	16.	last foreign people to control China (p. 471)
J	17.	ethnic Thai people who make up China's largest minority (p. 473)
I	18.	nomadic people of the plateaus north of China (p. 476)
A	19.	white-skinned original inhabitants of Japan (p. 486)

Short Answer

Write a question for each of the answers below. *Answers will vary.*

20. Answer: Shinto   *What Japanese religion promotes the worship of many gods which supposedly indwell mountains, trees, and rivers? (pp. 480-81)*

21. Answer: Cultural Revolution   *What do we call Mao Zedong's effort to "purify" the country by forcibly moving educated citizens to rural communes? (p. 470)*

22. Answer: Itsukushima Shrine   *What Japanese shrine in the Inland Sea has Japan's largest torii, or gateway, marking a sacred Shinto site? (p. 485)*

23. Answer: Diet   *What is the name of the Japanese parliament? (p. 482)*

24. Answer: intensive farming   *What type of farming in fertile areas allows many subsistence farmers to raise crops on a small plot of land? (p. 465)*

Multiple Choice

Write four choices for each problem below. Then write the correct choice in the blank. *Answers will vary.*

A (p. 466)   25. What Chinese philosophy teaches that harmony and order will exist when men begin to treat their fellow men properly?

A.	*Confucianism*	C.	*Shinto*
B.	*shamanism*	D.	*Taoism*

D (p. 466)   26. What religion emphasizes magic and presents the world as a competition between *yin* and *yang?*

A.	*ancestor worship*	C.	*Shinto*
B.	*Confucianism*	D.	*Taoism*

B (p. 470)   27. Under what disastrous program did Mao Zedong attempt to combine collective farms into productive communes?

A.	*Cultural Revolution*	C.	*kamikaze*
B.	*Great Leap Forward*	D.	*Meiji Restoration*

C (p. 480)   28. If the vast majority of people in a nation have the same ethnic background, that country is said to be

A.	*communal.*	C.	*homogeneous.*
B.	*heterogeneous.*	D.	*shaman.*

D (p. 466)   29. The ancient capital of China that was the center of dynasties for over a thousand years is

A.	*Beijing.*	C.	*Guangzhou.*
B.	*Chongqing.*	D.	*Xi'an.*

Geography

Comparison of Asia and Western Europe

Complete the chart showing some of the similarities and differences between the culture regions of Asia and Western Europe. Don't forget to look at the maps and statistical charts in Chapters 2-5.

Remind students to check information they wrote for the Unit Review after Chapter 15 (if they did it).

		Asia	Western Europe
Geography	Climate (pp. 48-49)	*variety of climates, including tropical rainy, but no polar, mediterranean, or marine west coast climates*	*every type of moderate climate, especially marine west coast, as well as cold climates in the north*
	Main Mountain Ranges	*great ranges of Asia in the interior, including the Himalayas, Karakoram, Trans-Himalayas, Kunlun, and Tien Shan*	*Alps in the south*
	High Point (p. 20)	*Mt. Everest (29,028 ft.)*	Mont Blanc (15,771 ft.)
	Nearby Oceans	*Pacific, Indian*	*Atlantic, Arctic*
	Longest River (p. 26)	*Chang (3,964 ft.)*	Danube (1,776 ft.)
Economy	Per Capita GDP (best and worst) (See tables on pp. 80, 349, 449.)	*Singapore ($22,900, 6th worldwide)* *Cambodia ($660)*	*Luxembourg ($24,800, 2nd worldwide)* *Greece ($9,500)*
	Population (p. 87)	*3,202,000,000*	*387,000,000*
	Population Density (p. 87)	*400 people per sq. mi.*	*276 people per sq. mi.*
	Largest City (p. 103)	*Tokyo (26,959,000), 1st worldwide*	Paris (1st metro, 9,523,000) London (1st city proper, 7,000,000)
	Most Populous Country (pp. 104, 332)	*China (1,210,004,956)*	*Germany (83,536,000)*
	Total Area of Region (p. 87)	*8,005,000 sq. mi.*	*1,400,000 sq. mi.*
	Largest Country in Size (pp. 96, 332)	*China (3,696,171 sq. mi., 3rd worldwide)*	*France (210,026 sq. mi.)*
Demography	Most Common Language Family (p. 89)	*Sino-Tibetan (see table, p. 91)*	*Indo-European*
	Main Religion (pp. 92, 95)	*Eastern religions (Hindu)*	*Christianity (Roman Catholicism)*
	Famous Buildings	*Taj Mahal, Golden Temple, Shwe Dagon Pagoda, Angkor Wat, Petronas Twin Towers, Borobudur, Great Wall, Forbidden City, Potola Palace, Itsukushima Shrine*	*Answers may vary (various castles, palaces, cathedrals, Stonehenge, the Eiffel Tower, Colosseum, Vatican, Parthenon)*

Geography

Map of the Persian Gulf

Fill in each blank with the correct letter or number from the map given. Countries are uppercase letters (A, B, C), cities are lowercase letters (a, b, c), and physical features are numbers. To complete the map work, refer to the map on page 491 of the student text.

Countries

_I_	1. Bahrain	_F_	5. Oman	_G_	8. United Arab Emirates		
_A_	2. Iran	_H_	6. Qatar				
_B_	3. Iraq	_D_	7. Saudi Arabia	_E_	9. Yemen		
_C_	4. Kuwait						

Cities

_j_	10. Abu Dhabi	_l_	14. Manama	_b_	18. Persepolis
_c_	11. Baghdad	_g_	15. Mecca	_e_	19. Riyadh
_k_	12. Doha	_f_	16. Medina	_h_	20. Sanaa
_d_	13. Kuwait	_i_	17. Muscat	_a_	21. Tehran

Physical Features

_4_	22. Euphrates River	_7_	25. Gulf of Oman	_3_	28. Tigris River
_1_	23. Elburz Mountains	_6_	26. Persian Gulf	_2_	29. Zagros Mountains
		_5_	27. Rub al Khali		
_8_	24. Gulf of Aden				

Map Work   Note: This section is optional.

30. Look at the chart on page 500. Draw the symbol for petroleum in each of the top five countries with crude oil reserves; place each country's rank in that list beside its symbol.

31. Draw these figures in the appropriate place.

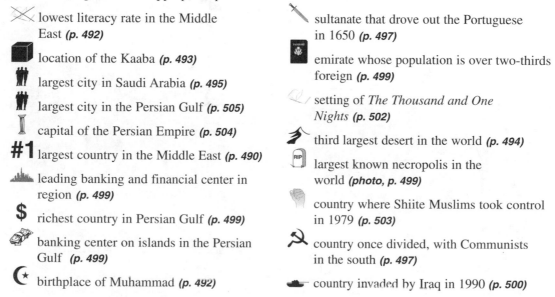

- lowest literacy rate in the Middle East (p. 492)
- location of the Kaaba (p. 493)
- largest city in Saudi Arabia (p. 495)
- largest city in the Persian Gulf (p. 505)
- capital of the Persian Empire (p. 504)
- #1 largest country in the Middle East (p. 490)
- leading banking and financial center in region (p. 499)
- $ richest country in Persian Gulf (p. 499)
- banking center on islands in the Persian Gulf (p. 499)
- birthplace of Muhammad (p. 492)

- sultanate that drove out the Portuguese in 1650 (p. 497)
- emirate whose population is over two-thirds foreign (p. 499)
- setting of *The Thousand and One Nights* (p. 502)
- third largest desert in the world (p. 494)
- largest known necropolis in the world (photo, p. 499)
- country where Shiite Muslims took control in 1979 (p. 503)
- country once divided, with Communists in the south (p. 497)
- country invaded by Iraq in 1990 (p. 500)

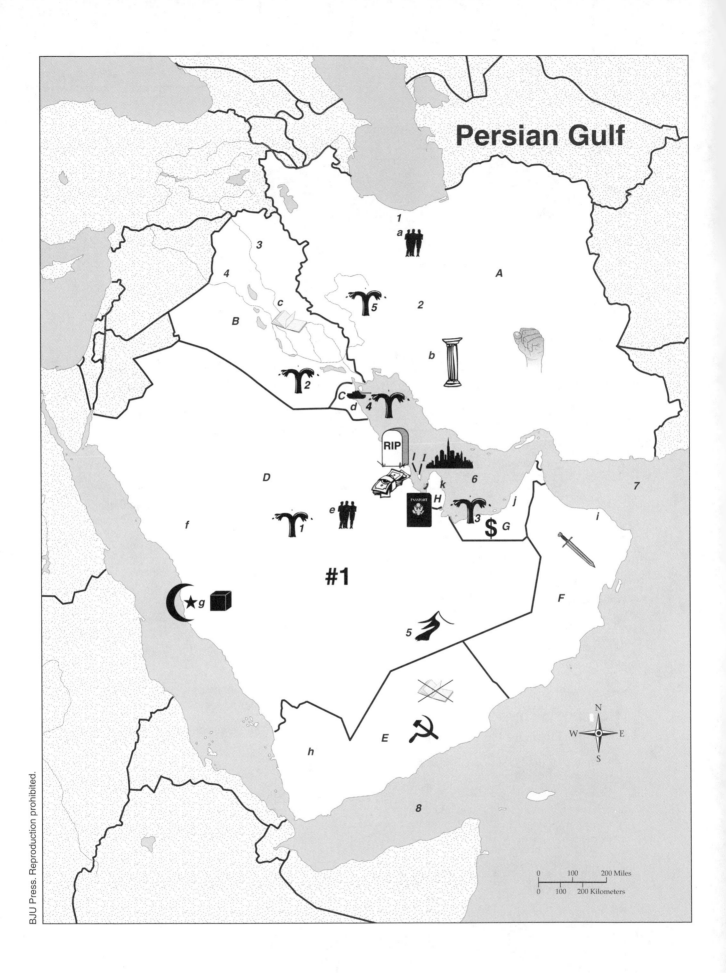

Persian Gulf

Geography

Survey of Islam

This chapter includes an extensive survey of Islam, one of the three great monotheistic (one-god) religions. (The other two are Christianity and Judaism.) Give the following basic facts about this religion and then evaluate it from Scripture.

1. Founder   *Muhammad (p. 493)*

2. Holy Book   *Koran (p. 493)*

3. Requirement to become a Muslim   *Repeat the declaration, "There is no God but Allah, and Muhammad is His Messenger" (p. 492).*

4. Five Pillars of Islam

    • *Declare that there is no god but Allah (above, p. 492).*

    • *Pray five times a day.*

    • *Give alms to the poor.*

    • *Fast during the month of Ramadan.*

    • *Make a pilgrimage to Mecca at least once.*

5. Most holy place   *Kaaba at the Great Mosque in Mecca (Muhammad's birthplace, p. 493)*

6. Second most holy place   *Prophet's Mosque (over Muhammad's tomb) in Medina (p. 493)*

7. First day on the Muslim calendar   *1 Anno Hegirae (July 16, 622), day Muhammad fled to Medina (p. 493)*

8. Month of fasting   *Ramadan (p. 492)*

9. Islamic worship building   *mosque (p. 492)*

10. Religious police   *mutawa (p. 494)*

11. Black cloak that strict Muslim women wear   *abaaya (p. 494)*

12. Islamic pilgrimage   *hajj (p. 492)*

13. Ancient religious law of Islam   *sharia (p. 503)*

14. Highest title of honor of a Shiite Muslim   *Ayatollah (p. 503)*

15. Two main rival Muslim groups and their key doctrinal differences

    • *Sunni—orthodox, conservative followers of the caliphs, the appointed successors to Muhammad (p. 501)*

    • *Shiite—honor the imam, the hereditary successor of Muhammad who claims to be a divine manifestation and qualified to interpret the holy writings (p. 501)*

16. Minor Islamic religion begun in Persia by renegades   *Baha'i (p. 506)*

17. Minor Islamic religion begun in Persia and followed by peace-loving mystics who believe nothing exists except God   *Sufism (p. 506)*

18. For each passage, summarize the similarity between Islam and Christianity; then discuss the difference.

- Deuteronomy 6:4-5   *Both are monotheistic, but the triune God of Christianity is not the same as Allah, and Christianity requires repentance and faith, not just a declaration.*

- Matthew 6:1-4   *Both encourage giving, but Christianity does not require it as a tax and demands that it be done in secret.*

- Matthew 6:5-8   *Both emphasize regular prayer, but Christianity does not see it as a good work done at preset times with preset words; it should be secret, and not with vain repetitions.*

- Matthew 6:16-18   *Both encourage fasting, but Christianity does not require it at a preset time and demands that Christians fast in secret.*

- John 2:13-21   *Both have a holy place, but Christians no longer worship in the temple at Jerusalem. They go to Christ and worship in their own temple—in their own bodies (I Cor. 6:19-20).*

Geography

Developed or Developing?

As you learned in Chapter 4, a country with a high per capita GDP is not always a developed country. Many countries in the Middle East have high per capita GDPs but fall short in other areas. Complete the chart by referring to page 492 as well as a world almanac. Then answer the questions that follow. *Show students how to use information in the* World Almanac *to calculate televisions per 1,000 people and infant mortality.*

Country	Economy		Demography			
	Per Capita GDP	**Televisions per 1,000 People**	**Literacy Rate**	**Natural Increase**	**Life Expectancy**	**Infant Mortality**
United States	$27,900	835	96%	0.6%	76	0.7%
Saudi Arabia	$10,100	256	63%	3.3%	70	4.4%
Iraq	$2,000	77	58%	3.6%	67	5.8%
Iran	$4,700	63	72%	2.6%	68	5.1%
Minor Arabian States						
Farmers on the Arabian Sea						
Yemen	$2,520	28	43%	3.6%	60	6.8%
Oman	$10,800	667	59%	3.3%	71	2.6%
Emirates on the Persian Gulf						
United Arab Emirates	$24,000	106	79%	1.5%	75	1.6%
Qatar	$20,820	400	79%	1.7%	74	1.9%
Bahrain	$12,000	435	85%	2.0%	75	1.6%
Kuwait	$17,000	385	79%	1.7%	76	1.1%

Statistics given match those in the textbook or those in the World Almanac *at the time of publication. If you wish, you could supply students with this information and then discuss the questions as a class.*

1. Use the map on page 81 to answer these questions.

   • What is the level of development in most of the Middle East?   *developing countries*

   • What is the only "least-developed country" in the Middle East? Why this country?   *Yemen; it is a poor farming country that lacks oil wealth and has been wracked by civil war.*

2. On the chart above, highlight in red the statistics for the least-developed country.

   • How many of these statistics are the worst on the chart?   *all (Note: a low level of television ownership is not bad, and a high rate of natural increase is not bad—they are simply more common in least-developed countries.)*

   • Find the country that has the most in common with the red statistics. Explain why this country is in such bad shape.   *Iraq has relatively little oil wealth compared to its populations, and it has been embroiled in costly wars with its neighbors.*

3. On the chart, highlight in green the statistic under each category that is most similar to the statistics for the United States (an example of a developed country).

   • Which country do you think is most like the United States? Explain why this might be the most developed country.   *Answers may vary, but they should be one of the emirates on the Persian Gulf. Qatar, for example, has great oil wealth and a small population, and it depends on cheap foreign labor.*

   • Which of Oman's statistics is higher than that of any other country in the region? Why is this unusual?   *Oman has more televisions per 1,000 people, even though it is a "farming country" that does not match the per capita wealth of the oil states.*

4. Compare and contrast the statistics for the farming countries on the Arabian Sea and the minor emirates of the Persian Gulf region.   *The emirates are better off in every category except Oman's surprisingly high number of televisions.*

Geography

Words from the Middle East

The Middle East has had a profound impact on Western civilization, including its language. Look up each word below in a dictionary. Give the original Middle Eastern language it came from and tell what it originally meant. Be ready to explain why Englishmen adopted each word from the Middle East.

The West learned about many things through the Arabs, Persians, and Turks—plants and animals, mathematical concepts, new products, concepts of war, and mythology.

1. admiral   *Arabic, "high commander"*

2. alchemy   *Arabic, "the chemistry"*

3. alcohol   *Arabic, "the powder of antimony" (see "Word History" under "alcohol" in American Heritage Dictionary)*

4. algebra   *Arabic, "the (science of) reuniting"*

5. apricot   *Arabic, "the plum"*

6. arsenic   *Old Iranian, "golden"*

7. assassin   *Arabic, "hashish users"*

8. bazaar   *Old Iranian, "sale-traffic"*

9. candy   *Arabic, "sugar candied"*

10. caravan   *Persian, same meaning as today*

11. chess/check   *Persian, "king, king in chess" (note: the West got the word through Arabic)*

12. coffee   *Arabic, same meaning as today*

13. cotton   *Arabic, same meaning as today*

14. elixir   *Arabic, "the elixir"*

15. ghoul   *Arabic, "demon"; "to seize suddenly"*

16. horde   *Old Turkic, "residence, court"*

17. jar   *Arabic, "earthen jar"*

18. khaki   *Persian, "dust"*

19. lemon   *Persian, same meaning as today*

20. mummy   *Arabic, "wax"*

21. paradise   *Avestan (Persian), "enclosure, park"*

22. safari   *Arabic, "journey"; "to travel, set out"*

23. scarlet   *Arabic, "rich cloth, scarlet cloth" (note: adopted by Persian)*

24. shawl   *Persian, same meaning as today*

25. sherbet   *Arabic, "drink" (note: adopted by Ottoman Turks)*

26. sofa   *Arabic, "carpet, divan" (note: adopted by the Turks)*

27. spinach   *Persian, same meaning as today (note: adopted by Arabic)*

28. syrup   *Arabic, same meaning as today "to drink"*

29. tiger   *Iranian, same meaning as today*

30. tulip   *Ottoman Turk, "muslin, gauze, turban"*

31. zero   *Arabic, "nothing, cipher"*

Geography

Name _____

Chapter 22   **Activity 5**

Finding Treasure in the Desert

You have discovered a diary in an old trunk that you bought at a local bazaar. Much information is in the diary. To understand the diary entries, you need your trusty GEOGRAPHY textbook. Look closely at Chapter 22, particularly the relief map on page 491. In the blank, write the name of the person, place, or thing described.

<u>Mecca, p. 491</u> 1. Start my vacation in the city that was Muhammad's birthplace.

<u>Jiddah, p. 492</u> 2. Travel west to the "Bride of the Red Sea."

<u>Aden, p. 497</u> 3. Take passage on a boat going south. Pass through Bab el Mandeb and stop at the city that gives its name to the gulf between the Red Sea and the Arabian Sea.

<u>khat, p. 497</u> 4. Do *not* buy any of those shrub leaves chewed as a narcotic.

<u>Gulf of Oman, p. 498</u> 5. Continue by ship eastward into the gulf between the Arabian Sea and the Persian Gulf.

<u>sultanate, p. 498</u> 6. See the ruler of Oman, whose form of government is unusual.

<u>desalination, p. 499</u> 7. Visit Qatar and observe the complicated process of removing salt from saltwater.

<u>Bahrain, p. 499</u> 8. Spend a day at the island country in the Persian Gulf famed for its natural springs and oil refinery.

<u>Riyadh, p. 495</u> 9. Land at Ad Dammam and continue inland to the capital of Saudi Arabia.

<u>ibn-Saud, p. 495</u> 10. Overhear a discussion of the first king of Saudi Arabia, who united the desert tribes early in the twentieth century.

<u>Bedouins, p. 496</u> 11. Spend a night outside the city, enjoying the traditional hospitality of the desert nomads.

<u>Mesopotamia, p. 501</u> 12. With some fear, proceed by car north to the "land between the rivers."

<u>Saddam Hussein, p. 501</u> 13. The people of Iraq live in terror of the dictator who has plunged their country into disastrous wars.

<u>Shatt al Arab, p. 501</u> 14. Stop in Iraq among the Shiites living in the marshy area formed at the confluence of the Tigris and Euphrates Rivers.

<u>Baghdad, p. 502</u> 15. Catch a boat going upriver to the exotic capital, the setting of the *Thousand and One Nights.*

<u>Iran-Iraq War, p. 504</u> 16. See many beggars on the roadside who lost their limbs in the tragic war against Iran that lasted eight years.

<u>Nineveh, p. 502</u> 17. Rent a jeep to see the ruins of the capital of the ancient Assyrian Empire in northern Iraq.

<u>Kurds, p. 503</u> 18. Spend the night among the poverty-stricken minority in Iraq's northeast corner.

<u>Zagros Mountains, p. 504</u> 19. Cross the border into Iran and travel through the mountain range where the Persian Empire began.

<u>Persepolis, p. 505</u> 20. Make an unplanned detour to see the ruins of the Persian capital, including the Hall of a Hundred Columns.

<u>Tehran, p. 505</u> 21. Stop in the largest city among the Persian Gulf nations.

<u>Ayatollah, p. 503</u> 22. Everywhere are murals and pictures of the highest official among Shiite Muslims.

<u>Elburz Mountains, p. 505</u> 23. In the distance from the capital loom the northern mountains of Iran, but I have no time to climb them.

Geography

Map of the Eastern Mediterranean

Refer to the maps on pages 509 and 523 to complete the map.

1. Label these features of physical geography:
   Rivers—Jordan River, Nile River
   Seas—Dead Sea, Mediterranean Sea, Red Sea
   Other bodies of water—Bosporus, Dardanelles, Gulf of Aqaba, Gulf of Suez
   Mountains—Pontic Mountains, Taurus Mountains
   Miscellaneous—Golan Heights, Negev

2. Label these features of human geography:
   Cities—Alexandria, Istanbul
   Miscellaneous—Anatolia, Aswan High Dam, Gaza Strip, Suez Canal, West Bank

3. Label all the countries and their capitals in the Eastern Mediterranean.

4. Draw these figures in the appropriate place. **Note: This section is optional.**

    first true democracy in the Middle East *(pp. 524-25)*

    largest proportion of Christians *(p. 516)*

    Wailing Wall *(p. 519)*

    world's oldest continuously inhabited city *(p. 515)*

   largest city in Africa *(p. 532)*

   largest city in the Middle East *(p. 510)*

   country with largest population in this region *(p. 531)*

   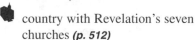 country with Revelation's seven churches *(p. 512)*

   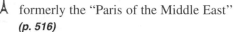 formerly the "Paris of the Middle East" *(p. 516)*

   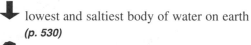 lowest and saltiest body of water on earth *(p. 530)*

    headwaters of Tigris and Euphrates *(p. 513)*

   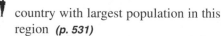 location of the Knesset *(p. 524)*

5. Look up the pictures on the following pages and identify their approximate location on the map by writing the page number and a short description of the site. Use the maps on page 509, 520, and 523 of your textbook. You may also use outside sources for clues. Assume that you are to identify all pictures on a page unless otherwise indicated.
   page 510
   page 511
   page 515
   page 516
   page 517
   page 532
   page 533 (not Mount Sinai)

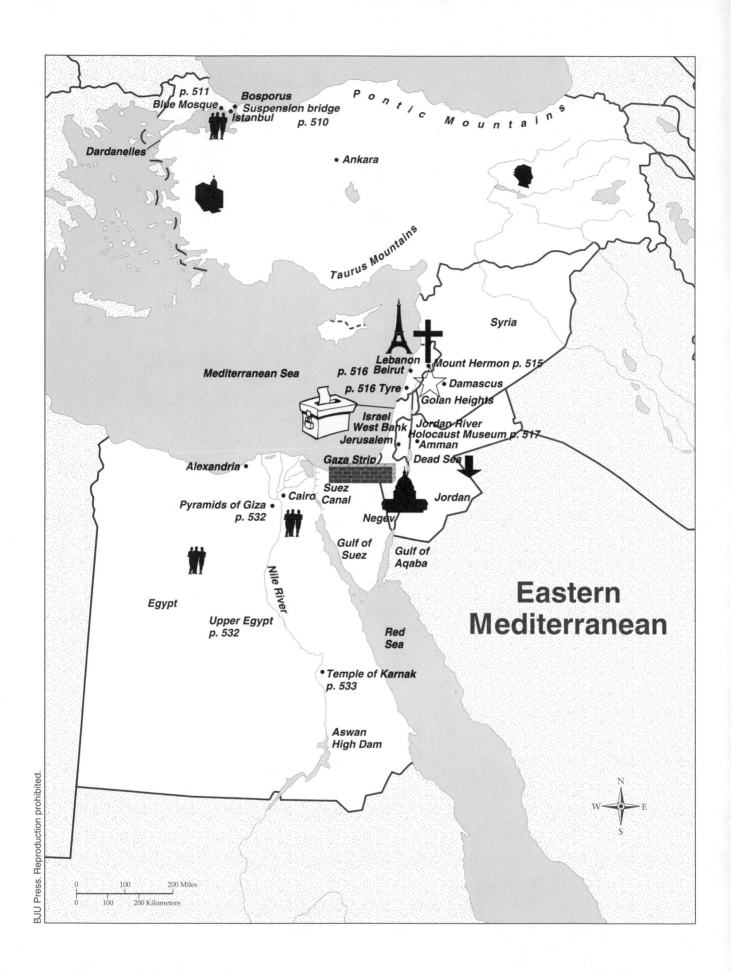

p. 511
Blue Mosque
Bosporus
Suspension bridge
p. 510
Istanbul

Pontic Mountains

Dardanelles

• Ankara

Taurus Mountains

Mediterranean Sea

Syria

Lebanon
p. 516 Beirut

• Mount Hermon p. 515

p. 516 Tyre •

• Damascus

Golan Heights

Israel
West Bank
Jerusalem

Jordan River
Holocaust Museum p. 517
• Amman

Gaza Strip

Dead Sea

Alexandria •

Suez
Canal

Jordan

Pyramids of Giza •
p. 532

Negev

Gulf of
Suez

Gulf of
Aqaba

Nile River

Eastern
Mediterranean

Egypt

Upper Egypt
p. 532

Red
Sea

• Temple of Karnak
p. 533

Aswan
High Dam

N
W   E
S

0   100   200 Miles
0   100   200 Kilometers

Geography

Photos of Palestine

Look up the photos on the pages below and identify the approximate location of the various sites by writing an X along with a short description of each site. Use the map on page 523 of your textbook. You may look for clues from outside sources. Assume that you are to identify all pictures on a page unless otherwise indicated.

1. page 516 (**not** Beirut)
2. page 517
3. page 521 (**not** Yasir Arafat)
4. page 522

5. page 524
6. page 525
7. page 527 (**not** Nehemiah's "broad wall")
8. page 530

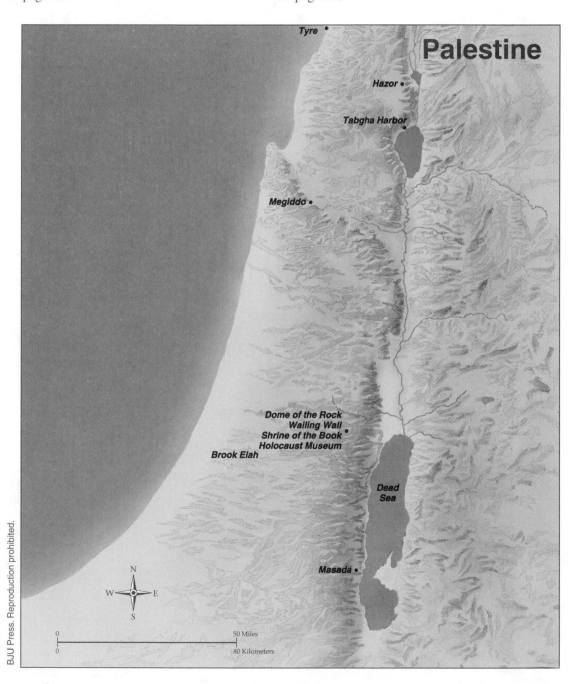

Geography

Tour of the Holy City

You are a young Israeli professor living in the Old City section of Jerusalem. You know all about your city—and you love to share your knowledge with anyone who will listen. As you are returning home, a string of tourists stop to ask you to help them find points of interest in the city. Identify and locate each of them. (All of the places are included in the photo spread on pages 527-29. Using the captions, the pictures, and the map on page 526, fill in the blanks below. Answers may vary slightly.)

Tourist 1: "Can you tell me where the large Islamic mosque is?"

Professor: "You must be talking about _____the Dome of the Rock_____ [site]. It's built over the former site

of _____Solomon's Temple_____ [fact from caption]. You'll find it at the top of _____Mt. Moriah_____

[mount]. Look for a _____golden_____ [detail from photo] roof."

Tourist 2: "I'm looking for the passageway that diverts water under a city wall."

Professor: "You're looking for _____Hezekiah's Tunnel_____ [site]. It takes water from the

_____Gihon Spring_____ [fact from caption]. That's just east of _____Mt. Zion_____ [mount].

If you're going to visit there, beware. You might get _____wet_____ [detail from photo]!"

Tourist 3: "I'd like to find the spot where Jesus ate His Last Supper with His disciples."

Professor: "That would be the _____Upper Room_____ [site]. You'll find it south of

_____the Western Hill_____ [mount]. Another close landmark to look for is _____the Zion Gate_____

[gate] to the northeast. You won't be able to walk all the way into the room because of

_____the metal barrier_____ [detail from photo]."

Tourist 4: "Can you tell me how to get to the wall that Nehemiah built?"

Professor: "Sure. People call it the _____"broad wall"_____ [fact from caption]. It's immediately

west of _____the Fortress of Antonia_____ [landmark]. You could also look for _____Mt. Moriah_____

[mount] southeast of the wall. You'll want to be careful walking in front of the wall because the path is

paved with _____stones_____ [detail from photo].

Tourist 5: "I want to visit the site of Jesus' crucifixion."

Professor: "Many people visit _____Golgotha_____ [name of site]. It's located at

_____Mt. Calvary or Gordon's Calvary_____ [name of mount]. Exit the Modern Wall at _____Herod's Gate_____

[name of gate] and travel northwest. If you look closely at the rugged hillside, you'll understand why it's

called "the place of the _____skull_____ [fact from caption]."

Tourist 6: "Could you tell me how to get to the spot where Jesus prayed before being arrested?"

Professor: "Yes. You're looking for _____the Garden of Gethsemane_____ [site], located on

_____the Mount of Olives_____ [mount]. Many colorful _____flowers_____ [detail from photo]

are there. The mount is _____east_____ [compass direction] of the Old City."

Tourist 7: "Where are the remains of the Jewish temple?"

Professor: "You must be talking about _____the Wailing Wall_____ [site]. It's at the top of

_____Mt. Moriah_____ [mount]. Look for _____the Dome of the Rock_____ [detail from photo and map]

above it, and you should be able to find your way. To the west will be _____the First North Wall_____ [wall]."

Tourist 8: "Where do Roman Catholics believe Jesus' tomb was?"

Professor: "Well, it's covered up now by ___*the Church of the Holy Sepulchre*___ [site]. The site is immediately northeast of ___*the Patriarch's Pool*___ [landmark] and west of ___*the Second North Wall or the Broad Wall*___ [wall]. Look for an old ___*stone*___ [detail from photo—building material] structure."

Tourist 9: "I'd like to see the pool that was created by diverted water."

Professor: "That's called ___*the Pool of Siloam*___ [site]. It's where ___*Hezekiah's Tunnel*___ [fact from caption] empties out the water it has brought from the Gihon Spring. It's in the southeast corner of the city, to the west of ___*the Fountain Gate*___ [gate]. Often you'll see ___*tourists or girls or people*___ [detail from photo] taking a break by the water."

Tourist 10: "Where was the church's first martyr dragged out of the city?"

Professor: "Tradition says that it was at ___*St. Stephen's Gate*___ [gate]. To the east of the gate is ___*the Mount of Olives*___ [mount]. Directly west is ___*the Pool of Israel*___ [landmark] and slightly northwest is ___*the Pool of Bethesda*___ [landmark]."

Tourist 11: "Where should I go to see where Jesus was held under arrest before Pilate?"

Professor: "The place you're looking for is called ___*the Pavement*___ [site]. It was probably in ___*the Fortress of Antonia*___ [fact from caption]. Two good landmarks are ___*the Pool of Israel*___ [landmark] to the east or ___*Mt. Moriah*___ [mount] to the south."

Tourist 12: "Where can I find the likely spot of Jesus' tomb?"

Professor: "You're talking about the garden tomb at ___*Mt. Calvary or Gordon's Calvary*___ [mount]. You're right. It fits the ___*biblical*___ [fact from caption] description very well. You'll need to go ___*north*___ [compass direction] of the city to find the tomb. It's carved into the side of ___*a rock or the hillside*___ [detail from photo]."

Tourist 13: "From where do people believe Christ ascended?"

Professor: "The traditional site is at the top of ___*the Mount of Olives*___ [mount]. To commemorate the event, ___*the Chapel of the Ascension*___ [site] was built. You'll find the mount ___*east*___ [compass direction] of the city. The closest city gate will be ___*St. Stephen's Gate*___ [gate]."

Tourist 14: "Can you help me find the pool where Jesus healed a crippled man?"

Professor: "I'd be glad to. I'm sure you're talking about ___*the Pool of Bethesda*___ [site]. It's a little decayed today, but many handicapped people used to wait there for ___*the stirring of the waters*___ [fact from caption]. You'll find it directly north of a larger pool, ___*the Pool of Israel*___ [pool]. It's northeast of ___*the Fortress of Antonia*___ [landmark]."

Geography

Ancient Cities

City life in ancient times was radically different from city life today. Pick one ancient city below. Then find as much information as you can about the city from a Bible dictionary, an encyclopedia, or other resources. **Assign one city to each student. With larger classes, have students work in teams or assign other ancient cities not listed.**

Acre	Beersheba	Damascus	Joppa	Smyrna
Aleppo	Beth-shan	Ephesus	Megiddo	Thebes
Alexandria	Byzantium	Haran	Palmyra	Troy

1. Location _____

2. Date founded _____

3. Land area _____

4. Unusual geographic features _____

   _____

5. Total population _____

6. Original ethnic makeup _____

7. Religious background _____

8. Main water source _____

9. Famous landmarks of the city _____

10. Closest trade route _____

11. Major items of trade _____

    _____

12. Main occupations _____

    _____

13. Famous resident(s) _____

    _____

14. Famous sieges or defeats _____

    _____

15. Other interesting facts from history _____

    _____

16. Condition of the city today _____

    _____

Geography

Nuggets from *National Geographic*

Look up the following articles in *National Geographic* and answer the questions about them.

"The Three Faces of Jerusalem" (April 1996)

1. Read pages 8-17. Explain why the Temple Mount in Jerusalem is sacred to each of the three main religions mentioned in the article.

   - *Jews—The Jewish temple was located here, and Jews would like to rebuild the temple here.*

   - *Christians—Tradition says that Abraham almost sacrificed Isaac here.*

   - *Muslims—Muslims believe that the Prophet Muhammad ascended to heaven from here.*

2. Why would some Jews support the plan to give Arabs part of Israel's land? Do you think their hope is well founded? *They hope giving away land will bring peace; answers will vary.*

3. What group of religious Jews has a rapidly increasing population? Why? (See page 20.)
   ultra-Orthodox; immigration from around the world and a high birthrate

"Egypt's Old Kingdom" (January 1995)

4. Read pages 26-31. How are the scrolls in the Abusir Papyri important for knowledge of both the past and the future? *They are the most detailed written documents from the Old Kingdom ever found; they list names of royal palaces and temples not yet discovered.*

5. Look at the maps on pages 22-23. Why did the construction of pyramids increase trade in Egypt? How did the construction affect the economy? *The materials needed for the pyramids came from several cities in the kingdom and some from outside the kingdom; the economy improved because the construction required workers to collect the materials and build the pyramids and farmers to grow food to feed the workers.*

6. In what way do the pyramids still affect the economy of Egypt? *Egypt's ancient wonders bring tourists to the country.*

Geography

The Jewish and Muslim Calendars

Both Jews and Muslims have their own systems of reckoning dates. After you have read about each system, answer the questions below.

Jewish Calendar

The Jewish calendar is lunisolar. Months are set up to follow the cycles of the moon, and years follow the revolutions of the earth around the sun. The problem with this system is that twelve lunar months (each with twenty-nine or thirty days) fall short of a full revolution of the sun by eleven days. To correct this problem, Jews add an extra month of thirty days seven times every nineteen years. So some of their years are shorter than ours, and some are longer.

The beginning of the Jewish year occurs around our month of September. The first day of the new year may be set back a day or two to make sure that certain Jewish holy days do not fall on the wrong days of the week.

The Jewish calendar does not base its numbering of years on the birth of Christ. Instead, it starts with the supposed date of Creation (3761 B.C. by the Christian calendar). Years are followed by A.M., meaning *anno mundi* or "year of the world."

Jewish Month	Date of Holy Day	Selected Holy Day
Tishri	1-2 10	Rosh Hashanah (New Year) Yom Kippur (Day of Atonement)
Heshvan		
Kislev	25	Beginning of Hanukkah
Tevet	2 or 3	End of Hanukkah
Shevat		
Adar (First and Second Adar in leap years)	13 14-15	Fast of Esther Purim
Nisan	15-22	Passover
Iyyar	5	Israel Independence Day
Sivan	6-7	Feast of Weeks
Tammuz	17	Fast (Mishna)
Av	9	Fast (Mishna)
Elul		

1. What is the problem with the way the Jewish calendar is organized? _**Months are arranged by the**_

   **moon and years by the sun. A solar year is eleven days longer than twelve lunar months.**

2. How is this problem corrected? _**An extra month of thirty days is added seven times every nineteen**_

   **years.**

3. What event begins the Jewish numbering of years? _**the supposed date of Creation, 3761 B.C. by our**_

   **calendar**

4. Assuming that Jewish and Christian calendars contain roughly the same number of years, what would

   be the Christian equivalent of the Jewish year 5735 A.M.? _**A.D. 1974**_

💡 Find a current calendar or an entry in the world almanac that includes Jewish holidays. What will be the date (on your calendar) of the Jewish New Year? Hanukkah? Passover? (Before you look up Hanukkah and Passover, try to calculate their approximate dates using the chart given above.)

Answers will vary.

💡 Which of the selected holidays were instituted in the Old Testament, and which ones are extrabiblical (originated outside of the Bible)? *Fast of Esther, Purim, Passover, and the Feast of Weeks are from the Old Testament. Hanukkah is the most well known of the extrabiblical holidays.*

Muslim Calendar

The Muslim calendar is based entirely on the cycles of the moon. The Muslim year has twelve months that alternate between twenty-nine and thirty days. Each year typically has 354 days. Because the calendar is never corrected to match the solar year, seasons do not always occur in the same months.

Muslims start their year with the *Hegira,* or the flight of Muhammad from Mecca to Medina (A.D. 622 by the Christian calendar). The month of Ramadan is the Muslims' holy month. Faithful Muslims fast each day of Ramadan from sunrise to sunset.

Muslim Months and Number of Days

Muharram (30 days), Safar (29 days), Rabī' I (30 days), Rabī' II (29 days), Jumādā I (30 days), Jumādā II (29 days), Rajab (30 days), Sha 'bān (29 days), Ramadān (30 days), Shawwāl (29 days), Dhū al-Qa 'dah (30 days), Dhū al-Hijjah (29 days)

1. What is the basis for the Muslim calendar? *the cycles of the moon*

2. How does this situation (from #1) affect the seasons in a Muslim country? *Seasons do not occur in the same months every year.*

3. What is the event that begins the Muslim numbering of years? *the Hegira, or the flight of Muhammad from Mecca to Medina*

4. If the Muslim New Year began on January 1 of the Christian calendar this year, how many years would pass before the next time it occurred around January 1? (Remember how many days the 354-day Muslim calendar loses each year compared to the 365-day Christian calendar.) *at least thirty-three years*

💡 The first year of the Muslim calendar starts with the Christian date of July 16, 622. If you were using the present Christian calendar, what would be the date for the start of the first Ramadan?

March 9, 623

Geography

Modified True/False

If the statement is true, write the word *true* in the blank. If it is false, change the underlined words to make the statement true.

true, p. 508	1. Kemal Atatürk is called the "Father of the Turks."
the Dardanelles, p. 510	2. The Greek name for the Bosporus was the Hellespont.
Thrace, p. 510	3. Turkey's corner of the Balkan Peninsula is called Anatolia.
true, p. 510	4. The largest city in the Middle East is Istanbul.
Byzantine Empire, p. 511	5. After the Roman Empire collapsed in the West, the remaining eastern segment was called the Ottoman Empire.
Turkey, p. 512	6. Modern Israel contains the sites of the seven key churches of Revelation.
Damascus, p. 515	7. Jerusalem claims to be the oldest continuously inhabited city in the world.
true, p. 516	8. The Druze formed around the testimony of an eleventh-century Egyptian ruler, Al-Hakim, who claimed to be God.
Lebanon, p. 516	9. Cyprus has the largest proportion of Christians in the Middle East.
true, p. 517	10. Both Jews and Christians call Palestine the Holy Land.
true, p. 517	11. Palestine was given to Britain as a mandate after the collapse of the Ottoman Empire.
Reconstructionists, p. 518	12. Modernist Jews see Judaism as a social identity rather than a religion.
true, p. 518	13. The Ashkenazim were early Jewish settlers who came from northern and eastern Europe.
true, p. 518	14. Branches of Judaism can be distinguished by their devotion to tradition.
Arabs, p. 518	15. The Sephardim tend to live and think like Europeans.
true, p. 520	16. Palestinians are descendants of the Philistines.
Yasir Arafat, p. 520	17. Yitzhak Rabin received the Nobel Peace Prize for negotiations he undertook as leader of the Palestine Liberation Organization.
wadis, p. 521	18. Dry stream beds that fill up with water after rainstorms are called shephelah.
the Golan Heights, p. 521	19. Israel captured Mount Hermon from Syria during the Six-Day War.
true, p. 524	20. A tell is a huge mound that forms as cities are built over ruins.
the West Bank, p. 524	21. Israel captured the Negev from Jordan during the Six-Day War.
true, pp. 524-25	22. Israel established the first true democracy in the Middle East.
true, p. 525	23. Historical Negev, the wilderness of Zin, and Arabah are all part of the modern Negev.
kibbutz, p. 525	24. A Knesset is a Jewish community in which the people share everything in common.
true, p. 531	25. Egypt has the largest population in the Eastern Mediterranean.
Lower, p. 532	26. The Nile Delta is also called Upper Egypt.
true, p. 532	27. Dams have ended the flood patterns of the Nile.
Cairo, p. 532	28. Alexandria is the largest city in Africa.
true, p. 533	29. Copts believe that Jesus has only a divine nature.
true, p. 533	30. Israel captured the Sinai Peninsula from Egypt during the Six-Day War.

Geography

A Second Look: The Middle East

In the first column list the eight culture regions of the world. In the second column list the five seas that touch Middle Eastern shores.

1. *Northern America*
2. *Latin America*
3. *Europe*
4. *Central Eurasia*
5. *Asia*
6. *Middle East*
7. *Africa*
8. *Oceania*

9. *Aegean Sea*
10. *Arabian Sea*
11. *Black Sea*
12. *Mediterranean Sea*
13. *Red Sea*

Underline the word or phrase that best completes each sentence.

14. The first true democracy in the Middle East was established by (<u>Israel</u>, Jordan).

15. The biggest city in the Middle East is (Cairo, <u>Istanbul</u>).

16. Most people in the Middle East practice the religion of (Christianity, <u>Islam</u>).

17. The largest country in the Middle East is (Iran, <u>Saudi Arabia</u>).

18. According to its inhabitants, the oldest continuously inhabited city in the world is (Baghdad, <u>Damascus</u>).

19. The most-spoken language family in the Middle East is (<u>Afro-Asiatic</u>, Uralic and Altaic).

Give the term that fits each description.

20. Muslim holy book that records Muhammad's revelations *Koran*

21. nomads in the Arabian desert *Bedouins*

22. Jewish community in which everything is shared in common *kibbutz*

23. dry stream beds that fill up with water after rainstorms *wadis*

24. huge mound formed as cities are built over ruins *tell*

In the blank beside each descriptive phrase, write *P.G.* for the Persian Gulf, *E.M.* for the Eastern Mediterranean, or *both* if it describes both regions.

both 25. deserts
both 26. Islam
both 27. mountains
E.M. 28. Judaism
E.M. 29. mandates of European powers
P.G. 30. oil

Geography

Map of North Africa

Fill in each blank below with the correct location. Countries are uppercase letters (A, B, C), cities are lowercase letters (a, b, c), and physical features are numbers (1, 2, 3). Refer to the relief map on page 539 to complete the activity.

Countries

A. __Morocco__

B. __Algeria__

C. __Tunisia__

D. __Libya__

E. __Chad__

F. __Niger__

G. __Mali__

H. __Mauritania__

Cities

a. __Tangier__

b. __Rabat__

c. __Casablanca__

d. __Algiers__

e. __Tunis__

f. __Tripoli__

g. __N'Djamena__

h. __Niamey__

i. __Tombouctou__

j. __Bamako__

k. __Nouakchott__

Physical Features (bodies of water and mountains)

1. __Strait of Gibraltar__

2. __Atlas Mountains__

3. __Ahaggar Mountains__

4. __Tibesti Mountains__

5. __Lake Chad__

6. __Aïr Mountains__

7. __Niger River__

Map Work *This section is optional.*

1. Look at the map on page 536. Label and draw a line between the two cultural subregions of North Africa: Barbary Coast and Sahel. Shade red those countries referred to as the Maghreb (see p. 541).

2. Draw these figures in the appropriate place.

   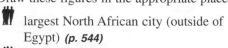 largest North African city (outside of Egypt) *(p. 544)*

   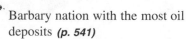 largest city on the Barbary Coast *(p. 543)*

   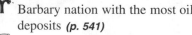 Barbary nation with the most oil deposits *(p. 541)*

    phosphate-rich territory occupied by Morocco *(p. 545)*

   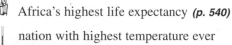 Africa's highest life expectancy *(p. 540)*

   nation with highest temperature ever measured *(p. 540)*

   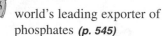 world's leading exporter of phosphates *(p. 545)*

North Africa

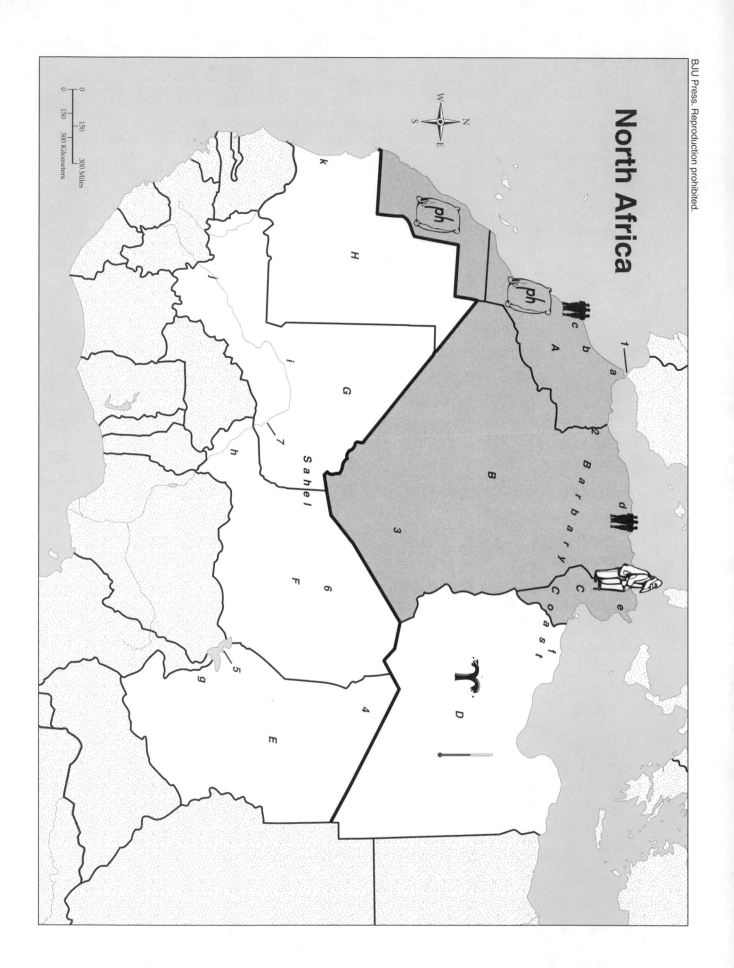

Geography

Great Deserts of the World

The seventeen largest deserts, listed on the next page, appear on the "Dry Climates" map on page 545, but they are not named. Find these deserts on the relief maps on pages 1, 218, 247, 272, 415, 430, 442, 491, and 597. (You can find the Chihuahuan Desert by finding the Mexican state of Chihuahua on page 254.) Write the rank of each desert on the map below. Then look up these deserts in the index and complete the chart on the next page. Finally, answer the questions below.

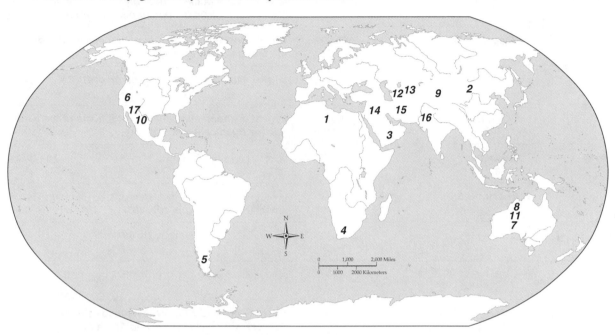

1. Which two continents have no great deserts? **Europe and Antarctica [Technically, Antarctica is a cold desert.]**

2. Which continent has the most great deserts? How many? **Asia; eight**

3. Compare the area of the Sahara to the areas of the next sixteen deserts combined. **The Sahara is slightly larger.**

4. Many of these deserts are joined together into larger "desert areas," visible on the climate map (p. 545). List the deserts that are apparently part of the following desert areas:

   • Australian Desert (1,300,000 sq. mi.) **Great Victoria, Great Sandy, and Gibson Deserts**

   • Arabian Desert (900,000 sq. mi.) **Rub al Khali, Syrian Desert**

   • Turkestan Desert (750,000 sq. mi.) **Kyzyl-Kum, Kara Kum**

   • North American Desert (500,000 sq. mi.) **Great Basin, Chihuahuan Desert, Sonoran Desert**

5. Which two countries include parts of at least *three* great deserts? **United States and Australia**

6. Which of the great deserts has the same name as a country? **Syrian**

7. Look at the African climate map on page 566. How many North African countries share part of the Sahara, including Egypt? **all of them**

8. What body of water separates the Sahara and Arabian Deserts? **Red Sea**

💡 Why do you think the Atacama Desert is considered one of the great deserts, even though it is not on this list? _Though its area is small, it stretches over a thousand miles and has a reputation as the driest desert on earth (p. 284)._

The Namib Desert in Southern Africa is a great, long desert, but it is too narrow to appear on this list. Areas may vary slightly.

Desert	Location (Main Country)	Area (sq. mi.)	Interesting Facts
1. Sahara	North Africa	3,500,000	_largest desert in the world; only desert that spans a continent; highest temperature on record (pp. 538, 540)_
2. Gobi	_Mongolia (China)_	_500,000_	_world's coldest and most northerly desert; discovery of the first dinosaur eggs (p. 477)_
3. Rub al Khali	Saudi Arabia	250,000	_largest sand desert in the world (p. 494)_
4. Kalahari	Southern Africa	_200,000_	_largest diamond mine in the world; home of the hardy San (or Bushmen) (pp. 586-87)_
5. Patagonia	_Argentina_	200,000	plateau named for the "Big Feet" of native Indians _(p. 288)_
6. Great Basin	_Western U.S._	190,000	lowest point in the Western Hemisphere (at Death Valley); driest state Nevada _(pp. 192, 203)_
7. Great Victoria	Australia	150,000	sandy desert in the outback _(p. 607)_
8. Great Sandy	Australia	150,000	sandy desert in the outback _(p. 607)_
9. Taklimakan	_China_	140,000	_possibly the driest desert in Asia; lowest point (Turpan Depression) outside Israel and Africa (p. 475)_
10. Chihuahuan	Western U.S.—Mexico	140,000	first atomic bomb test; largest state in Mexico _(pp. 206, 255)_
11. Gibson	Australia	120,000	stony desert in the outback _(p. 607)_
12. Kara Kum	_Turkmenistan_	120,000	location of the Aral Sea environmental disaster, created when rivers were drained for cotton _(p. 420)_
13. Kyzyl-Kum	_Uzbekistan_	100,000	historic oasis at Bukhara, where the philosopher Avicenna lived _(p. 421)_
14. Syrian	Middle East	100,000	oldest continuously inhabited city—Damascus _(p. 515)_
15. Dasht-e-Kavir	_Iran_	100,000	last stronghold of Zoroastrianism _(p. 505)_
16. Thar (Great Indian)	_India (Pakistan)_	100,000	also known as the Great Indian Desert _(p. 437)_
17. Sonoran	_Western U.S. (Mexico)_	70,000	_only American desert with saguaro cacti; most U.S. copper deposits (p. 206)_

Geography

The Mediterranean Sea—Waterway of the World

At this point, you have completed your study of every nation that touches the Mediterranean Sea, the world's greatest "inland waterway." The nations of the Mediterranean have some surprising similarities in climate and industry, and their histories are closely linked. Look at the maps in your book to answer the questions below.

1. Look at the culture region map on pages 58-59. How many of the eight world culture regions touch the Mediterranean? ___*four*___

2. What strait is the narrowest water route between Western Europe and North Africa? ___*Strait of Gibraltar*___

3. What is the largest and most populated island in the Mediterranean? What country owns it? ___*Sicily is owned by Italy (p. 360).*___

4. What island is divided between Turks and Greeks? ___*Cyprus (pp. 513-14)*___

5. Look at the empire maps (listed in the "Ready Reference to Maps" on page vii) as well as the colonial Africa map on page 554. List all the empires that once controlled lands in North Africa. Do you know the most recent empire that lost its land here? ___*empires—Nazi, Roman, Greek (part of Libya), Arab, Persian, Byzantine, Ottoman; colonial empires—Italy, France, and Spain (p. 554). France had the most recent empire, which broke up after World War II.*___

6. Look at the climate map on page 49. List all of the climates found along the Mediterranean Sea. What climate appears to be most common on the coast? Which climates occur in North Africa? ___*dry (semiarid and desert) and moderate (mediterranean, marine west coast, humid subtropical, and humid continental on the Black Sea); mediterranean is most common on the coast; North Africa has semiarid, desert, and mediterranean climates.*___

7. Look at the land-use maps on pages 63 and 340. What is the most common use of land on the Mediterranean coast? ___*commercial (mediterranean) farming*___

8. Look at the language map on page 89. What three language families are spoken on the Mediterranean coast? Describe the most common language families spoken in the different culture regions. ___*Indo-European is spoken on the north coast in Western Europe and Central Eurasia; Afro-Asiatic is spoken in North Africa; and a mix of Afro-Asiatic (Arabic) and Uralic-Altaic (Turkic) is spoken in the Middle East.*___

9. Look at the religion map on page 95. What religions are followed in the Mediterranean region? How does this breakdown compare to the language map on page 89? ___*four—Roman Catholic, Eastern Orthodox, Sunni Muslim, and Jewish; religion unites the Turks and Arabs but divides the Indo-Europeans (Roman Catholic and Eastern Orthodox). Jews belong to the same language family as Arabs.*___

10. Look at the population density maps on pages 333, 534, and 560. How many metropolitan areas with a population above 2 million have ports on the Mediterranean coast? How many of these cities are in North Africa? ___*eight metropolitan areas (four in Europe excluding Istanbul, three in the Middle East including Istanbul and Alexandria, and only one—Algiers—in Africa)*___

Look at the relief maps for the Mediterranean countries on pages 349, 372, 394, 509, and 539. How many countries touch this sea or one of its seven arms, including the Black Sea? (Don't forget about the islands and ministates.) How many of these countries are in North Africa? ___*twenty-six, with only four in North Africa (ten in Central Eurasia, six in the Middle East, and six in Western Europe)*___

Geography

Name _____

Chapter 24   Activity 4

Crossword Puzzle

Across

1. country once ruled by Mansa Musa
3. African empire that lasted one thousand years
5. tall desert nomads in Niger
6. Arabic for "the desert"
8. only Sahel nation with a seacoast
10. region that includes Tunisia, Algeria, and Morocco
12. area of drifting, blowing sand
13. country that once ruled all of the Sahel and Maghreb
14. key lake in the Kanem-Bornu empire
17. valuable resource in Libya and Algeria
18. flat desert areas covered with pebbles
19. most common religion in North Africa

Down

2. isolated mountain range in Algeria
4. most important river in the Sahel
6. largest of the African empires
7. solid mass of barren, windswept rock
9. savanna region in the southern Sahara
10. country that now occupies Western Sahara
11. early people of the Maghreb
14. Arabic for "a shallow salt lake"
15. name for a person of Berber and Arab descent
16. mountain range near the Barbary Coast

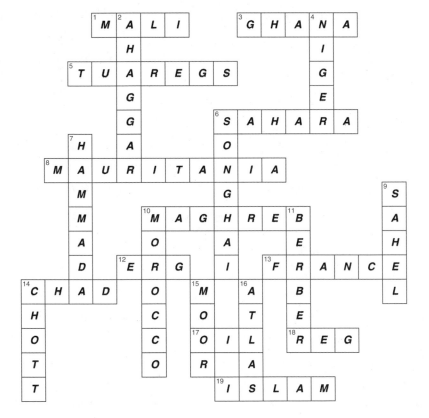

Skill: Recognition

Geography

Map of West Africa

Refer to the map on page 555 to complete the map on the next page. Using the letters and numbers given, label the following features.

Countries

A. Benin
B. Burkina Faso
C. Côte d'Ivoire
D. Gambia
E. Ghana
F. Guinea

G. Guinea-Bissau
H. Liberia
I. Nigeria
J. Senegal
K. Sierra Leone
L. Togo

Cities

a. Abidjan
b. Abuja
c. Accra
d. Banjul
e. Bissau
f. Conakry
g. Dakar

h. Freetown
i. Lagos
j. Lomé
k. Monrovia
l. Ouagadougou
m. Porto-Novo
n. Yamoussoukro

Physical Features

1. Benue River
2. Fouta Djallon

3. Gulf of Guinea
4. Senegal River

Map Work *This section is optional.*

1. Shade yellow the smallest country on the African continent. *(p. 554)*

2. Shade red the two countries that were established as settlements for freed slaves. *(p. 556)*

3. Draw these figures in the appropriate place.

   most populous nation in Africa *(p. 559)*

   former Gold Coast *(p. 557)*

   Britain's first African possession *(p. 554)*

   former Portuguese colony *(p. 555)*

   former German colony *(p. 558)*

   an important slave market formerly *(p. 556)*

   a leading producer of diamonds *(p. 556)*

   largest commercial fleet in the world *(p. 556)*

   nation with largest church in the world *(p. 557)*

   most important industrial center in West Africa *(p. 560)*

   Africa's leader in hardwoods *(p. 561)*

   Africa's leader in petroleum *(p. 561)*

   Africa's leader in bauxite *(p. 564)*

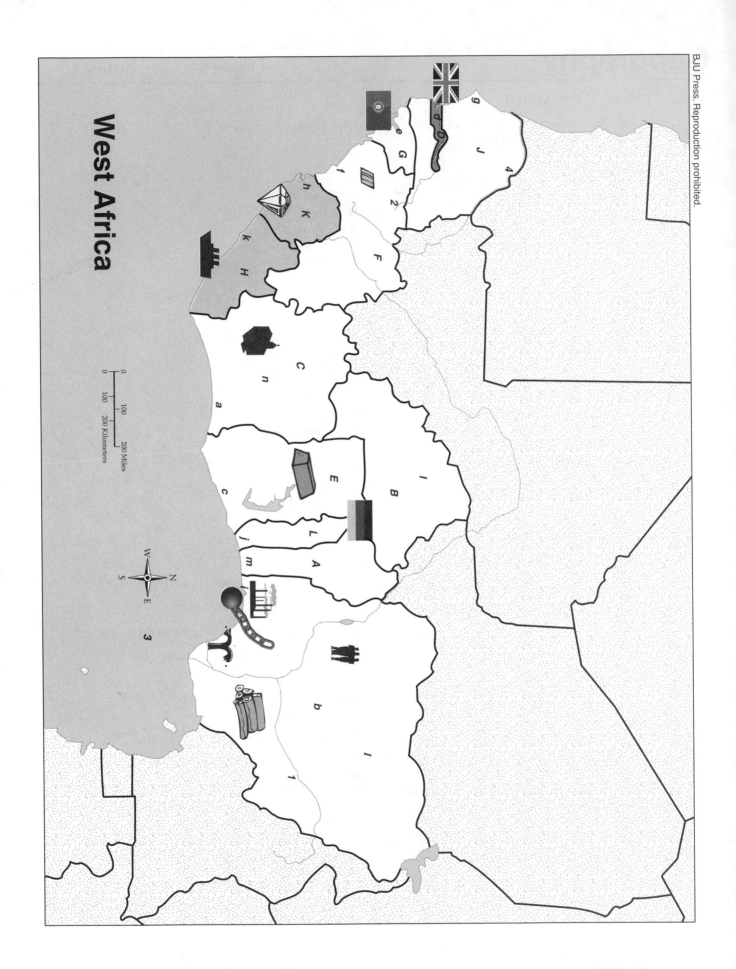

West Africa

Skill: Maps

Geography

Map of Central Africa

Refer to the map on page 562 to complete the map below.

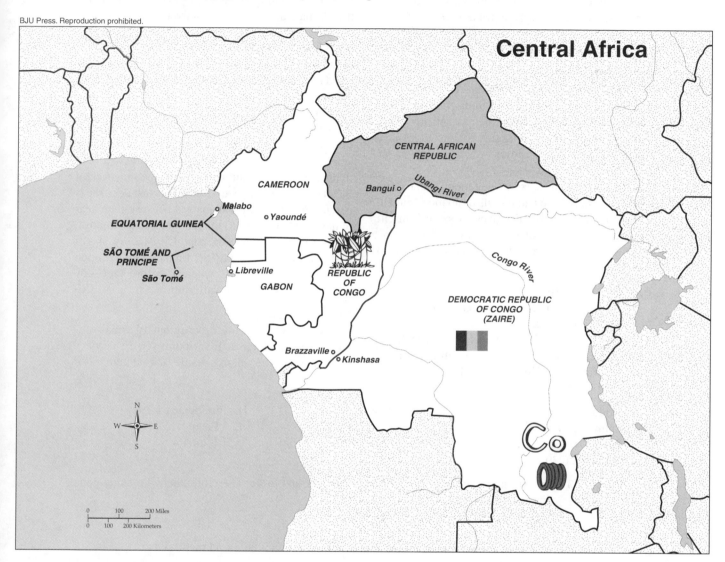

1. Label these features of physical geography: Congo River, Ubangi River.

2. Label all the countries and their capitals in Central Africa.

3. Shade green the only landlocked country in Central Africa. *(p. 567)*

4. Draw these figures in the appropriate place. *This section is optional.*

   ▮▯▯ former Belgian colony *(p. 564)*   ℂ⊙ world's leader in cobalt *(pp. 565-66)*

   ◉◉◉ Africa's largest copper deposits *(p. 565)*   🗻 largest and least explored jungle wilderness *(p. 566)*

Tribal Religions *For more information, see* Communicating Christ in Animistic Contexts *by Gailyn Van Rheenen (Grand Rapids, Michigan: Baker Book House, 1991).*

Spirit worship has no holy books and many varieties. However, nearly all tribes hold to a few of the same fundamental doctrines, similar to the false religions in Old Testament times.

Basic Tribal Beliefs

The basic concept in tribal religions is the belief in spirits—that everything has spiritual power, including both living beings and nonliving spiritual forces. The tribalist's goal is to control spirits for his own purposes, whether blessing or cursing.

Tribal religions lack a strong moral foundation. Their gods may have bad morals or no morals at all. Consequently, the tribalist lives to serve himself. Religion is a means of getting power. Sin is anything that upsets human relations, causing tension in a society.

Biblical Response

The Bible supports the existence of spirits. In fact, God Himself is a Spirit (John 4:24). Angels and demons are spiritual beings. Even man has a spirit that can respond to God and will live forever (I Corinthians 5:5). However, the Bible rejects the views that everything is part of a spiritual force and that man should manipulate the spirit world. God is the ultimate authority in the universe.

When witnessing to a person with a tribal background, missionaries must remember several things. First, sin is ultimately an offense against the one true God. Sin affects more than society; it separates man from God eternally. Second, evil spirits do exist and have, for a limited time, been given some power on earth. But God's solution to the problems of both sin and satanic activity lies in the cross. Christ died for sin so that man could renew a relationship with God, and He defeated the kingdom of Satan by triumphing over death. This last doctrine is crucial in witnessing to tribalists because their fear of harm and death holds them under Satan's control. Warn tribalists, however, that Christianity has a cost—those who accept Christ may be called upon to suffer for their faith, whereas before they saw religion as a way to end suffering.

Scriptural Support

Read the following descriptions of tribal religions. Then look up each Scripture verse and place the letter in the blank beside the statement it refutes.

A. Exodus 20:3-5
B. Psalm 51:4
C. Isaiah 57:21
D. Matthew 26:39

E. Mark 10:45
F. I Corinthians 15:54-57
G. Ephesians 2:8-9

H. Philippians 1:29
I. I Peter 1:15
J. I John 4:4

___A___ 1. Everything around me is part of one great spiritual force. Therefore, there are many gods that I can worship.

___E___ 2. I use religion to get things for myself.

___I___ 3. Gods do not set moral standards because they may not be moral themselves.

___D___ 4. I try to force God (the gods) to do what I want.

___B___ 5. Sin refers to offenses between men.

___G___ 6. I can do something to make up for my sin.

___C___ 7. By my works I can restore peace in society.

___J___ 8. I fear the power of evil spirits over me.

___F___ 9. The spirits control me with the threat of death.

___H___ 10. Religion should relieve me of suffering.

Geography

More on an African Tribe

Pick one tribe below. Then find as much information as you can about it from an almanac, an encyclopedia, or another resource. **Assign one tribe to each student. With larger classes, have students work in teams or assign other tribes not listed.**

Akan	Bassa	Hausa	Malinke	Peuhl
Balanta	Fon	Ibo	Mende	Temne
Bariba	Fula	Luba	Mongo	Yoruba

1. Country (where majority of tribe lives) _____

2. Percentage of population _____

3. Location within country _____

4. Other countries where tribe members live _____

5. Total population of tribe _____

   _____

6. Language _____

7. Religion _____

8. Main occupations _____

   _____

9. Major cities _____

   _____

10. History _____

    _____

    _____

    _____

11. Unusual customs/traditions _____

    _____

    _____

    _____

12. Other cultural notes of interest _____

    _____

    _____

    _____

Geography

Moving to Sub-Saharan Africa

You are moving to a city in West or Central Africa. You want to research the area so that you have some idea of what to expect ahead of time. Using your book or another resource, answer the following questions about your new home.

1. Why are you going to Africa?

   ☐ business   ☐ missions   ☐ teaching

2. What city will be your new home?

   ☐ Dakar, Senegal   ☐ Kinshasa, Democratic   ☐ Lagos, Nigeria
                               Republic of Congo

3. How many people live in your new city?

   ☐ less than one million ☐ one to three million   ☐ over three million

4. How many people can read? Identify the literacy rate of your new country.

   ☐ 0-33%   ☐ 34-66%   ☐ 67-100%

5. How do most people earn their living?

   ☐ agriculture   ☐ government   ☐ private industry/service

6. Approximately how much money do your new neighbors make? Identify the per capita GDP (gross domestic product) of the country.

   ☐ less than $1,000   ☐ $1,000-$2,000   ☐ over $2,000

7. How will you pay for purchases? Identify the national currency.

   ☐ dollar   ☐ franc   ☐ other

8. What is (are) the major health problem(s) in your region?

   ☐ drought/famine   ☐ tropical disease   ☐ war/fighting

9. What language should you use for official business?

   ☐ English   ☐ French   ☐ other

10. In what area do you anticipate the most culture shock?

    ☐ dress   ☐ food   ☐ government services
    ☐ time schedule   ☐ work habits   ☐ other

11. What everyday food(s) do you expect to eat?

    ☐ beans   ☐ corn   ☐ grain
    ☐ meat   ☐ rice   ☐ other

12. What, if any, problems is the government experiencing?

    ☐ civil war   ☐ corrupt or repressive   ☐ disunity
                             leadership

13. What religion do most of the people practice?

    ☐ Christianity   ☐ Islam   ☐ native religions

14. What will the weather be like generally?

    ☐ hot and dry   ☐ tropical wet

15. What body of water is near your city?

    ☐ Atlantic Ocean   ☐ Congo River   ☐ Gulf of Guinea

Geography

Headline News

What terms and places are described in the underlined portion of the following news headlines? See how many answers you can give without looking in your book.

sub-Sahara, p. 551

1. "Floods Destroy Crops Throughout the Region South of the Sahara"

Liberia, p. 556

2. "Nation Never Colonized by Europeans Erupts in Bloody Civil War"

Bight of Benin, p. 558

3. "Boating Accident in Bay North of the Gulf of Guinea"

animism, p. 552

4. "Spirit Worship Increasing"

autocrat, p. 553

5. "Ruler with Unlimited Authority Takes Over"

French West Africa, p. 553

6. "Dakar Becomes Capital of the New French Region in North and West Africa"

Volta, p. 557

7. "Burkina Faso and Ghana Dispute River Rights on their Border"

voodoo, p. 558

8. "Benin Declares Its Form of Animism the Official State Religion"

Berlin Conference, p. 559

9. "Africa Carved Up at Meeting of Western Nations"

Hausa tribe, p. 559

10. "Largest Ethnic Group in Nigeria Attacks Ibo Christians"

Biafran War, p. 561

11. "A Million Ibo Die in a Bloody Conflict"

African sleeping sickness, p. 561

12. "Tsetse Fly Spreads Dreaded Tropical Killer"

yellow fever, p. 561

13. "Plague of Mosquitoes Causes Rise in Malaria and Other Disease"

HIV, p. 562

14. "Over Nineteen Million Africans Infected with Virus that Causes AIDS"

French Equatorial Africa, p. 563

15. "France Dissolves Its Colonial Empire on the Equator"

Democratic Republic of Congo, p. 564

16. "Former Belgian Colony Wins Independence"

Mobutu Sese Seko, p. 564

17. "Aging Military Dictator Overthrown in Zaire"

São Tomé and Príncipe, p. 564

18. "Island Nation Gains Independence from Portugal"

Ubangi River, p. 566

19. "New Animal Discovered on the Northern Tributary of Congo River"

Central African Republic, p. 567

20. "Malarial Epidemic Rages in Central Africa's Only Landlocked Country"

Geography

Map of East Africa

Refer to the map on page 570 to complete the map below.

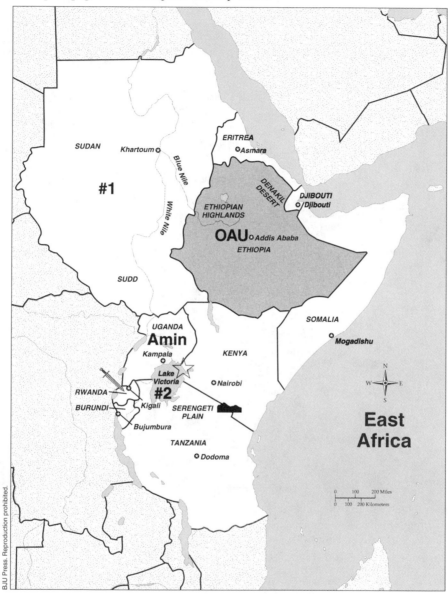

1. Label these features of physical geography:
   Bodies of Water—Blue Nile, Lake Victoria, White Nile
   Miscellaneous—Denakil Desert, Ethiopian Highlands, Serengeti Plain, Sudd

2. Label all the countries and their capitals in East Africa.

3. Shade red the country never successfully colonized by foreigners. *(p. 573)*

4. Draw these figures in the appropriate place. **Note: This section is optional.**

   #2 world's second largest freshwater lake *(p. 576)*

   #1 Africa's largest country *(p. 572)*

   site of massacres between Hutus and Tutsis *(p. 581)*

   OAU headquarters of the OAU *(p. 574)*

   highest mountain in Africa *(p. 580)*

   ☆ source of the Nile *(pp. 576-77)*

   Amin nation ruled by Idi Amin *(p. 580)*

Geography

Map of South Africa

Refer to the map on page 582 to complete the map below.

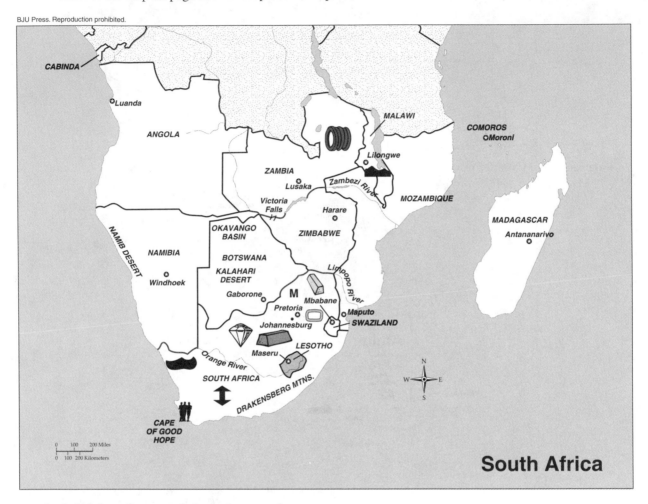

1. Label these features of physical geography:
   Rivers—Limpopo River, Orange River, Zambezi River
   Deserts—Kalahari Desert, Namib Desert
   Miscellaneous—Cape of Good Hope, Drakensberg Mountains, Victoria Falls, Okavango Basin

2. Label these features of human geography:
   City—Johannesburg
   Region—Cabinda

3. Label all the countries and their capitals in South Africa.

4. Shade red the country that is entirely surrounded by another country. *(p. 586)*

5. Draw these figures in the appropriate places. *This section is optional.*

   ![] largest city in eastern and southern Africa *(p. 582)*

   ![] nation infamous for its policy of apartheid *(p. 585)*

   ![] country where Boers settled *(p. 584)*

   ![] "Switzerland" of Africa *(p. 590)*

   ![] world's largest diamond mines *(p. 583)*

   ![] Africa's leader in copper *(p. 589)*

6. Look at the chart on page 66 of your textbook to find South Africa's leading products. Draw the appropriate symbols (see page 64) for each product in South Africa.

Journal of the Discovery of the Source of the Nile
by John Hanning Speke

In 1857 the British explorers and army officers John Hanning Speke and Richard Francis Burton set out on their second African expedition to search for the source of the Nile River. After they reached Lake Tanganyika in Tanzania, Speke continued on alone and became the first European to see Lake Victoria. He concluded that the lake was the source of the Nile, but Burton questioned Speke's conclusion because Speke did not travel around the lake or see the Nile flowing from the lake. Speke returned to Africa in 1860, this time traveling with James Grant. On this expedition, Speke journeyed along the northwest side of Lake Victoria and viewed the Nile's exit from the lake. In his book *Journal of the Discovery of the Source of the Nile,* published in 1863, Speke describes his final trip to Lake Victoria. Read the following excerpts, and then answer the questions that follow.

Purpose of the Expedition

My third expedition in Africa, which was avowedly for the purpose of establishing the truth of my assertion that the Victoria N'yanza [Lake], which I discovered on the 30th of July, 1858, would eventually prove to be the source of the Nile, may be said to have commenced on the 9th of May, 1859, the first day after my return to England from my second expedition, when, at the invitation of Sir R. I. Murchison [president of the Royal Geographical Society], I called at his house to show him my map for the information of the Royal Geographical Society. Sir Roderick, I need only say, at once accepted my views; and, knowing my ardent desire to prove to the world, by actual inspection of the exit, that the Victoria N'yanza was the source of the Nile, seized the enlightened view that such a discovery should not be lost to the glory of England and the society of which he was president; and said to me, "Speke, we must send you there again."

The Journey

[Speke and Grant sailed from London in April 1860 and arrived in Zanzibar in August 1860. Then they traveled through many villages and kingdoms in Tanzania and Uganda. Many tribal chiefs demanded payment before allowing Speke to pass through their land.]

October 4, 1860. A short stage brought us to . . . the district of Nzasa, where there is another small village presided over by Phanzé, Khombé, la Simba, meaning Claw of Lion. He, immediately after our arrival, sent us a present of a basket of rice, value one dollar, of course expecting a return. . . . Not being aware of the value of the offering, I simply requested the sheikh to give him four yards of American sheeting, and thought no more about the matter, until presently I found the cloth returned. The "sultan" could not think of receiving such a paltry present from me, when on the former journey he got so much; if he showed this cloth at home, nobody would believe him, but would say he took much more and concealed it from his family, wishing to keep all his goods to himself. I answered that my footing in the country had been paid for on the last journey, and unless he would accept me as any other common traveler, he had better walk away.

June 16, 1861. [At another district in Tanzania, Speke met with a chief who wanted gifts in return for information about African lakes.] . . . A fine-looking man of about thirty, [the chief] wore the butt-end of a large sea-shell cut in a circle, and tied on his forehead, for a coronet [crown]. . . . After passing the first compliment, I gave him a barsati [cloth], as my token of friendship, and asked him what he saw when he went to the Masai country. He assured me "that there were two lakes, and not one"; for, on going from Usoga to the Masai country, he crossed over a broad strait, which connected the big N'yanza with another one at its northeast corner. Fearfully impetuous, as soon as this answer was given, he said "Now I have replied to your questions, do show me all the things you have got, for I want to see every thing, and be very good friends." . . . My guns, clothes, and every thing were then inspected, and begged for in the most importunate manner.

[By July 1862, the expedition had traveled through the jungles around the western side of Lake Victoria and was just north of the lake.]

July 18, 1862. . . . As Grant's leg was considered too weak for traveling fast, we took counsel together and altered our plans. I arranged that Grant should go to Kamrasi's direct with the property, cattle, and women [Kamrasi was the ruler of a kingdom north of Lake Victoria who was not friendly to the explorers' desire to open a northern route for trade]

. . . while I should go up the river to its source or exit from the lake, and come down again navigating as far as practicable.

July 21, 1862. Here at last I stood on the brink of the Nile. Most beautiful was the scene; nothing could surpass it! It was the very perfection of the kind of effect aimed at in a highly-kept park; with a magnificent stream from 600 to 700 yards wide, dotted with islets and rocks, the former occupied by fishermen's huts, the latter by sterns and crocodiles basking in the sun. . . .

July 25, 1862. Nango, an old friend, and district officer of the place . . . took us to see the nearest falls of the Nile—extremely beautiful, but very confined. The water ran deep between its banks, which were covered with fine grass, soft cloudy acacias [a variety of trees or shrubs with small flowers], and festoons of lilac convolvuli [trailing plants]. . . . The whole was more fairy-like, wild, and romantic than . . . any thing I ever saw outside of a theatre.

July 28, 1862. At last, with a good push for it, crossing hills and threading huge grasses, as well as extensive village plantations lately devastated by elephants . . . we arrived at the extreme end of the journey, the farthest point ever visited by the expedition. . . .

We were well rewarded; for the "stones," as the Waganda call the falls, was by far the most interesting sight I had seen in Africa. Every body ran to see them at once, though the march had been long and fatiguing, and even my sketch-block was called into play. Though beautiful, the scene was not exactly what I expected; for the broad surface of the lake was shut out from view by a spur of hill, and the falls, about 12 feet deep, and 400 to 500 feet broad, were broken by rocks. Still it was a sight that attracted one to it for hours—the roar of the waters, the thousands of passenger-fish, leaping at the falls with all their might, the Wasoga and Waganda fishermen coming out in boats and taking post on all the rocks with rod and hook, hippopotami and crocodiles lying sleepily on the water, the ferry at work above the falls, and cattle driven down to drink at the margin of the lake, made, in all, with the pretty nature of the country—small hills, grassy-topped, with trees in the folds, and gardens on the lower slopes—as interesting a picture as one could wish to see.

The expedition had now performed its functions. I saw that old Father Nile without any doubt rises in the Victoria N'yanza, and, as I had foretold, that lake is the great source of the holy river which cradled the first expounder of our religious belief. I mourned, however, when I thought how much I had lost by the delays in the journey having deprived me of the pleasure of going to look at the northeast corner of the N'yanza. . . . But I felt I ought to be content with what I had been spared to accomplish; for I had seen full half of the lake, and had information given me of the other half, by means of which I knew all about the lake, as far, at least, as the chief objects of geographical importance were concerned. . . .

I now christened the "stones" Ripon Falls, after the nobleman who presided over the Royal Geographical Society when my expedition was got up. . . .

[Because of delays, Speke and Grant traveled directly to Khartoum and then Egypt, without inspecting the Nile's route downstream into and out of Lake Albert.]

1. Why did Sir Murchison encourage Speke to return to Africa?   *to inspect Lake Victoria and prove that the lake is the source of the Nile River, for the glory of England and the Royal Geographical Society*

2. In the July 28 entry, Speke refers to previous delays on his journey. How was the expedition delayed?
The kings and chiefs of the African kingdoms and districts demanded payment before allowing Speke to pass.

3. How much of Lake Victoria did Speke see on his second expedition there?   *half*

4. Explain why the discovery of the source of the Nile was considered so important.   *The Nile is the lifeblood of Egypt and the longest river in the world; philosophers and explorers for centuries had wondered where its source lay.*

5. Several explorers disagreed with Speke's conclusion, even after his second expedition to Lake Victoria. List some possible arguments they might have had.   *Speke did not trace the shore of Lake Victoria as he traveled up the western side, so he couldn't prove that the lake from which the river flowed was indeed Lake Victoria; he did not follow the river to prove that it flowed to Egypt.*

In 1937, the German explorer Dr. Burkhart Waldecker discovered that the southernmost source of the Nile is the Ruvubu River, which begins in Burundi.

Geography

The Journals of David Livingstone

Born in Scotland in 1813, David Livingstone began working in a cotton mill at the age of ten. He taught himself Latin and loved to read, especially the classics, scientific books, and travel books. At the age of twenty-three he entered medical school because he desired to be a medical missionary to China. The Opium Wars prevented Livingstone's original plan; he finished medical school in 1840 and left for southern Africa instead. There he established missions and explored the interior of the "Dark Continent." Livingstone was the first European to see Victoria Falls and several African lakes, and he faithfully recorded his observations in his journals. Livingstone did not believe that Speke had discovered the true source of the Nile. The following excerpts are from his books *Missionary Travels and Researches in South Africa* and *The Last Journals of David Livingstone in Central Africa.* Read the excerpts, and then answer the questions.

Victoria Falls

I resolved on the following day [November 16, 1855] to visit the falls of Victoria, called by the natives *Mosi-oa-tunya,* or more anciently Shongwe ["Place of the Rainbow"]. Of these we had often heard since we came into the country. . . . They [the natives] did not go near enough to examine [the falls], but, viewing them with awe at a distance, said, in reference to the vapor and noise, "Mosi oa tunya" (smoke does sound there). . . .

After twenty minutes' sail from Kalai, we came in sight, for the first time, of the columns of vapour appropriately called "smoke," rising at a distance of five miles, exactly as when large tracts of grass are burned in Africa. Five columns now arose, and bending in the direction of the wind, they seemed placed against a low ridge covered with trees. The tops of the columns at this distance appeared to mingle with the clouds. They were white below, and higher up became dark, so as to simulate smoke very closely.

The whole scene was extremely beautiful; the banks and islands dotted over the river are adorned with sylvan [forest] vegetation of great variety of color and form. . . . There, towering over all, stands the great burly baobab, each of whose enormous arms would form the trunk of a large tree, beside groups of graceful palms, which, with their feathery-shaped leaves depicted on the sky lend beauty to the scene. . . . No one can imagine the beauty of the view from anything witnessed in England. . . .

When about half a mile from the falls, I left the canoe by which we had come down thus far, and embarked in a lighter one with men well acquainted with the rapids, who, by passing down the center of the stream in the eddies and still places caused by many jutting rocks, brought me to an island situated in the middle of the river, and on the edge of the lip over which the water rolls. In coming hither there was danger of being swept down by the streams which rushed along on each side of the island, but

the river was now low, and we sailed where it is totally impossible to go when the water is high. But though we had reached the island, and were within a few yards of the spot, a view from which would have solved the whole problem, I believe that no one could perceive where the vast body of the water went. It seemed to lose itself in the earth, the opposite lip of the fissure into which it disappeared being only eighty feet distant.

At least I did not comprehend it until, creeping with awe to the verge, I peered down into a large rent which had been made from bank to bank of the broad Zambezi, and saw that a stream of a thousand yards broad leaped down a hundred feet, and then became suddenly compressed into a space of fifteen or twenty yards. The entire falls are simply a crack made in a hard basaltic rock. . . .

In looking down into the fissure on the right side of the island, one sees nothing but a dense white cloud, which, at the time we visited the spot, had two bright rainbows on it. . . . From this cloud rushed up a great jet of vapour exactly like steam, and it mounted 200 or 300 feet high; there condensing, it changed its hue to that of dark smoke, and came back in a constant shower which soon wetted us to the skin. This shower falls chiefly on the opposite side of the fissure, and a few yards back from the lip there stands a straight hedge of evergreen trees whose leaves are always wet. From their roots a number of little rills run back into the gulf, but, as they flow down the steep wall there, the column of vapour, in its ascent, licks them clean off the rock and away they mount again. They are constantly running down but never reach the bottom.

Having feasted my eyes long on this beautiful sight, returned to Kalai. Next day I saw the falls at low water and the columns of vapour when five or six miles distant. When the river is in flood the columns, it is said, can be seen ten miles off, and the sound is quite distinct about the same distance away.

Search for the Source of the Nile

[Livingstone was on his way to Ujiji—modern Tanzania—on an expedition to discover the source of the Nile.]

November 8th 1868. The discovery of the sources of the Nile is somewhat akin to the discovery of the North-west Passage [water route north of Canada that connects the Atlantic to the Pacific], which called forth, though in a minor degree, the energy, the perseverance, and the pluck of Englishmen; and any thing that does that is beneficial to the nation and to its prosperity. The discovery of the sources of the Nile possesses, moreover, an element of interest which the North-west Passage never had. The great men of antiquity have recorded their ardent desires to know the fountains of what Homer called "Egypt's heaven-descending spring."

The Slave Trade

October 17th 1861. The Lake [Nyasa] slave-trade was going on at a terrible rate. Two enterprising Arabs had built a dhow [ship], and were running her, crowded with slaves, regularly across the lake. We were told that she sailed the day before we reached their headquarters. . . . We did not see much evidence of a wish to barter. Some ivory was offered for sale, but the chief traffic was in human chattels [slaves].

Would that we could give a comprehensive account of the horrors of the slave-trade, with an approximation of the number of lives it yearly destroys! For we feel sure that were even half the truth told and recognized, the feelings of men would be so thoroughly roused that this devilish traffic in human flesh would be put down at all risks. But neither we, nor anyone else, have the statistics necessary for a work of this kind.

Let us state what we do know of one portion of Africa. We were informed by Colonel Rigby, late H. M. [Her Majesty] political agent, and consul at Zanzibar, that 19,000 slaves from this Nyasa country alone pass annually through the custom-house of that island. This is exclusive, of course, of those sent to Portuguese slave ports. Let it not be supposed for an instant that this number, 19,000, represents all the victims. Those taken out of the country are but a very small section of the sufferers. We never realized the atrocious nature of the traffic until we saw it at the fountain-head. There truly "Satan has his seat." Besides those actually captured, thousands are killed and die of their wounds and famine, driven from their villages by the slave raid proper. Thousands perish in internecine [mutually destructive] war waged for slaves with their own clansmen and neighbors, slain by the lust of gain. . . . It is our deliberate opinion, from what we know and have seen, that not one-fifth of the victims of the slave-trade ever become slaves. . . . We should say that not even one-tenth arrive at their destination.

Stanley and Livingstone

October 24th 1871. . . . When my spirits were at their lowest ebb, the Good Samaritan was close at hand, for one morning Susi [one of Livingstone's servants] came running, at the top of his speed, and gasped out: "An Englishman! I see him," and off he darted to meet him. The American flag at the head of a caravan told of the nationality of the stranger. Bales of goods, baths of tin, huge kettles, cooking pots, tents, etc., made me think: "This must be a luxurious traveler, and not one at his wits' end like me."

October 28th. It was Henry Moreland [Morton] Stanley, the traveling correspondent of the *New York Herald,* sent by James Gordon Bennett, Jr. [owner of the newspaper] . . . to obtain accurate information about Dr. Livingstone, if living, and if dead, to bring home my bones.

The news that he had to tell one who had been two full years without any tidings from Europe made my whole frame thrill. The terrible fate that had befallen France, the telegraphic cables successfully laid in the Atlantic, the election of General Grant, the death of the good Lord Clarendon, my constant friend, the proof that Her Majesty's Government had not forgotten me in voting 1,000 pounds for supplies, and many other points of interest, revived emotions that had remained dormant. . . . Appetite returned; and instead of the spare tasteless two meals a day, I ate four times daily, and in a week began to feel strong.

Near the End

[Livingstone continued his search for the source of the Nile until his death near Lake Bangweulu in Zambia.]

March 19th 1873. [Livingstone's last birthday] Thanks to the Almighty Preserver of men for sparing me thus far on the journey of life! Can I hope for ultimate success [finding the source of the Nile]? So many obstacles have arisen. Let not Satan prevail over me, oh! my good Lord Jesus!

April 19th. . . . I am excessively weak, and but for the donkey, could not move a hundred yards. It is not all pleasure, this exploration. . . . No observations now, owing to great weakness: I can scarcely hold a pencil, and my stick is a burden. Tent gone: the men build a good hut for me and the luggage. South-west one hour and a half.

April 21st. Tried to ride, but was forced to lie down, and they carried me back to village exhausted.

April 22nd. Carried on kitanda [wooden platform] over Buga south-west two and a quarter [two hours and fifteen minutes].

April 27th. Knocked up [exhausted] quite, and remain—recover—sent to buy milch-goats. We are on the banks of the Molilamo.

[Livingstone died three days later.]

1. What danger did Livingstone face in order to see Victoria Falls?   *possibly going over the falls*

2. What reasons does Livingstone give for the importance of the search for and the discovery of the Nile's source?   *The search brought out energy and perseverance in Englishmen, which helped to prosper their nation; it had baffled men for hundreds of years.*

3. According to Livingstone, what harmed the African slaves even more than the actual slavery?   *wounds, famine, and war among themselves*

4. Why was Livingstone glad to see Stanley?   *He brought supplies and news from outside Africa.*

5. Even in his last days, Livingstone kept a journal. Why are his journals important to the study of geography?   *He made careful and detailed observations of the things he saw, many of which had never been recorded before; his journals show us what Africa was like during the late 1800s.*

6. Livingstone was the first to explore parts of Africa. What factors had discouraged exploration previously?   *the difficulty of getting supplies to the interior, heat, humidity, and especially the diseases carried by insects*

7. Why is Livingstone considered such a great explorer?   *He went where no other explorer had gone, and he recorded his explorations; he survived for many years of exploration.*

Geography

Let's Explore Africa

Africa remains a mystery to many Westerners. If you were to visit the continent, what would you know about the countryside?

1. What deep valley that starts in the Middle East would you see cutting through the landscape of East Africa? *Great Rift Valley, p. 571*

2. In what country would you find five of the Nile's six falls (cataracts)? *Sudan, p. 572*

3. What large marsh would you see in southern Sudan? *Sudd, p. 572*

4. In what modern country could you possibly find traces of the ancient kingdom of Nubia? *Sudan, p. 572*

5. What modern coastal country would you need to visit to see the main port of the ancient Axum kingdom? *Eritrea, p. 575*

6. In what East African valley would you find five great lakes? *Western Rift, p. 576*

7. What *lingua franca* would you expect to hear in East Africa? *Swahili, p. 577*

8. What country should you visit to find the nomadic Masai? *Kenya, p. 579*

9. What country would you be in if you were on the island of Zanzibar? *Tanzania, p. 579*

10. In what part of South Africa might you notice the lingering influence of the fierce warrior Shaka? *Zululand or Natal, p. 583*

11. What blend of Dutch and Zulu words would you hear in the Orange Free State? *Afrikaans, p. 584*

12. What escarpment would you see on the coastal plain of Natal? *Drakensberg Mountains, p. 584*

13. What vast savanna would take you all across the interior of southern Africa? *the veldt, p. 584*

14. What landmark (a body of water) would you find at the northern border of South Africa? *Limpopo River, p. 584*

15. In what country would you expect to hear debate on the horrors of apartheid? *South Africa, p. 585*

16. What former rebel leader might you hear credited with working to end apartheid? *Nelson Mandela, p. 585*

17. Where would you have to go to watch South Africa's administrative government at work? *Pretoria, p. 585*

18. Regardless of where you go in South Africa, you are likely to meet people of what type of tribes? *Bantu, p. 585*

19. In what landlocked country would you find the San peoples? *Botswana, p. 586*

20. If you take a boat ride, you should watch for fog along what Namibian coast? *Skeleton Coast, p. 587*

21. In what barren region of Namibia should you search for Hottentots? *Namib Desert, p. 587*

22. If you followed the course of the Zambezi River, you could find what famous waterfall? *Victoria Falls, p. 588*

23. What country, named for a wealthy Englishman, would you no longer find on Africa's map? *Rhodesia, p. 588*

24. That country (see #23) has been renamed for what large stone monument? *Great Zimbabwe, p. 589*

25. In what country could you visit the area in which David Livingstone died? *Zambia, p. 590*
    Livingstone's faithful aides buried his heart in Africa.

Geography

Africa's Cultural Subregions

Follow the directions below to create your own "Culture Map of Africa." It should look like a mini-version of the "Culture Map of Africa" on page 536.

- Label on the map the five main culture regions of Africa: North, West, Central, East, and South.
- Write "#1 in size" in Africa's largest country, and write "#1 in pop." in the most populous country. **(pp. 572, 579)**
- Choose a variety of colors for the cultural subregions below, and color the respective regions on the map. (You should use one color for each letter on the map.) Then match each letter on the map with the correct cultural subregion below.

A	1. Sahara	**E**	7. Ivory Coast	**K**	12. Horn of Africa
B	2. Sahel	**G**	8. Slave Coast	**P**	13. Indian Ocean islands
J	3. Sudan	**H**	9. Lower Guinea Coast	**L**	14. Lakes Region
F	4. Volta	**C**	10. West Atlantic Coast	**N**	15. Southwest Plateau
M	5. South Africa	**I**	11. Congo Basin	**O**	16. Zambezi River nations
D	6. "Free" Coast				

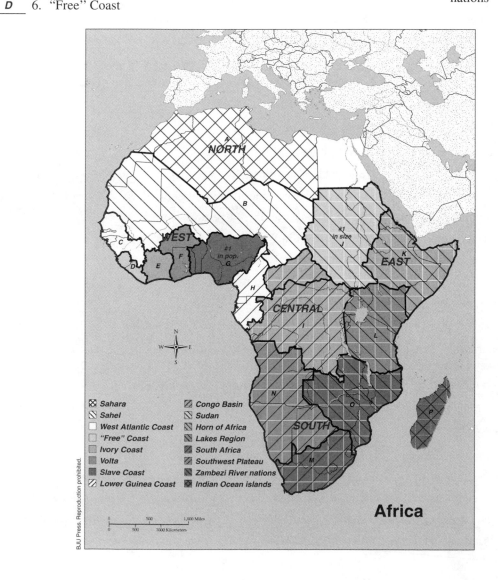

Geography

☆ **European Legacy in Africa**

Europe has had a significant influence on Africa, and that influence continues to this day. Answer the following questions about Europe's legacy in this important region. ☆ *Class discussion.*

Common Misconceptions About Africa Among Europeans

For each misconception about Africa, explain the basis for this misconception and then explain the truth.

1. Africa consists almost entirely of desert and jungle. *Europe's first exposure to Africa was its desert in the north and later its jungles in the west. But in fact, savanna is the main biome, which continues across the Sahel and the plateaus of the east and south. See the vegetation map on page 53.*

2. Sub-saharan Africa had no great civilizations. *Europe was unable to penetrate the great civilizations in Africa's interior, particularly the empires on the Niger River. Instead, it dealt with weak, warring tribes on the coast. But today we have been learning more about these empires, shown on the map on page 547.*

3. Europeans spread slavery across sub-Saharan Africa. *Europeans used their superior weapons to expand their control of the slave trade on the coast of West Africa, shipping slaves to colonies around the world. But in fact, Africans had enslaved Africans for centuries, and they traded them, along with ivory and gold. The Muslim slave trade preceded that of Europeans in the north and east, and it was the European colonists who finally banned slavery. See the discussion on pages 555-56 and the map on page 558.*

4. All Africans are black. *Certainly the majority of sub-Saharan Africans are black, but North Africa consists mostly of Arabs and Berbers, while East Africa has many of mixed Arab and Black descent. South Africa has a large minority of Whites, coloreds, and even Indians.*

Cultures in Conflict

Answer these questions about African cultures.

5. At what infamous conference in 1884 did Europe essentially "steal Africa"? *Berlin Conference, p. 559*

6. What policy of racial separation did the Afrikaner minority impose in South Africa? *apartheid, p. 585*

7. Look at the imperialism map on page 554 to answer these questions.

   a. What was the predominant European power in West Africa? *France*

   b. What was the predominant European power in East and South Africa? *Britain*

   c. Name two modern countries that were once divided between European powers. *Morocco, Cameroon, Somalia (any two)*

   d. What was the only country completely free of European invasion? *Liberia*

8. In addition to native languages, what European language is an official language in each of the following key countries?

   Nigeria *English, p. 559*   Kenya *English, p. 577*

   Democratic Republic of Congo (Zaire)   South Africa *English (and Afrikaans), p. 585*
   French, p. 564

💡 What is the most "European" country in Africa? *Answers will vary, but South Africa has more Whites than all other countries in Africa combined, and it is often considered the only industrialized nation.*

💡 Would Africa be better off if it had never come in contact with Europeans? *Answers will vary. The West brought hospitals, schools, industries, entertainment, and the gospel (in various forms). But it also worsened the slave problem, and its arbitrary borders created a nightmare for modern countries.*

Geography

Map of Australia and New Zealand

Fill in each blank with the correct letter or number from the map below. Regions are uppercase letters (A, B, C), cities are lowercase letters (a, b, c), and physical features are numbers (1, 2, 3). To complete the map work, refer to pages 597, 602, and 611 of the student text.

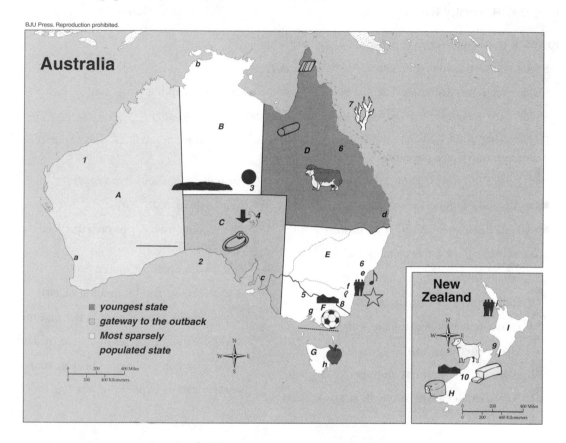

Regions

_E_	1. New South Wales		_H_	6. South Island
_I_	2. North Island		_G_	7. Tasmania
_B_	3. Northern Territory		_F_	8. Victoria
_D_	4. Queensland		_A_	9. Western Australia
_C_	5. South Australia			

Cities

_c_	10. Adelaide		_h_	15. Hobart
_i_	11. Auckland		_g_	16. Melbourne
_d_	12. Brisbane		_a_	17. Perth
_f_	13. Canberra		_e_	18. Sydney
_b_	14. Darwin		_j_	19. Wellington

Physical Features

9	20. Cook Strait		4	25. Lake Eyre
2	21. Great Australian Bight		10	26. Mount Cook
7	22. Great Barrier Reef		8	27. Mount Kosciusko
6	23. Great Dividing Range		5	28. Murray River
1	24. Hamersley Range		3	29. Simpson Desert

Map Work *Note: This section is optional.*

30. Shade yellow the youngest state in Australia. *(p. 604)*

31. Shade green the Australian state that is considered the gateway to the outback. *(p. 606)*

32. Shade red the largest but most sparsely populated Australian state. *(p. 607)*

33. Draw these figures in the appropriate place. Try where possible to place products in their correct areas within a country (see page 602).

Australia's lowest point *(p. 607)*

Australia's highest point *(p. 601)*

New Zealand's highest point *(p. 613)*

world's largest freestanding rock *(p. 608)*

flattest landform on earth *(p. 607)*

Red Center of Australia *(p. 608)*

sports center of Australia *(p. 601)*

Opera House *(p. 600)*

Australia's largest city *(p. 599)*

New Zealand's largest city *(p. 612)*

Australia's first settlement *(p. 599)*

Apple Isle *(p. 603)*

in Queensland, *two* ores that lead the world *(p. 605)*

state where opals are mined *(p. 607)*

world's largest coral formation *(p. 604)*

world's leading exporter of butter *(p. 610)*

world's leading exporter of cheese *(p. 610)*

world's leading exporter of beef *(p. 605)*

world's leading exporter of wool *(p. 610)*

Geography

☆ ## Comparison of Australia and the United States

In the blanks below, write as many similarities and differences as you can between Australia and the United States. Don't forget to look at the statistical charts in the student text. ☆ *Class discussion.*

Physical Geography

Climate   *The United States has a wide variety of climates. Australia also has some variety, but the majority of the land area is desert (tropical and temperate dry).*

Main Mountain Ranges   *Both have north-south systems (Appalachians and Pacific Mountain System versus the Great Dividing Range), and both have scattered systems (Ozark-Ouachitas versus Darling and Hamersley Ranges).*

High Point   *Alaska's Mt. McKinley, at 20,320 feet, is close to three times as tall as Australia's 7,316-foot Mt. Kosciusko.*

Plateaus   *The United States has major interior plateaus (Appalachian, Colorado, and Columbia Plateaus). The western two-thirds of Australia is taken up with the dry, flat Western Plateau.*

Main Lakes   *The United States has the largest system of freshwater lakes in the world (Great Lakes). Australia's largest lake, Lake Eyre, though the lowest point on the continent, is dry most of the time.*

Rivers   *Both have long river systems—the Mississippi-Missouri and the Murray. The Murray is the only major system in Australia because many other rivers are dry most of the year.*

Economy

Per Capita GDP   *The U.S. ($27,607) is #1 in the world, while Australia ($22,100) is #9.*

Agricultural Products   *The United States is a world leader in wheat, corn, dairy products, tobacco, cotton, and fruit. Australia's main agricultural product is beef. Coastal areas also produce varieties of fruits and vegetables, and there is an area of wheat production in the south to the west of the Great Dividing Range.*

Major Mining Products (See chart on p. 66.)   *Both have large mineral reserves. The U.S. is among the top two nations in gold, copper, lead, phosphates, nitrates, sulfur, and coal. Australia is among the top two nations in lead and bauxite and also has significant reserves of other metals and coal.*

Major Ports   *The United States has ports with access to both the Atlantic and Pacific. Because Australia is an island country with a dry interior, most of its major cities are located along the coast and serve as ports. Australia has access to the Indian and South Pacific Oceans, but it is far from the main ocean lanes. Its main port is Sydney.*

Demography

Total Population   *The U.S. at 267,954,767 is over 14 times larger than Australia at 18,438,824.*

Population Density   *Though the U.S. has a low population density (72) compared to several other countries, Australia is significantly lower with a density of only 6.*

Natural Increase   *The rates are essentially the same (Australia, 0.7%; U.S., 0.6%).*

Life Expectancy   *Both have high life expectancies—U.S. (76) and Australia (80).*

Literacy Rate   *Both countries have a high literacy rate (96% in the United States, 100% in Australia).*

Largest City   *New York (7 million) and Sydney (3.7 million) have the largest populations. They are located at key junctures for trade. But New York is part of a megalopolis that includes 19.5 million people.*

History

First Settlement   *Earliest settlements in the U.S. (Jamestown, 1607, or St. Augustine, 1565) were overshadowed by later cities. Sydney, established in 1788, is still the main city in Australia.*

Creation of the Country   *Both countries were colonies of England. Some American colonists were transported convicts, but many more came for religious or economic opportunity. The majority of early Australian colonists were British prisoners. America overthrew the mother country while Australia maintained loose ties.*

Government

Area   *Both are among the largest countries in the world; the U.S. is fourth, and Australia is sixth. The U.S. has 3,675,031 sq. mi.; Australia has 2,942,000.*

Form of Government   *The U.S. is a federal republic with a strong presidency. Australia also has a federal system of state government but is a constitutional monarchy with the British monarch as the symbolic head of state, represented in Australia by a governor-general. Both have divided legislatures, a House of Representatives and a Senate. Australians are scheduled to vote to determine whether they want to remain part of the British Commonwealth or become a republic with a president as head of state.*

Political Divisions   *The U.S. has fifty states, while Australia has six states and two territories.*

Society

Cultural Subregions   *The United States is divided between the Northeast (population center and historic cities), South (regionalism), Midwest (breadbasket), and West (frontier). Australia doesn't have groups of states that exactly parallel these regions. However, Australia's coast east of the Great Dividing Range has major population centers like the Northeast; rivalries between New South Wales and Victoria may be compared roughly to the rivalry between the Old North and South; farming and ranching occur in the Central Lowlands as in the Midwest; and the Western Plateau may be looked on as Australia's frontier, although it covers a significantly larger portion of the country than America's West does.*

Main Minorities   *Both countries have large ethnic majorities—peoples of European descent. The main minorities in the U.S. are Blacks, Hispanics, Asians, and Indians; Australia has a small minority of Asians. It also has a population of Aborigines, native Australian peoples. Though only 1 percent of the population, the Aborigines have been given much land by the Australian government.*

Main Religion   *Both countries consist mostly of "Christians." They are divided among Roman Catholics and a wide range of Protestant denominations.*

Sister States

Which U.S. state is most similar to each Australian state? Be prepared to defend your answers.
Answers will vary.

New South Wales _____

Victoria _____

Tasmania _____

Queensland _____

South Australia _____

Western Australia _____

Geography

Aboriginal Peoples

Using your textbook and encyclopedias, complete the following chart comparing these aboriginal peoples: Australia's Aborigines, New Zealand's Maoris, and America's Indians.

Answers may vary.

	Aborigines	Maoris	Indians
Country	Australia	New Zealand	United States
Origins	Southeast Asia	Polynesian islands north of New Zealand	Asia (across to present-day Alaska and then throughout North America)
Means of Survival	hunting and gathering (nomads)	fishing and hunting, later farming	hunting and gathering, some farming
Weapons	spear and boomerang	guns from Europeans	bow & arrow, spears & clubs, tomahawk, guns from Europeans
Interaction with Europeans	pushed into interior, many were killed or died of disease	fought bloody wars though outnumbered, violations of Treaty of Waitangi led to Land Wars, Europeans won and took land	pockets of fierce resistance, were settled on reservations, many died of disease
Domestic Animals	dingo (type of dog)	dogs, pigs	dogs (horses came later)
Group Organization	tribes divided into bands and clans	many small, competing chieftainships	tribes divided into bands or clans and associations, sometimes joined together in federations
Religion	superstitious, spirits control life and created world in Dreamtime	impersonal, spiritual force (mana) flows through people and things; those with too much force are dangerous, declared taboo	spirit power throughout nature influences lives, Great Spirit joined by other spirits
Current National Status	many on reservations, but the government has returned large tracts of land	many in cities, have been integrated into European way of life	many on reservations, face significant social problems
Current Population	about 206,000	about 300,000	over 2 million

Geography

Name _____

Chapter 27   Activity 4

Word Search

Write the answers to each question in the blank, and then circle the answer in the puzzle. Answers can be found in any direction: backwards, forwards, or diagonally.

1. What term describes the islands in the Pacific far from the main landmasses? __*Oceania*__

2. What type of mammals raise their young in a pouch? __*marsupial*__

3. Where was Australia's first settlement? __*Sydney*__

4. What do Australians call sheep? __*jumpbucks*__

5. What is brown coal called? __*lignite*__

6. What Australian city name comes from the Aboriginal word for "meeting place"? __*Canberra*__

7. What is Australia's smallest state? __*Tasmania*__

8. What river system of the Central Lowlands is the most important on the Australian continent?
   __*Murray*__

9. What is formed from the skeletons of polyps? __*coral*__

10. What is the "frontier state" of Australia? __*Queensland*__

11. What do Australians call a ranch? __*station*__

12. What do you call a spot where warm water bubbles up to the surface without a pump?
    __*artesian well*__

13. What is the sparsely populated interior of Australia called? __*outback*__

14. What desert is sometimes called the Red Center of Australia for its waves of red sand? __*Simpson*__

15. Who were the first inhabitants of New Zealand? __*Maori*__

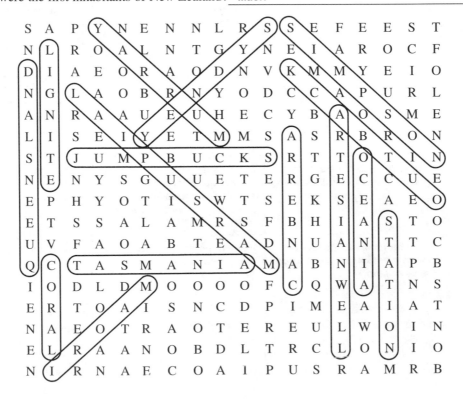

252   Chapter Review

Skill: Recognition

The Life and Voyages of Captain James Cook

Born in England in 1728, James Cook entered the Royal Navy in 1755. While a navy officer, he took three voyages to explore the Pacific Ocean. His findings helped him become the most famous British navigator. He recorded many new plants and animals, as well as the native customs of the lands he visited. On his second journey, Cook stopped at Easter Island. He discovered the Hawaiian Islands (which he named the Sandwich Islands) on his third voyage. Read the following selections from Cook's journals and letters, and then answer the questions that precede each selection.

1. Look up *plantain* in a dictionary. What is it? Why was it common? _a fruit similar to the banana; it_

   grew well in the Polynesian climate

   _____

2. What reason does Cook give for the statues' existence on Easter Island? What other possibilities can

   you think of? _He believed they were burial places; they may have been idols, or they may have been_

   placed around the island to scare would-be intruders.

   _____

3. Why did Cook believe that the statues had been built by a previous generation? _Many of the statues_

   had fallen down, and the natives did not repair the foundations, which were decaying.

   _____

Easter Island

March 14th, 1774. I went ashore, accompanied by some of the gentlemen, to inform myself if any refreshments or water were to be got. We landed at a sandy beach, where about 100 of the natives were collected. They gave us no disturbance at landing; on the contrary hardly one had so much as a stick in their hands. After distributing among them some medals and other trifles, they brought us sweet potatoes, plantains, and some sugar cane which they exchanged for nails and etc; after having found a small spring or rather well made by the natives, of very brackish water, I returned on board and anchored the ship. . . .

March 15th. [Cook sent a party to explore the island on this date. The party returned in the evening and reported their findings to Cook.] . . . They observed that this side of the island was full of gigantic statues, some placed in groups on platforms of masonry, others single, being fixed only in the earth, and that not deep; these latter are, in general, much larger than the others. They measured one which had fallen down, and found it very near twenty-seven feet long; . . . and yet this appeared considerably short of the size of one they saw standing. . . .

The stupendous stone statues erected in different places along the coast are certainly no representation of any Deity or places of worship; but most probably burial places for certain tribes or families.

I myself saw a human skeleton lying in the foundation of one just covered with stones. . . .

[The platforms of masonry] are built, or rather faced, with hewn stones of a very large size; and the workmanship is not inferior to the best plain piece of masonry we have in England. They use no sort of cement; yet the joints are exceedingly close, and the stones morticed and tenanted one into another in a very artful manner. . . .

The statues, or at least many of them, are erected on these platforms, which serve as foundations. . . . The workmanship is rude, but not bad; nor are the features of the face ill-formed, the nose and chin in particular; but the ears are long beyond proportion; and as to the bodies, there is hardly anything like a human figure about them. . . .

We could hardly conceive how a nation of people like these, wholly unacquainted with any mechanical power, could raise such stupendous figures, and afterwards place the large cylindric stones upon their heads. The only method I can conceive is by raising the upper end by little and little, supporting it by stones as it is raised, and building about it till they got it erect; thus, a sort of mount or scaffolding would be made, upon which they might roll the cylinder, and place it upon the head of the statue, and then the stones might be removed from about it. . . . But let them have been made and set up by this or any other method, they must have been a work of immense time, and sufficiently show the ingenuity and perseverance of the age in which they were built; for the present inhabitants have most certainly had no hand in them, as they do not even repair the foundations of those which are going to decay.

March 16th. I sent a boat ashore to purchase such refreshments as the natives might have brought to the waterside. Not one of them had so much as a stick or a weapon of any sort in their hands. After distributing a few trinkets amongst them, we made signs for something to eat, on which they brought down a few potatoes, plantains, and sugar cane and exchanged for nails, looking-glasses and pieces of cloth. We presently discovered that they were as expert thieves and as tricking in their exchanges as any people we had yet met with. It was with some difficulty that we could keep the hats on our heads, but it was hardly possible to keep anything in our pockets, not even what themselves had sold us; for they would watch every opportunity to snatch it from us, so that we sometimes bought the same thing two or three times over, and after all did not get it.

4. The longitude of the island Cook saw on January 18 was actually 159° 19′ W. Why did he record it as 200° E? *He didn't break the longitudes into two 180° halves; instead, he numbered longitude to 360°.*

5. Look at the map on page 220 of the text. As Cook was traveling north, which Hawaiian island was the "nearest land" he saw on January 18, 1778? *Kauai*

6. Give possible reasons for the Hawaiian natives' reaction to Cook. *They might have thought he was a god, or they may have just been treating him with the respect they gave their chiefs.*

7. Why would the islanders be attracted to iron nails? *They had only a little iron; it is a strong material for building.*

8. Do you think the Hawaiians would have been surprised to hear Europeans speaking in Otaheite? *No, they probably figured Otaheite was the language of the world.*

9. Underline all references that Cook makes to previous voyages. How was his experience helpful? *He was able to compare the various cultures, and he learned how to deal with the natives.*

10. Cook is considered one of the most skilled leaders in naval history. What evidence do you see of his leadership skills? *care for details, insight into people, concern for provisions, cautious, generous*

11. Compare and contrast the natives of Easter Island and the Hawaiian Islands. *Both groups traded with Cook and stole from him, though the Hawaiian natives did not cheat him while trading; the natives of Hawaii were more impressed with Cook's ship (reluctant to board the ship) and with Cook himself (bowing to him and presenting him with gifts).*

Hawaiian Islands

We were seeing birds every day, sometimes in greater numbers than others, and several turtles. All these are looked upon as signs of the vicinity of land. In the morning of January 18th, 1778, an island made its appearance, and soon after we saw more land, entirely detached from the former. We had light airs and calms by turns, so that at sunset we were not less than nine or ten leagues [a league equals three miles] from the nearest land. Our latitude was 21° 12′ N, and longitude 200° 41′ E.

January 19th. When we were about two leagues distant, we were in some doubt whether or not the land before us was inhabited; this doubt was soon cleared up by seeing some canoes coming off from the shore towards the ships. I immediately brought to, to give them time to come up. There were three and four men in each canoe, and we were agreeably surprised to find that they spoke the language of Otaheite [a Polynesian language]. It required but very little address to get them to come alongside; but we could not prevail upon any one to come on board. They exchanged a few fish they had in the canoes for any thing we offered them, but valued nails, or iron, above every other thing. The only weapons they had were a few stones in some of the canoes and these they threw overboard when they found they were not needed.

Seeing no signs of an anchoring-place at this part of the island, I bore away to leeward [with the wind], and ranged along the south-east side, at the distance of half a league from the shore. . . . We passed several villages, some seated near the sea, and others farther up the country. The inhabitants of all of them crowded to the shore, and collected themselves on the elevated places to view the ships.

January 20th. We stood in for the land, and were met by several canoes filled with people, some of whom took courage and ventured on board. I never saw Indians so much astonished at the entering a ship before; their eyes were continually flying from object to object, the wildness of their looks and gestures fully expressing their surprise and astonishment at the several new objects before them and evidencing that they never had been on board a ship before.

At nine o'clock, being pretty near the shore, I sent three armed boats to look for a landing-place and fresh water. As the boats put off an Indian stole the butcher's cleaver, leaped over board with it, got into his canoe and made for the shore. The boats pursued him but to no effect.

About noon the boats returned, and the officer reported that he had seen a large pond behind a beach near one of the villages, which the natives told him was fresh water; and that there was anchoring ground before it.

As soon as the ships were anchored, I went ashore to look at the water and try the disposition of the inhabitants, several hundred of whom were assembled on a sandy beach before the village. The very instant I leaped on shore, they all fell flat upon their faces, and remained in that humble posture till I made signs to them to rise. They then brought me a great many small pigs, which they presented to me, with plantain trees, in a ceremonious way as is usual on such like occasions, and I ratified these marks of friendship by presenting them with such things as I had with me. After things were a little settled, I left a guard upon the beach and got some of the Indians to shew me the water, which proved to be very good and convenient to come at. Our guides proclaimed our approach and every one whom we met fell on their faces and remained in that position till we had passed. This, as I afterwards understood, is done to their great chiefs.

January 21st. [Cook and his men spent the day collecting water and transporting it to the ship.] At sunset I brought everybody on board, having got during the day nine tons of water, and, by exchanges, chiefly for nails and pieces of iron, about sixty or eighty pigs, a few fowl, a quantity of potatoes, and a few plantains and taro roots. No people could trade with more honesty than these people, never once attempting to cheat us, either ashore or alongside the ships. Some indeed at first betrayed a thievish disposition, or rather they thought they had a right to any thing they could lay their hands upon, but this conduct they soon laid aside.

[Cook left the Hawaiian Islands five weeks later and sailed along the western coast of North America and into the Arctic Ocean looking for the fabled southern continent. On his return trip he stopped again at the Hawaiian Islands, where he was killed by natives in a dispute over the theft of a boat from his ship the *Discovery*.]

Geography

Map of the Pacific Islands

Refer to the map on page 616 to complete the map below. Using the letters given, label the following features.

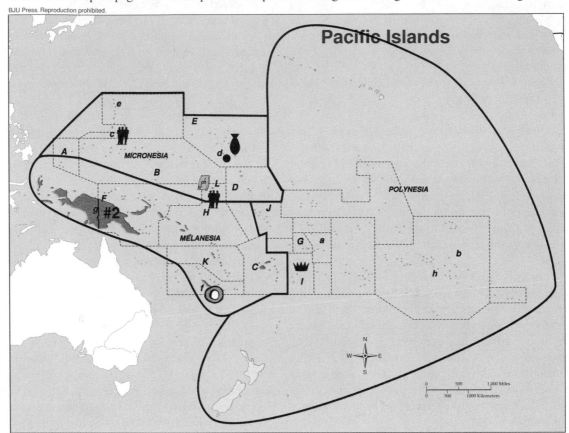

Countries

A. Belau	E. Marshall Islands	J. Tuvalu
B. Federated States of Micronesia	F. Papua New Guinea	K. Vanuatu
	G. Samoa	L. Nauru
C. Fiji	H. Solomon Islands	
D. Kiribati	I. Tonga	

Islands

a. American Samoa	d. Kwajalein	g. New Guinea
b. French Polynesia	e. Mariana Islands	h. Tahiti
c. Guam	f. New Caledonia	

Map Work Note: This section is optional.

1. Label and draw borders around the three cultural subregions of the Pacific Islands: Melanesia, Micronesia, and Polynesia. Use a different color for each region.

2. Draw these figures in the appropriate place.

   ● largest atoll in the world *(p. 624)*

    most populous island in Micronesia *(p. 623)*

   ◎ a world leader in nickel *(p. 622)*

    highest population density in the Pacific *(p. 624)*

    high-quality phosphates *(p. 625)*

   #2 second largest island in world *(p. 618)*

    testing of U.S. nuclear bombs *(p. 624)*

    only kingdom in the Pacific *(p. 626)*

Geography

Final Survey of Missions

You have now completed your survey of missions. Answer the questions below based on what you have learned in the textbook's ten "Missions" features.

1. *Page 93.* What is the name of Christ's commandment for us to be witnesses for Him (Matt. 28:19-20, Mark 16:15-16, Luke 24:46-48, John 20:21, Acts 1:8)? __*Great Commission*__

2. The two branches of missions are home missions and _____*foreign*_____ missions.

3. *Page 174.* Name two special groups that could be targeted by home missions in your area. __*Possible answers include alcoholics, the deaf, the blind, orphans, the sick, college students, the homeless, soldiers, foreign immigrants, and Indians.*__

4. Is it ever appropriate to adjust the gospel message to please your hearers (II Tim. 4:2-3)? __*The basic truths should never change.*__

5. *Page 236.* What basic sacrifice must all missionaries make in order to minister to foreign peoples, such as Canadians (I Cor. 9:22)? __*Missionaries must sacrifice their heritage to overcome the national pride of their hearers.*__

6. *Page 267.* What special type of missions is desperately needed in poor, neighboring countries like Haiti (Matt. 25:35-36)? __*medical missions*__

7. *Page 341.* What is the most common missionary work, patterned after the apostle Paul (I Cor. 3:6-7)? __*church planting*__

8. *Page 400.* When missionaries face government persecution, what truth should protect them from discouragement (II Cor. 5:20)? __*We are ambassadors for Christ, the King of kings, who rules over all governments.*__

9. *Page 461.* How many of the world's language groups do not have a single verse of Scripture in their own language? How many have a complete Bible? __*Of 6,600 language groups, two-thirds do not have a single verse; complete Bible translations appear in only 341 languages.*__

10. What five languages do most Bible translators need to learn? __*English, Greek, Hebrew, the national trade language, and the tribal language*__

11. Name two sources of conflict on the mission field. What truth gives missionaries strength to continue (Phil. 4:13)? __*Missionaries have conflicts with nationals and with coworkers; Christ gives them strength to accomplish His will.*__

12. *Page 495.* What kind of missionary work is possible in closed countries, such as Saudi Arabia? What kind of career could you use on the mission field? __*tent making; closed countries still desire teachers and skilled technicians*__

13. According to Paul, what causes missionaries to suffer persecution (II Tim. 3:12)?   *living godly lives*

14. *Page 579.* What missionary opportunity fulfills Paul's commission in II Timothy 2:2?   *Bible College professor*

15. *Page 623.* What type of mission field requires missionary pilots?   *remote, primitive lands in which climates are hostile and where normal transportation is impossible*

16. Why is preparation for missionary aviation more difficult than most types of missionary work?
    extra cost and mechanical training

17. What principle in II Corinthians 4:7 helps missionaries to juggle their obligations to family and ministry?   *We are "earthen vessels" dependent on God to meet our daily needs.*

Remind students that the first features covered the five stages of mission work (call, deputation, visa/adjustment, term, and furlough) and the last five covered the main challenges to mission work (governments, coworkers, lost people, inner self, and family).

Geography

☆ **Lost Islands**

Below is a list of key Pacific islands and island chains. Sort them out according to their main region (Melanesia, Micronesia, or Polynesia), their countries, and their island groups. See how much you can do without looking at your textbook or the map (page 616). ☆ *Class discussion.*

American Samoa	French Polynesia	Nauru	Solomon Islands
Belau	Hawaiian Islands	New Caledonia	Tonga
Caroline Islands	Kiribati	Papua New Guinea	Tuvalu
Chuuk Islands	Kosrae	Pitcairn Island	Vanuatu
Easter Island	Mariana Islands	Pohnpei	Yap Islands
Fiji	Marshall Islands	Samoa	

I. Melanesia—name means "black islands"

    A. _**Papua New Guinea**_ includes Bismarck Archipelago, New Britain, and Bougainville

    B. _**Solomon Islands**_ include Guadalcanal

    C. _**Vanuatu**_ includes New Hebrides

    D. _**Fiji**_ includes Vitu Levu (Big Island)

    E. _**New Caledonia**_ is famous for nickel mines

II. Micronesia—name means "small islands"

    A. _**Caroline Islands**_

        1. Federated States of Micronesia

            a. _**Kosrae**_

            b. _**Pohnpei**_

            c. _**Chuuk Islands**_

            d. _**Yap Islands**_

        2. _**Belau**_

    B. _**Mariana Islands**_ include Guam

    C. _**Marshall Islands**_ include Kwajalein

    D. _**Nauru**_ is famous for phosphates

    E. _**Kiribati**_

III. Polynesia—name means "many islands"

    A. _**Tuvalu**_, world's fourth smallest nation

    B. Samoan Islands

        1. _**Samoa**_

        2. _**American Samoa**_ includes Pago Pago

    C. _**Tonga**_, last kingdom in the Pacific

    D. _**French Polynesia**_ includes Tahiti

    E. _**Hawaiian Islands**_ is one of the fifty United States

    F. _**Pitcairn Island**_ was the last stop for the HMS *Bounty* mutineers

    G. _**Easter Island**_ is Chile's island with mysterious *moai*

Memory Aids

It is very difficult to remember the differences between all the Pacific Islands. To answer the following questions, carefully examine your outline, the map on page 616, and the table on page 617. These should become "memory aids" for you.

1. Melanesia and Micronesia consist mostly of independent countries, with one significant exception apiece. What island group is the major exception, and what foreign country controls that region?

    • foreign-controlled region of Melanesia _**New Caledonia (French)**_

    • foreign-controlled region of Micronesia _**Mariana Islands (United States)**_

2. Unlike Melanesia and Micronesia, Polynesia is mostly controlled by foreign countries. What Polynesian territories do these foreign countries control?

- France   *French Polynesia*
- United Kingdom   *Pitcairn Island*
- Chile   *Easter Island*
- United States   *American (Eastern) Samoa and the Hawaiian Islands [plus the Midway Islands and others not shown]*

3. Melanesia and Micronesia each have *five* main parts, and Polynesia has "the rest." List the parts below, and then think of a few key words that summarize the most significant fact about each.
Answers will vary. It will also help students if they can visualize the relative location of these places on the map.

Five Parts of Melanesia and Their Foremost Facts

a.   *Papua New Guinea: birds of paradise; four Cs (cacao, copra, coffee, copper); huge population; 1,200 languages*

b.   *Solomon Islands: blackbirders; World War II battlefields at Guadalcanal*

c.   *Vanuatu* : Captain Cook named these volcanic islands New Hebrides

d.   *Fiji: crossroads of the Pacific*

e.   *New Caledonia: nickel mines*

Five Parts of Micronesia and Their Foremost Facts

a.   *Caroline Islands: four federated states of Micronesia; Belau*

b.   *Mariana Islands: Guam (the most populous island in Micronesia)*

c.   *Marshall Islands: nuclear tests and missile target practice; Kwajalein (largest atoll in the world)*

d.   *Nauru: wealth from phosphates; third smallest country in the world*

e.   *Kiribati: straddles the international date line and Micronesia and Polynesia*

Seven Parts of Polynesia and Their Foremost Facts

a.   *Tuvalu: lowest population and per capita GDP in the Pacific; fourth smallest country in the world*

b.   *Samoan Islands: divided between independent Samoa and American Samoa (with Pago Pago)*

c.   *Tonga: last and oldest kingdom in the Pacific*

d.   *French Polynesia: large French territory with the cultural center in Tahiti*

e.   *Hawaiian Islands: U.S. state*

f.   *Pitcairn Island: populated by descendants of those who mutinied on the* Bounty

g.   *Easter Island: mysterious moai stone faces*

4. Complete the simple table comparing the three broad groups of the Pacific Islands.

Group	Main Type of Island—Continental, High (Volcanic), Low (Coral)	Physical Characteristics of the Native People	Cultural Traits	Vegetation and Resources
Melanesia	*continental*	*short and black-skinned*	*most remote and primitive; many small, independent societies where a "big man" rose to power based on prowess in battle*	*rich variety similar to the continents*
Micronesia	*low (coral)*	*taller and lighter-skinned than Melanesians*	strict ranks in society, with titles that distinguish the "value" of people from different islands	*poor soil and no resources (except copra)*
Polynesia	*high (volcanic)*	*light-skinned and wavy hair*	*common language and culture, with a complex system of hereditary chiefs*	*good soil [but little variety of native animals]*

Geography

The Race Between Amundsen and Scott

In 1911 both Roald Amundsen and Robert Falcon Scott set out on expeditions to the South Pole. The Norwegian Roald Amundsen had originally been on his way to the North Pole, but he turned around mid-trip and headed to Antarctica when he learned that someone else had already arrived at the North Pole. Amundsen started his expedition sixty miles closer to the South Pole than Scott and used dogs to pull his sledges, while Scott insisted on manhauling his supplies. Amundsen reached the Pole a little over a month before Scott. Read the following excerpts from *The South Pole* (Roald Amundsen's account of his expedition) and the journals of Captain Robert Scott. Then answer the questions below.

Roald Amundsen: *The South Pole*
Near the Pole

[December 9, 1911] Every step we now took in advance brought us rapidly nearer the goal. . . . None of us would admit that he was nervous, but I am inclined to think that we all had a little touch of that malady. What should we see when we got there? A vast, endless plain, that no eye had yet seen and no foot yet trodden; or—No, it was an impossibility; with the speed at which we had travelled, we must reach the goal first, there could be no doubt about that. And yet—and yet—Wherever there is the smallest loophole, doubt creeps in and gnaws and gnaws and never leaves a poor wretch in peace.

At the Pole

[December 14, 1911] At three in the afternoon a simultaneous "Halt" rang out from the drivers. They had carefully examined their sledge meters, and they all showed the full distance—our Pole by reckoning. The goal was reached, the journey ended. I cannot say—though I know it would sound much more effective—that the object of my life was attained. That would be romancing rather too barefacedly. I had better be honest and admit straight out that I have never known any man to be placed in such a diametrically opposite position to the goal of his desires as I was at that moment. The regions around the North Pole—well, yes, the North Pole itself—had attracted me from childhood, and here I was at the South Pole. Can anything more topsy-turvy be imagined? . . .

After we had halted we collected and congratulated each other. We had good grounds for mutual respect in what had been achieved, and I think that was just the feeling that was expressed in the firm and powerful grasps of the fist that were exchanged. After this we proceeded to the greatest and most solemn act of the whole journey—the planting of our [Norwegian] flag. Pride and affection shone in the five pairs of eyes that gazed upon the flag, as it unfurled itself with a sharp crack, and waved over the Pole. I had determined that the act of planting it—the historic event—should be equally divided among us all. It was not for one man to do this; it was for *all* who had staked their lives in the struggle and held together through thick and thin. This was the only way in which I could show my gratitude to my comrades in this desolate spot. I could see that they understood and accepted it in the spirit in which it was offered. Five weatherbeaten, frostbitten fists they were that grasped the pole, raised the waving flag in the air, and planted it as the first at the geographical South Pole.

Departure

[December 17, 1911] . . . We began our preparations for departure. First we set up the little tent we had brought with us in case we should be compelled to divide into two parties. . . . Inside the tent, in a little bag, I left a letter, addressed to H.M. [His Majesty] the King, giving information of what we had accomplished. The way home was a long one, and so many things might happen to make it impossible for us to give an account of our expedition. Besides this letter, I wrote a short epistle to Captain Scott, who, I assumed, would be the first to find the tent.

[Amundsen's well-planned and well-executed expedition made it safely back from the South Pole.]

The Journals of Robert Falcon Scott
[Scott's polar party included four other men: Henry Bowers, Edgar Evans, Lawrence ("Titus") Oates, and Edward Wilson.]

Night, January 15.—It is wonderful to think that two long marches would land us at the Pole. We left our depot today with nine days' provisions, so that it ought to be a certain thing now, and the only appalling possibility the sight of the Norwegian flag forestalling ours. . . . Only 27 miles from the Pole. We *ought* to do it now.

Tuesday, January 16.—Camp 68. Height 9760. T. [temperature] –23.5°. The worst has happened, or nearly the worst. . . . About the second hour of the march Bowers' sharp eyes detected what he thought was a cairn [a pile of stones built as a marker]; he was uneasy about it, but argued that it must be a sastruga. Half an hour later he detected a black speck ahead. Soon we knew that this could not be a natural snow feature. We marched on, found that it was a black flag tied to a sledge bearer; near by the remains of a camp; sledge tracks and ski tracks going and coming and the clear trace of dogs' paws—many dogs. This told us the whole story. The Norwegians have forestalled us and are first at the Pole. It is a terrible disappointment, and I am very sorry for my loyal companions. Many thoughts come and much discussion have we had. To-morrow we must march on to the Pole and then hasten home with all the speed we can compass. All the day-dreams must go; it will be a wearisome return. . . .

Wednesday, January 17.—Camp 69. T. –22° at start. Night –21°. The Pole. Yes, but under very different circumstances from those expected. We have had a horrible day—add to our disappointment a head wind 4 to 5, with a temperature –22°, and companions laboring on with cold feet and hands. . . . This is an awful place and terrible enough for us to have labored to it without the reward of priority. Well, it is something to have got here. . . . Now for the run home and a desperate struggle. I wonder if we can do it.

Thursday morning, January 18.—[Scott and his men discover the tent left by Amundsen.] . . . In the tent we find a record of five Norwegians having been here. . . . The tent is fine—a small compact affair supported by a single bamboo. A note from Amundsen, which I keep, asks me to forward a letter to King Haakon [the King of Norway]! . . .

Sights at lunch gave us ½ to ¾ of a mile from the Pole, so we call it the Pole Camp. (Temp. Lunch –21°.) We built a cairn, put up our poor slighted Union Jack, and photographed ourselves—mighty cold work all of it. . . .

Well, we have turned our back now on the goal of our ambition and must face our 800 miles of solid dragging—and good-bye to most of the daydreams!

[Over the next several weeks, bad weather and dwindling food and supplies of oil for cooking plagued the team. By March, one expedition member had died, probably from injuries from a fall, and things looked grim for the rest of the party.]

Sunday, March 4.— . . . All the morning we had to pull with all our strength, and in 4½ hours we covered 3½ miles. Last night it was overcast and thick, surface bad; this morning sun shining and surface as bad as ever. . . . A colder snap is bound to come again soon.

Monday, March 5.—Lunch. Regret to say going from bad to worse. . . . Marched for 5 hours this morning over a slightly better surface covered with high moundy sastrugi. Sledge capsized twice; we pulled on foot, covering about 5½ miles. We are two pony marches and about 4 miles from our depot. Our fuel dreadfully low and the poor Soldier [Oates, who was suffering from severe frostbite] nearly done. It is pathetic enough because we can do nothing for him; more hot food might do a little, but only a little, I fear. We none of us expected these terribly low temperatures, and of the rest of us Wilson is feeling them most; mainly, I fear, from his self-sacrificing devotion in doctoring Oates' feet. We cannot help each other, each has enough to do to take care of himself. . . .

Tuesday, March 6.— . . . Poor Oates is unable to pull, sits on the sledge when we are track-searching—he is wonderfully plucky, as his feet must be giving him great pain. . . . If we could have kept up our 9-mile days we might have got within reasonable distance of the depot before running out [of oil], but nothing but a strong wind and a good surface can help us now, and though we had quite a good breeze this morning, the sledge came as heavy as lead. If we were all fit I should have hopes of getting through, but the poor Soldier has become a terrible hindrance, though he does his utmost and suffers much I fear.

Sunday, March 11.—Titus Oates is very near the end, one feels. What we or he will do, God only knows. We discussed the matter after breakfast; he is a brave fine fellow and understands the situation, but he practically asked for advice. Nothing could be said but to urge him to march as long as he could. One satisfactory result to the discussion; I practically ordered Wilson to hand over the means of ending our troubles to us, so that any one of us may know how to do so. Wilson had no choice between doing so and our ransacking the medicine case. We have 30 opium tabloids apiece and he is left with a tube of morphine. So far the tragical side of our story.

Friday, March 16 or Saturday 17.—Lost track of dates, but think the last correct. . . . [Oates] has borne intense suffering for weeks without complaint, and to the very last was able and willing to discuss outside subjects. He did not—would not—give up hope till the very end. He was a brave soul. This was the end. He slept through the night before last, hoping not to wake, but he woke in the morning—yesterday. It was blowing a blizzard. He said, "I am just going outside and may be some time." He went out into the blizzard and we have not seen him since. I take this opportunity of saying that we have stuck to our sick companions to the last. . . . We knew that poor Oates was walking to his death, but though we tried to dissuade him, we knew it was the act of a brave man and an English gentleman. We all hope to meet the end with a similar spirit, and assuredly the end is not far.

Monday, March 19.— Today we started in the usual dragging manner. Sledge dreadfully heavy. We are 15½ miles from the depot and ought to get there in three days. What progress! We have two days' food, but barely a day's fuel. All our feet are getting bad—Wilson's best, my right foot worse, left all right.

There is no chance to nurse one's feet till we can get hot food into us. Amputation is the least I can hope for now, but will the trouble spread? That is the serious question. The weather doesn't give us a chance—the wind from N. N.W. and –40° temp. today.

Wednesday, March 21.—Got within 11 miles of depot Monday night; had to lie up all yesterday in a severe blizzard. Today forlorn hope, Wilson and Bowers going to depot for fuel.

[March] 22 and 23.—Blizzard bad as ever—Wilson and Bowers unable to start—tomorrow last chance—no fuel and only one or two of food left—must be near the end. Have decided it shall be natural—we shall march for the depot with or without our effects and die in our tracks.

[In November, a relief expedition found Scott, Wilson, and Bowers dead in their tent. The searchers also found Scott's diary, letters he had written, and thirty-five pounds of geological specimens the party had pulled on the sledge.]

1. What fears did both expeditions share?   *being beaten to the Pole; not making it back from the Pole*

2. What hardships did both parties face?   *extreme cold, frostbite, strong wind, blizzards, lack of communication with the rest of the world*

3. Contrast the arrival of the two parties at the Pole.   *Amundsen's party congratulated each other and felt respect, pride, affection for their nation's flag, and gratitude; Scott records no joy at reaching the Pole, only disappointment, doubts about reaching home, and the awfulness of the cold weather.*

4. Why would Amundsen leave a letter for Scott to deliver to King Haakon?   *Scott could deliver the letter if Amundsen died and Scott made it back alive.*

5. How far did Scott's party have to travel on the return trip?   *800 miles*

6. What problems with the sledge does Scott describe in the March 4, 5, and 6 entries? What could Scott have done to alleviate these problems?   *It was difficult to pull the sledge over bad surfaces, the sledge capsized twice and was heavy; he could have left behind the heavy geological specimens.*

7. Why did Oates walk into the blizzard?   *He knew he was holding up the rest of the expedition and that he would not live much longer.*

8. List the reasons that Scott and his men didn't reach their last depot.   *The men were weak and frostbitten, and a blizzard kept them from traveling the final miles to the depot.*

Geography

Map of Antarctica

Refer to the map on page 631 to complete the map work below.

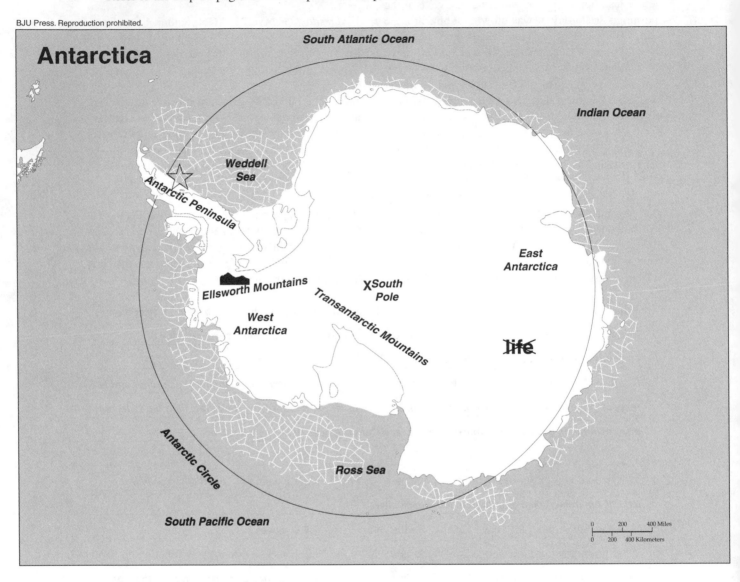

1. Label these features of physical geography:
   Oceans—Indian Ocean, South Atlantic Ocean, South Pacific Ocean
   Seas—Ross Sea, Weddell Sea
   Miscellaneous—Antarctic Peninsula, Transantarctic Mountains, Ellsworth Mountains, East Antarctica, West Antarctica

2. Draw and label the Antarctic Circle.

3. Draw an *X* to show the placement of the South Pole in Antarctica.

4. Draw these figures in the appropriate place. *Note: This section is optional.*

   ☆ most valuable property in Antarctica *(p. 632)*

   l̶i̶f̶e̶ coldest region that is unable to sustain life *(pp. 631-32)*

   ◣ highest mountain on the continent (Vinson Massif) *(p. 631)*

Geography

Journey into the Challenger Deep

On January 23, 1960, Jacques Piccard and U.S. Navy Lieutenant Don Walsh took the bathyscaph *Trieste* into Mariana Trench, the deepest trench in the ocean. Piccard's father, Auguste Piccard of Switzerland, had designed the *Trieste* to operate like an underwater balloon. The heavy steel passenger sphere would naturally sink, while gasoline in the float above the sphere would provide buoyancy. When Piccard and Walsh wanted to descend more quickly, they jettisoned gasoline. To ascend from the ocean floor, they dropped iron pellets held by electromagnets under the float. The *Trieste* could move only straight up and down, not horizontally.

The U.S. Navy bought the bathyscaph in 1958. Piccard remained with the *Trieste* as consultant. After several trial dives off the coast of San Diego, the *Trieste* was ready for the big dive to "the basement of the earth."

Read the following excerpts from Walsh's article "New Eyes for the Scientist" (*Frontiers,* October 1960) and Piccard's book *Seven Miles Down.* Then answer the questions.

Don Walsh: "New Eyes for the Scientist"

On the 23rd of January, 1960, the United States Navy bathyscaph *Trieste* dove almost seven miles down into the deepest known place on the ocean's floor. This dive into the Challenger Deep, 200 miles southwest of Guam, took nearly nine hours for the 14-mile round trip. . . .

Why does our Navy own and maintain a craft of this sort? It can never fire a shot in anger, and it will never evolve into a weapon. The answer to this question is science. Science is a vital factor in our defense effort, and it is only by staying ahead in all areas of the sciences that we can maintain the technical superiority needed for national security. It is this fact along with man's need for more knowledge about the oceans which cover 72% of the surface of his planet, Earth, that prompted the Navy to buy the *Trieste* from the craft's inventor, Auguste Piccard. . . . The Navy base at Guam would be our temporary home base for the duration of the project. The real objective of this program would not be merely to see how deep we could go but to make valuable measurements in the deepest known water column and to observe with the human eye the bottom of this vast trench. We would go where no man had ever gone before, and this alone was reason enough to make the dives. To see what had been unseen, and to measure that which had not been measured. . . .

Early in the morning of the 23rd, just after sunrise, Jacques and I slid down the entrance tube and squeezed into the steel sphere. After a few rapid tests and checks, we bolted the heavy door and commenced the dive.

Time went by very quickly, even though nine hours is a long time to sit in a 17-cubic foot space. We were kept very busy controlling the descent, taking measurements and observations, and com-municating with the surface on our underwater telephone.

The bottom, seven miles down, was distinctly different from the bottom seen on previous dives. It appeared to be made up of very fine white particles. Our landing stirred up the sediment, and we were engulfed in a white cloud. . . .

Just before landing we saw a flatfish lying on the bottom. He was white and about one foot long. After we had landed we saw him swim off into the cloud. The only other living thing of note was a small shrimp that Jacques saw as he glanced out of the window near the bottom.

The trip to the surface was fast, and we arrived in the late afternoon light. Shortly after we got up we committed an American Flag to the depths to commemorate the conquest of the last frontier on Earth. We could not plant the flag on the bottom, in the classical way of the explorer, due to the formidable technical problems involved; but we felt that this would be the next best thing. . . .

We had shown that our Navy is capable of investigating the ocean's floor, no matter what the depth; and we had discovered a great deal of useful scientific information to add to man's knowledge of the sea.

Jacques Piccard: *Seven Miles Down*

Now that we knew of the Challenger Deep, it could no longer be ignored. Until man placed himself on the bottom of the deepest depression on earth, he would not be satisfied. There is a driving force in all of us which cannot stop, if there is yet one step beyond. . . . The bathyscaph was designed to take that step beyond. Once she touched down in the Challenger Deep, there would be no place on earth, from the highest mountains to the frigid poles, that still thwarted man's entry. It would be the last great geographic conquest. Such an achievement focusing attention on this almost neglected realm would doubtless accelerate the building of deep research submersibles everywhere. . . .

[The following excerpts describe the *Trieste's* journey into the Challenger Deep.]

As we plummeted, there was an illusion of great speed. And we *were* falling fast—more than three feet per second (the speed of an average elevator). This was just about our terminal velocity. . . .

0920 [time], depth 2,400. . . . We broke out our first chocolate bars—the only food aboard. Walsh and I had a private joke about these "lunches." On the last dive I had provided lunch—Swiss Nestlé bars. This time Walsh offered to bring the lunch. He did—fifteen American Hershey bars.

1144-29,150 feet [time and depth]. Now we were as deep under the sea as Mt. Everest is high above it. . . . This was a vast emptiness beyond all comprehension. There was, perhaps, a mile of water still beneath us, but the possibility of collision with the trench wall was still on my mind. I pushed the ballast button, slowing us down to two feet per second; then, to one foot per second. . . .

We were landing on a nice, flat bottom. . . . Indifferent to the nearly 200,000 tons of pressure clamped on her metal sphere, the *Trieste* balanced herself delicately on the few pounds of guide rope that lay on the bottom, making token claim, in the name of science and humanity, to the ultimate depths in all our oceans—the Challenger Deep. The depth gauge read 6,300 fathoms—37,800 feet. The time—1306 hours. . . .

And as we were settling this final fathom, I saw a wonderful thing. Lying on the bottom just beneath us was some type of flatfish, resembling a sole, about 1 foot long and 6 inches across. Even as I saw him, his two round eyes on top of his head spied us—a monster of steel—invading his silent realm. Eyes? Why should he have eyes? . . . The flood light that bathed him was the first real light ever to enter this hadal realm [the deepest regions of the ocean]. Here, in an instant, was the answer that biologists had asked for decades. Could life exist in the greatest depths of the ocean? It could! . . .

Slowly, extremely slowly, this flatfish swam away. Moving along the bottom, partly in the ooze and partly in the water, he disappeared into his night. Slowly too—perhaps everything is slow at the bottom of the sea—Walsh and I shook hands. . . .

As the turbidity that we had stirred up in landing began to clear, I saw a beautiful red shrimp. The ivory ooze was almost flat. . . . No animal tracks could be seen anywhere. The bottom was not perfectly smooth, however. I noted some minor undulations suggestive of animal plowings. For twenty minutes we made our scientific observations. . . .

At 1326, I cut the current on the electro-magnet for thirty-six seconds, releasing 800 pounds of ballast. Slowly, the *Trieste* lifted her massive 150-ton hulk off the bottom. The long seven-mile return trip to the world of man began.

We were both chilled. The temperature in the sphere had dropped to 50° F. Our feet were especially cold. In our confined space there was no way to exercise and increase the circulation of blood. . . .

It was about then that, through the port, we noticed the bright flecks of paint that were caught in the burble of our wake. It was not unusual to see a few flecks in deep dives, for at great depths, the sphere is actually shrunk under pressure and some paint is bound to be loosened. But this was more than I usually noted before. . . .

At 1656—almost exactly on our ETA—the *Trieste* broke the surface. The rocking of the sphere told us we had returned to the heaving breast of the sea. Our seven-mile elevator ride was ended.

1. Why did the U.S. Navy buy the *Trieste*? <u>**for scientific research and national security**</u>

<u> </u>

2. List the reasons Walsh and Piccard give for searching the deep. How are they similar to Hunt's explanation of the urge to climb Mt. Everest? <u>**to gain more scientific knowledge, to increase national**</u>

<u>**security, to make measurements and observations, and because no one else had gone to the bottom**</u>

<u>**before; Hunt wanted to climb Everest because no one else had ever reached the peak**</u>

3. What time did the *Trieste* reach the bottom of the Mariana Trench? When did Piccard begin the ascent? Give the answers in nonmilitary time. <u>**1:06 P.M.; 1:26 P.M.**</u>

4. Why would Piccard be surprised that the fish at the bottom of the Mariana Trench had eyes? *He was an evolutionist and theorized that fish on the bottom of the ocean wouldn't evolve eyes because they didn't need them.*

5. What effect did traveling seven miles down have on the *Trieste?* *The temperature inside the Trieste dropped; the sphere shrunk and paint came off.*

6. Why did Piccard refer to the trip in the last line as a "seven-mile elevator ride"? *The bathyscaph could go only straight up or straight down, and it moved at approximately the speed of an elevator.*

7. How was this geographic conquest different from the conquests of Mt. Everest and the South Pole? Which event was the most important? Explain. *Unlike the Mt. Everest and South Pole expeditions, the journey to the bottom of the Challenger Deep was not a race; also, the Trieste's journey was more of a scientific experiment than a journey for the sake of adventure. Answers will vary regarding the most important event. Climbing Mt. Everest was a great feat but didn't add much to scientific knowledge or national defense. Reaching the South Pole included more scientific research, and Antarctica is important as a site for further research and for the possible development of its mineral resources. Exploring the ocean is important as well for scientific research, security, and developing resources.*

Geography

☆ **Arctic and Antarctic**

Complete the chart. You will need to research the Arctic in an encyclopedia or another resource.

Answers may vary. ☆ ***Class discussion.***

	Arctic	Antarctic
Climate	*Average temperature is less than 50°F in summer and has been as low as –87°F in winter. The south receives more precipitation (10 inches annually) than the extremely dry north.*	*Temperatures average –94°F in the winter in the high interior, and winds blow at up to 200 mph. Temperatures on the coast average –22°F. Summer temperatures are warmer (on the coast 32°F). The interior is very dry with less than 2″ of precipitation annually.*
Physical Geography	*An ocean (Arctic) surrounded by continents; ice masses are only "solid ground" at North Pole; four rivers drain into seas near Alaska and Russia.*	*A continent surrounded by oceans (polar waters border on Atlantic, Pacific, and Indian Oceans); pear-shaped land mass is divided by Transantarctic Mountains—high plateau in east, mountains in west; Antarctic Peninsula in west extends northward toward South America; Ross and Weddell Seas cut into the western section.*
Ice Pack	*The Arctic ice pack covers 90% of the Arctic Ocean during the winter and averages 6 ft. thick. The ice pack breaks up into ice floes in the summer.*	*The Antarctic ice pack covers the band of polar water that circles the Antarctic continent. It also breaks up into ice floes during the summer. The pack doubles in thickness in the winter, an annual variation that is six times that of the ice pack in the Arctic.*
Glaciers	*Glaciers are found primarily in Greenland; Arctic icebergs break off of these glaciers and pose dangers to passing ships.*	*Glaciers flow into the Ross and Weddell Seas and form ice shelves. The edges of these shelves break off in the summer to form large, flat icebergs.*
Wildlife	*There is more land life in summer—many insects and migratory birds. But a few birds and mammals stay in the Arctic region throughout the year. Marine life (seals, walruses) remains constant. Polar bears are the only land animals that venture onto the ice pack.*	*The eastern interior section of the Antarctic continent is unable to sustain life of any kind. There is much life in the coastal areas (sea creatures and birds, especially penguins).*
Exploration	*Vikings colonized Greenland before A.D. 1000. A Northeast Passage through the Arctic was successfully crossed in 1879. A Northwest Passage was cut through in 1903-6. Admiral Robert Peary reached the North Pole in 1909.*	*Three ships claimed first sight of the continent in 1820. Norwegian Henryk Johann Bull set foot on the continent in 1895. Norwegian Roald Amundsen was first to reach the South Pole on December 14, 1911.*
Countries with Territorial Claims	*The United States, Canada, Iceland, Denmark, Norway, Sweden, Finland, and Russia are part of an Arctic Council that cares for the Arctic region.*	*Australia, Argentina, Chile, France, New Zealand, Norway, United Kingdom (See chart on p. 631.) (Scientists from Cold War powers persuaded their governments to preserve the continent for science, resulting in the signing of the Antarctic Treaty by twelve nations.)*

Geography

Trivia Game: The Ocean Floor

Except for the bonus questions, the answers to these trivia questions are in this chapter. You need to check outside resources if you do not know the bonus "trivia."

The bonus section is optional. Use this activity any way you wish.

Five Points

1. What are the submerged edges of continents?   *continental shelves, p. 634*

2. What is the deepest trench on earth?   *Mariana Trench, p. 636*

3. Name a trench found in the Indian Ocean.   *Java Trench, p. 635*

4. What zone does adequate light reach in the upper seven hundred feet of the ocean?   *photic zone, p. 635*

5. What oceanic ridge has received the most attention from scientists because of its convenient location?   *Mid-Atlantic Ridge, p. 636*

6. What are deep-sea vents?   *hot springs, p. 636*

7. What are the coastal waters from which a nation may exclude foreign ships?   *territorial waters, p. 637*

8. What are the waters that are open to any vessel?   *high seas, p. 638*

Ten Points

9. What major feature lies on the continental shelf of Australia?   *Great Barrier Reef, p. 635*

10. What two abyssal plains lie off the coast of Antarctica?   *Amundsen and Weddell, p. 635*

11. What is the midsea zone of the ocean water?   *mesopelagic zone, p. 635*

12. Name an unusual fish discovered in the deep-sea zone of the ocean.   *angler fish, p. 635*

13. Which ocean has the most trenches?   *Pacific Ocean, p. 635*

14. Who invented the bathyscaph?   *Auguste Piccard, p. 636*

15. How deep is the Challenger Deep?   *35,800 feet below sea level, p. 636*

16. What wreck did the unmanned craft *Argo* discover?   *the Titanic, p. 637*

17. What treaty gives participating nations a two-hundred-mile exclusive economic zone for fishing and oil drilling?   *Law of the Sea Treaty (LOST), p. 638*

Bonus Questions (Fifteen Points)

18. What percentage of the earth's surface is covered by ocean?   *71 or 72%, p. 20*

19. How much area is covered by the world's largest ocean?   *about 70 million square miles (Pacific Ocean), p. 21*

20. What is a powerful wave caused by an earthquake?   *tsunami, p. 440*

21. On the average, what percentage of seawater is salt?   *3½%*

22. What are small marine organisms that drift with the ocean currents?   *plankton*

23. What are animals that can swim freely in the sea?   *nekton*

24. What are marine organisms that live on or near the sea floor?   *benthos*

25. What famous German battleship that sank in World War II was discovered on the ocean floor in 1989?   *the Bismarck*

Geography

What Am I?

Read each phrase and decide the term it describes. Write the correct answer in the blank.

plateau, p. 631	1. I am a basic geographic landform that covers most of East Antarctica.
iceberg, p. 631	2. I am a jagged chunk of ice that breaks off a glacier and lies mostly hidden underwater.
ice floe, p. 631	3. I am a broken-off piece of the polar ice pack.
pear, p. 631	4. I am a fruit shaped like Antarctica.
ice shelf, p. 632	5. I am an unbroken glacier that has flowed onto the sea.
mountain, p. 632	6. I am the dominant geographic landform of West Antarctica.
nunatak, p. 632	7. I am an isolated mountain in Antarctica.
continental slope, p. 634	8. I am the steep side of a continent under the ocean.
abyssal plain, p. 635	9. I am an extensive flat area of the ocean floor.
trench, p. 635	10. I am a deep canyon in the ocean floor.
photic zone, p. 635	11. I am the upper level of the ocean with enough light for plants to grow.
oceanic ridge, p. 636	12. I am a mountain range under the sea.
seamount, p. 636	13. I am an isolated underwater volcano.
deep-sea vent, p. 636	14. I am a hot spring that pours lava and sulfur into ocean waters.
bathyscaph, p. 636	15. I am an invention of Auguste Piccard that explored the lowest levels of the ocean.
deep, p. 636	16. I am the depths of the ocean below eighteen thousand feet.
high seas, p. 638	17. I am the ocean surface open to any nation's vessels.
exclusive economic zone, p. 638	18. I am the two-hundred-mile region in which a nation has sole rights to fish and drill for oil.

Where Am I?

Read each phrase and decide the place it describes. Write the correct answer in the blank.

Antarctic Circle, p. 630	19. I am the imaginary circle at 66½° S.
Transantarctic, p. 631	20. I am the mountains that divide Antarctica.
Antarctic Peninsula, p. 632	21. I am the most coveted piece of property in Antarctica.
Mariana Trench, p. 636	22. I am the deepest ocean canyon in the world.
troposphere, p. 638	23. I am the lower section of the atmosphere containing clouds and the air people breathe.
stratosphere, p. 639	24. I am the region of the atmosphere containing most of the ozone layer.

Geography

Geographical World Records

Create a list of geographical world records. Start by filling in the facts requested. Then try to find more world records that you can write in the blanks at the bottom. Check the charts in Chapters 2 and 5 for help with several of the answers.

Physical Records

1. largest continent *Asia*
2. smallest continent *Australia*
3. largest culture region in area *Africa*
4. largest ocean *Pacific Ocean*
5. smallest ocean *Arctic Ocean*
6. largest island *Greenland*
7. longest river *Nile*
8. largest lake *Caspian Sea*
9. highest mountain *Mount Everest*
10. lowest shoreline *Dead Sea*
11. deepest ocean trench *Mariana Trench*
12. highest waterfall *Angel Falls*
13. largest desert *Sahara*

Demographic Records

14. most populous country *China*
15. least populous country *Vatican City*
16. most populous culture region *Asia*
17. largest city *Tokyo, Japan*
18. most-spoken language family *Indo-European*
19. most-spoken language *Mandarin (China)*
20. largest world religion *Roman Catholicism*

Additional Records

21. _____
22. _____
23. _____
24. _____
25. _____

World Culture Regions

Complete the chart on the reverse side. First, look at the map on pages 58-59 and write the names of the twenty-four major cultural *sub*regions under the correct world culture regions. Then place the *physical features, countries, cities,* and *terms* beside the subregions with which they are most closely associated.

Physical Features

Andes	Danube River	Mediterranean Sea	Rhine River
Aral Sea	Ganges River	Mesopotamia	Sahara
Baltic Sea	Great Dividing Range	Mexican Plateau	Siberia
Canadian Shield	Great Rift Valley	Mississippi River	South China Sea
Congo River	Gulf of Guinea	New Guinea	Thames River
Cook Strait	Huang He	Palestine	veldt

Countries (or Regions)

Algeria	Germany	Kazakhstan	Ontario
Brazil	Greater Volga	Mexico	Papua New Guinea
China	India	New South Wales	Poland
Democratic Republic of Congo (Zaire)	Indonesia	Nigeria	South Africa
	Iran	North Island	Sweden
Egypt	Italy	Northeast	United Kingdom
Ethiopia			

Cities

Addis Ababa	Jakarta	Mexico City	Stockholm
Algiers	Kiev	Moscow	Sydney
Auckland	Kinshasa	New York	Tashkent
Bombay	Lagos	Paris	Tehran
Cairo	London	Port Moresby	Tokyo
Cape Town	Madrid	São Paulo	Toronto

Terms

ancestor worship	dissident	malaria	selva
apartheid	entrepot	Maori	shatter belt
Bedouin	European Union	mestizo	subcontinent
bight	federated republic	outback	Swahili
copra	fjord	Renaissance	Turkistan
desertification	House of Commons	ribbon development	Zionist

This would be a good place to review the "Four Foremost Facts" given in the teacher introduction to each of the world culture regions and subregions. You might want to read selected facts and ask students to name the region they describe, or ask students to name their own "foremost facts" and see how closely their lists match the lists in the teacher's manual.

	Cultural Subregion	Physical Feature	Populous Country (Region)	Largest City	Term
Northern America	United States	Mississippi River	Northeast	New York	federated republic
	Canada	Canadian Shield	Ontario	Toronto	ribbon development
Latin America	Middle America	Mexican Plateau	Mexico	Mexico City	mestizo
	South America	Andes	Brazil	São Paulo	selva
Western Europe	British Isles	Thames River	United Kingdom	London	House of Commons
	Scandinavia	Baltic Sea	Sweden	Stockholm	fjord
	Continental Europe	Rhine River	Germany	Paris	European Union
	Mediterranean Europe	Mediterranean Sea	Italy	Madrid	Renaissance
Central Eurasia	Eastern Europe	Danube River	Poland	Kiev	shatter belt
	Russia	Siberia	Greater Volga	Moscow	dissident
	Central Asia	Aral Sea	Kazakhstan	Tashkent	Turkistan
Asia	South Asia	Ganges River	India	Bombay	subcontinent
	Southeast Asia	South China Sea	Indonesia	Jakarta	entrepot
	East Asia	Huang He	China	Tokyo	ancestor worship
Middle East	Persian Gulf	Mesopotamia	Iran	Tehran	Bedouin
	Eastern Mediterranean	Palestine	Egypt	Cairo	Zionist
Africa	North Africa	Sahara	Algeria	Algiers	desertification
	West Africa	Gulf of Guinea	Nigeria	Lagos	bight
	Central Africa	Congo River	Congo (Zaire)	Kinshasa	malaria
	East Africa	Great Rift Valley	Ethiopia	Addis Ababa	Swahili
	South Africa	veldt	South Africa	Cape Town	apartheid
Oceania	Australia	Great Dividing Range	New South Wales	Sydney	outback
	New Zealand	Cook Strait	North Island	Auckland	Maori
	Pacific Islands	New Guinea	Papua New Guinea	Port Moresby	copra

Geography

☆ **What If You Ruled the World?** ☆ *Class discussion.*

Here are some of the worst problems facing the world today. Explain why these problems have been so hard to solve. If you were a trusted advisor to all the rulers of the world, what practical steps would you suggest they take to solve these problems? Of course, no solution will succeed without God's help. *Answers will vary. Ask students to come up with their own lists of the "Ten Most Serious Problems in the World Today."*

1. The **drug trade** is a growing industry that encourages crime and lawlessness (see p. 275).   *The drug trade lines the pockets of criminals and revolutionaries in poor countries where the people are willing to take risks in return for huge profits.*

    How I would try to solve this problem.   *Two approaches have been tried: cutting supplies and cutting demand. Governments have more control over the former.*

2. Democratic governments have proved to be very unstable in **Latin America** (see pp. 246, 251-52, 271-73).   *Democracy in this region was not planted in the same political soil as democracy in Northern America. It was inspired by the violence of the French Revolution, and violence begets violence (Matt. 26:52). Also, Latin America had no middle class, as in the north, and the sharp difference between the rich and the poor created unending debate about land reform.*

    How I would try to solve this problem.   *The end of violence requires a change of heart on all levels of society but particularly among the rich and the rulers. If leaders would serve rather than seek to be served, then the rule of law might have a chance.*

3. Roman Catholics and Protestants in **Northern Ireland** have suffered violence for decades (see pp. 314-15).   *The Irish Problem dates back almost five hundred years to when Britain took Ireland and began sending immigrants to settle in the north. The two sides have different world views and bear the weight of a bitter history and distrust.*

    How I would try to solve this problem.   *No government rests on a solid foundation unless it first demands respect for the rule of law and yet exhibits mercy. Terrorists should be rooted out and punished according to the law, but the laws should be changed to give equal rights to all people.*

4. **Prejudice** in Eastern Europe leads to mistreatment of weak minorities (see pp. 380-84).   *The shatter belt includes a dangerous mix of ethnic groups, religion, and politics. A history of despotic rule encourages a vicious cycle of abuses and revenge.*

    How I would try to solve this problem.   *The only hope for peace is popular acceptance of the rule of law and the dignity of individuals. Such a change of heart requires time and the good example of leaders.*

5. **Communism** retains a foothold in Asia, where it continues to threaten the peace and prosperity of its neighbors (see pp. 451-53, 469-70, 477-78).   *Communism is just an excuse for leaders to dominate their people for personal gain, and because this political view lacks any moral foundation, Communist leaders will resort to any evil means to accomplish their ends.*

    How I would try to solve this problem.   *Patience is the best ally of democracy, as was evident in Russia, where time proved the hollowness of Communist dogma. Foreign countries should continue to put all possible pressure on the Communists to face up to their evil and their failures.*

6. **Despots,** such as Saddam Hussein, continue to hold power in the Middle East and threaten peace and the world's supply of oil (see pp. 499-502).   *The Middle East is steeped in Muslim traditions and a history of despotic rule, which has no sympathy for Western ideas of liberty and human rights. As long as the common people tolerate injustice, it will spread.*

   How I would try to solve this problem.   *The West must recognize that democracy is not a simple answer to man's problems and that Muslims raise legitimate concerns about the debauchery of the West. Yet Western nations must continue to support universal truths about human rights and dignity. The sword is not the answer, and God does not give princes power so that they can use it for their own ends.*

7. Radical Muslims in the Middle East continue to harbor a desire to eliminate **Israel** from the map (see pp. 508, 520-21, 531).   *Muhammad sowed the seeds of modern discord when he promoted the idea of jihad, religious wars that guarantee paradise to warriors who fall while fighting them. Radical Muslims refuse to acknowledge the right of Israel to exist, while Israelis will defend their new state to the utmost.*

   How I would try to solve this problem.   *The leaders of Islam have made themselves the enemies of the triune God (Ps. 2:2-4) and the enemies of Abraham's descendants (Gen. 12:2-3). Israel is right not to trust its neighbors, but it should also be above reproach in its own dealings and trust in God to vindicate its policies.*

8. **Drought** and desert sands appear to be spreading in the Sahel (see p. 546).   *A combination of climatic change and poor land management appears to be causing desertification. Also, the people are Muslims who refuse to acknowledge the hand of God.*

   How I would try to solve this problem.   *It is important to change farming techniques and the lifestyle that has contributed to desertification. But the people themselves must see the need for change, and the government needs to give people the freedom to change (or move to cities and import food).*

9. Bad weather, ferocious diseases, and a series of civil wars have encouraged widespread famine and poverty in **sub-Saharan Africa** (see pp. 551-53, 561-62, 572-76).   *Sub-Saharan Africa has a difficult legacy of tribal religions that enslave the soul and tribal policies that encourage violence. On top of this was Europe's exploitation of its African colonies. The people lack experience with Western democracy.*

   How I would try to solve this problem.   *As in Latin America, the leaders and their people need a change of heart. History and the Bible support the view that hard work is more apt to bring prosperity than dependence on government assistance. The government needs to give people the freedom and responsibility to solve their own problems, beginning with a change of heart about work and trade.*

10. The **ozone layer** appears to be breaking down, allowing deadly radiation to reach the earth's surface (see p. 640).   *This conclusion is based on incomplete evidence about the relationship between the release of certain chemicals into the air and the chemical changes in ozone. A lack of knowledge about the complex cycles in nature makes solutions risky.*

   How I would try to solve this problem.   *It is possible that no solution to this problem exists. Continued research appears to be a worthwhile investment, but it is debatable whether changing chemicals in industry will help anything.*

Geography

☆ **Your Opinion Counts**

Now that you have studied geography in detail, how have your opinions changed? With the help of your textbook, give your opinion about the most memorable facts. **Answers will vary.** ☆ **Class discussion.**

Physical Geography

1. For each of the natural features below, which one in the world would you most like to see?

   mountain _____

   volcano _____

   waterfall _____

   other natural wonder _____

2. What climate would you prefer? _____

3. What environmental disaster concerns you the most? _____

Countries

4. What country is currently the most influential in the world? _____

5. What country is the greatest threat to world peace and prosperity? _____

6. Compared to other countries, how would you rate the United States's success in developing its

   resources (and fulfilling the dominion mandate)? _____

   _____

7. What country is the clearest example of God's blessing in the world? Explain. _____

   _____

8. What country is the clearest example of God's cursing in the world? Explain. _____

   _____

9. If you were assigned to read a book on any country, which country would you choose? _____

   _____

10. What is the greatest lesson about life that you have learned from the study of other countries?

    _____

    _____

11. What has been the greatest gift of each of the following countries to the world? (Or, what is the most memorable fact about each country?)

    Australia _____

    Brazil _____

    Canada _____

    China _____

    France _____

    Germany _____

    India _____

Book Review

Italy _____

Japan _____

Mexico _____

Russia _____

United Kingdom _____

12. Where would you most like to go as a missionary? _____

13. Where would you least like to go as a missionary? _____

World Culture Regions

14. What culture region has had the greatest impact on the shape and character of the other world culture regions? _____

15. Which of the world's eight culture regions is changing the fastest? _____

16. Which of the world's eight culture regions is changing the least? _____

17. Which culture region (unit) did you most enjoy studying? Why? _____

_____

_____

18. Which culture region (unit) did you least enjoy studying? Why? _____

_____

_____

19. What is the greatest work of architecture in the world? _____

20. What major religion is most similar to Christianity? What does Christianity offer that would make followers of this religion want to convert to Christ? _____

_____

_____

21. Which culture region offers the greatest opportunities for missionaries? _____

22. Which would be the hardest region to reach as a missionary? _____

Foreign Relations

23. What country (in the list above) is most like the United States? _____

24. What country (in the list above) is least like the United States? _____

25. What country has had the greatest impact on the culture of the United States? _____

26. What has been the United States's greatest gift to the world? _____

27. What has been the United States's greatest harm to the world? _____

28. What country is the greatest threat to the United States's peace and power? _____

29. If the United States had to choose one country as its main friend (ally), which should it be?

_____

30. Does the United Nations serve a useful purpose in the world today? Explain. _____

_____

_____

Miscellaneous

31. In which country would you most like to live? Why? _____
_____
_____

32. In which city would you most like to live? _____

33. What was the most amazing or unusual thing you learned in this course? _____
_____

34. What was the most useful thing you learned in this course? _____
_____

35. How can your knowledge of geography help you if you go into business? _____
_____

36. How can your knowledge of geography help your understanding of the following subjects?
    current events _____
    history _____
    literature _____
    political science _____
    economics _____
    biology _____

37. What type of missionary work interests you the most? _____
_____